ULTRA LONG FLIGHT PAPER AIRPLANES

20 Incredible Planes Designed for Record Breaking Flights

TAKUO TODA

TUTTLE Publishing
Tokyo | Rutland, Vermont | Singapore

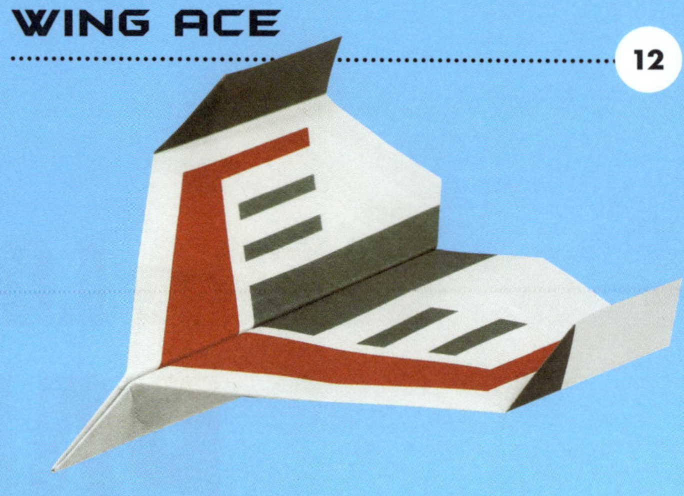

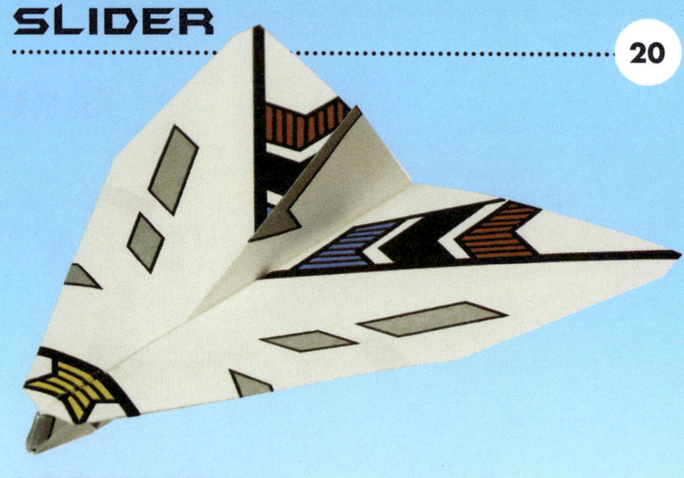

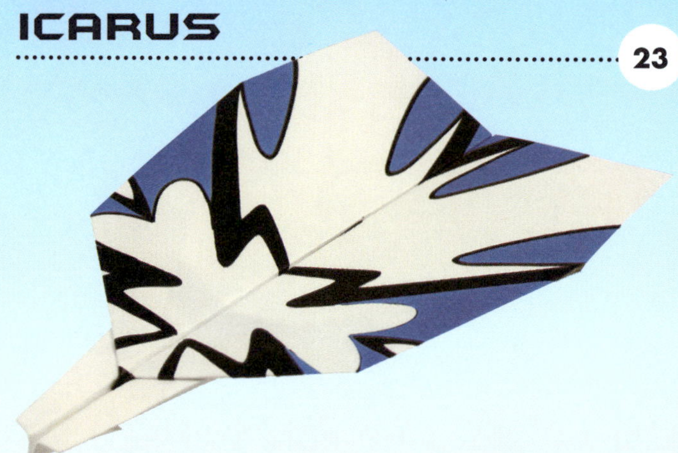

Let's fly airplanes that stay in the air for a long time! There's even an airplane design here that was used to break the record for the longest flight time in the world!

Why I Wrote This Book

"I want to hold the Guinness World Record for longest paper airplane flight time!" This is something that every paper airplane enthusiast aspires to at one time or another.

At one point, an enthusiast from a different paper airplane tradition once said to me in a condescending tone, "Origami airplanes don't really fly that well, do they?" However, the Guinness World Record for longest paper airplane flight duration is only recognized for *origami* airplanes. No matter how far planes assembled using scissors and adhesives and launched using rubber catapults can fly, the *Guinness World Records* books do not recognize those attempts.

As of 2008, only two people had managed to exceed 20-second flights. One of them barely surpassed a 20-second flight, after which he reportedly retired from launching paper airplanes due to a shoulder injury. But the Guinness World Record throw by the other individual was an astounding 27.6 seconds! To put this into perspective, it's like being asked to run 100 meters in under 8 seconds—a nearly impossible feat. It seemed like a record that couldn't be broken, and even attempting to do so felt meaningless, but I declared that I would absolutely break it.

Upon reexamining my folding techniques, I discovered a model with the potential to break the record—a plane I had previously dismissed for looking unattractive.

If one makes paper airplane wings as wide as possible, the performance advantage sought is lost to air resistance from the initial velocity when thrown to a height. To counter this, I meticulously refined the folding process and paper selection, eventually discovering that *bagasse* paper (paper made from spent sugarcane pulp) offered the best performance.

The next step was improving my throwing form. I analyzed footage of my best throws and perfected a form where I start with the plane held just above the floor as I step forward slightly with my dominant leg and spring upward in a twirling motion, releasing the plane. This form had the potential needed to achieve my goals. While it did place significant strain on my shoulders, waist and knees, it allowed me to launch the paper airplane at maximum speed.

This book serves as your guide to breaking my Guinness World Record! I hope that someone will build upon my methods, make further improvements and ultimately shatter the record.

—Takuo Toda
Chairman of the Origami Airplane Association

You can watch the footage of the epic flight that broke the Guinness World Record on my YouTube channel: *www.youtube.com/user/OriplaneChannel*

Folding Symbols Used in This Book

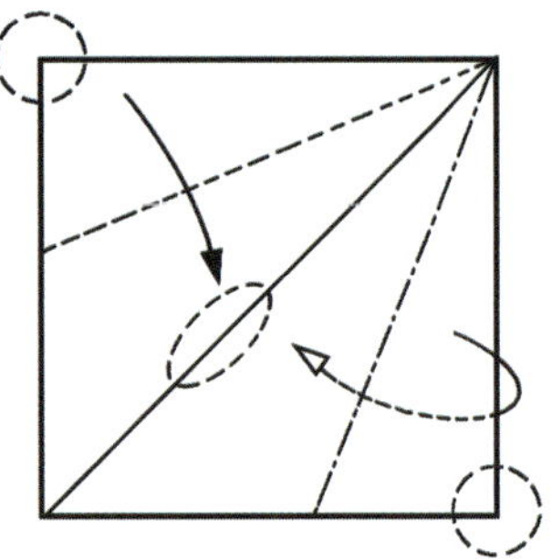
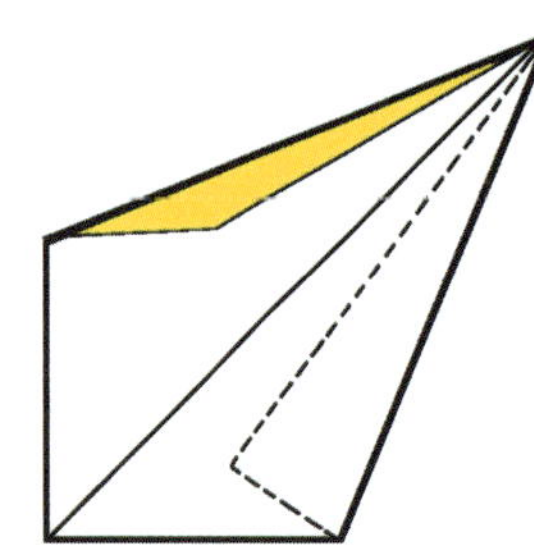
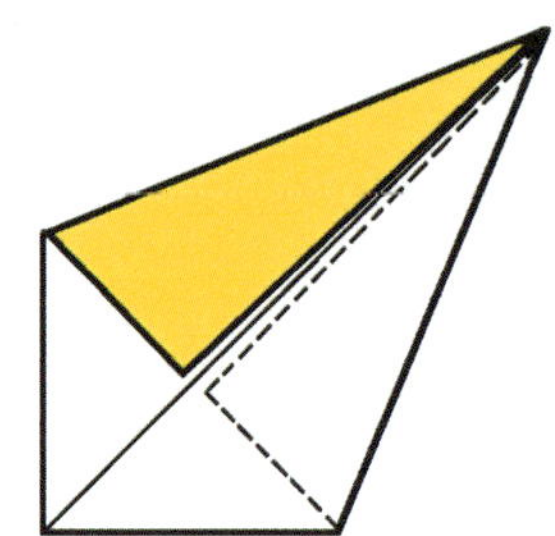

Valley fold line (after folding, it's hidden inside)

Fold toward the front side

Mountain fold line (after folding, it remains outside)

Fold toward the back side

Crease line (indicated only when necessary)

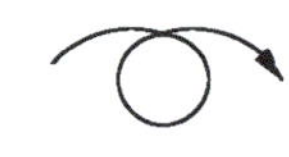
Flip the entire paper over

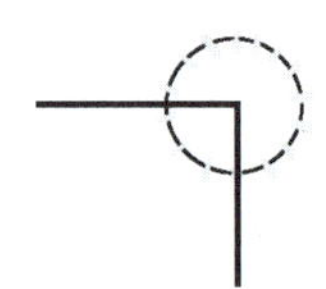
Reference point

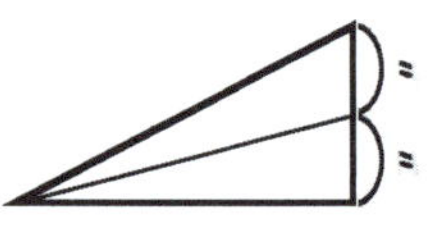
Indicates spans of equal length

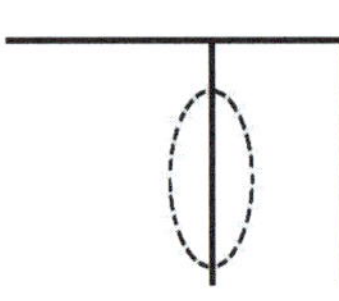
Reference line

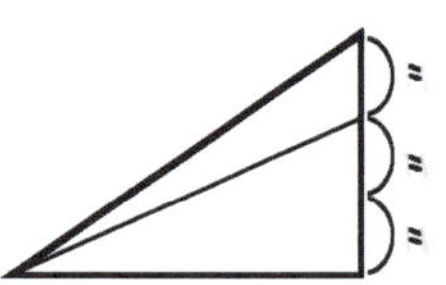
Indicates a span of twice the length

Inside Reverse Fold

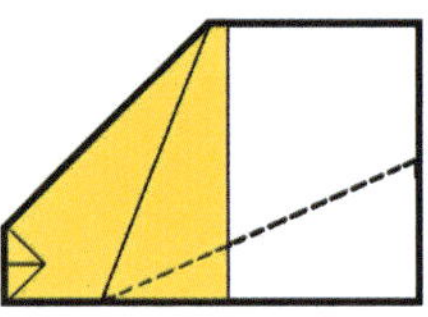
Make a crease. ➡

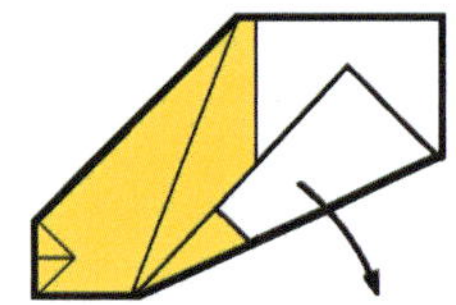
Unfold. ➡

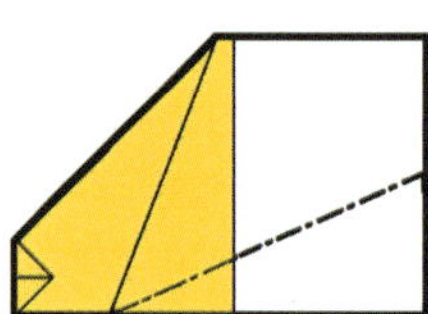
Fold the crease you made into a mountain fold, open the paper slightly, and push the corner inside. ➡

Flatten the paper.

How to Make Firm, Accurate Creases

Your results will vary, depending on the size of the paper and the direction in which it's being folded.

1. Take hold of the bottom left corner and lift it, bringing it toward the top left corner.

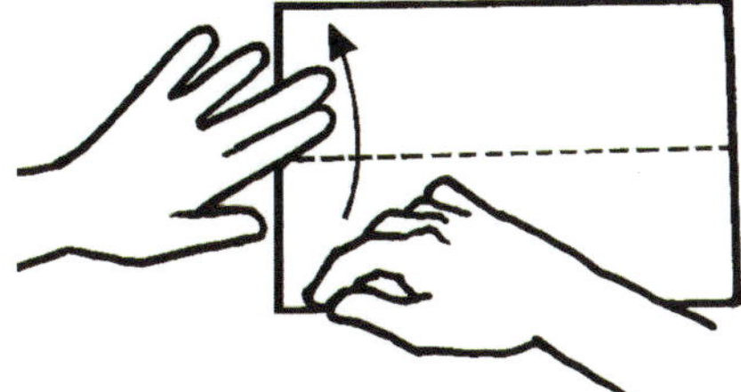

2. Once the top left corners are aligned, keep your right hand still and withdraw your left hand.

3. Gently flatten the bottom left corner of the paper with your left hand.

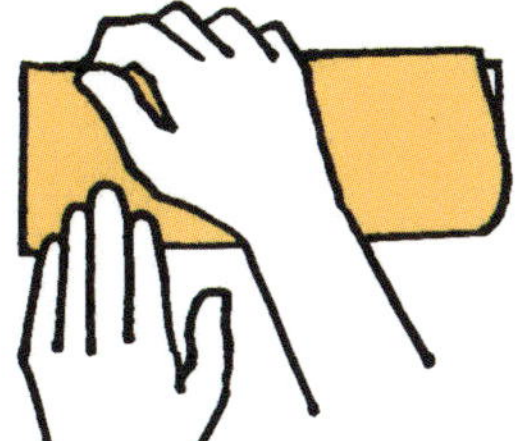

4. While pressing down firmly on the bottom left corner with the tips of your left-hand fingers, release your right hand.

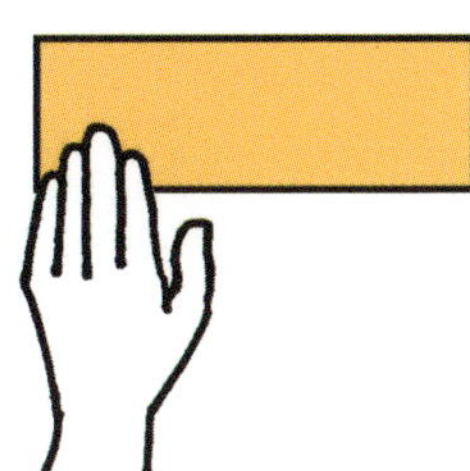

5. Take hold of the upper right corner and pull it toward the direction of the arrow, aligning the edges of the paper.

6. With your left pinky finger as the anchor, crease the bottom left half by spreading your other left-hand fingers.

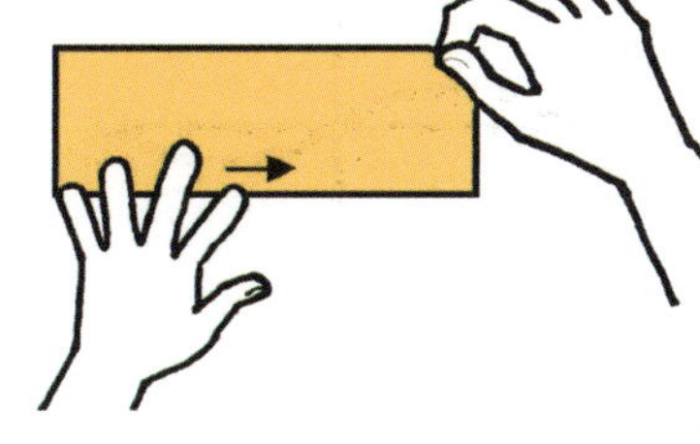

7. Keep pressing down on the paper with the tips of your left-hand fingers while you release your right hand.

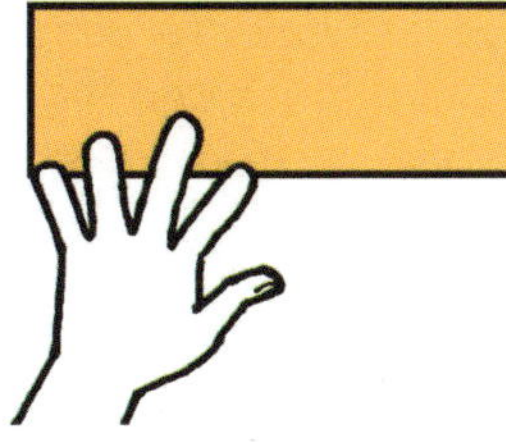

8. Gently press down the bottom right portion with your right hand and lightly make a crease.

9. With the pad of your right thumb, make a strong crease on the bottom right half of the paper.

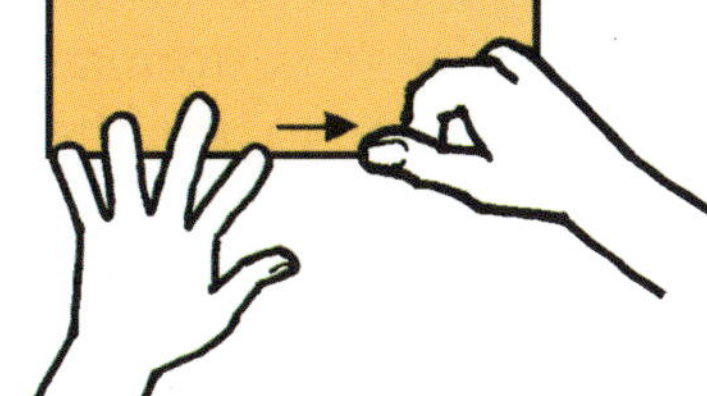

10. Do the same on the bottom left to complete the crease.

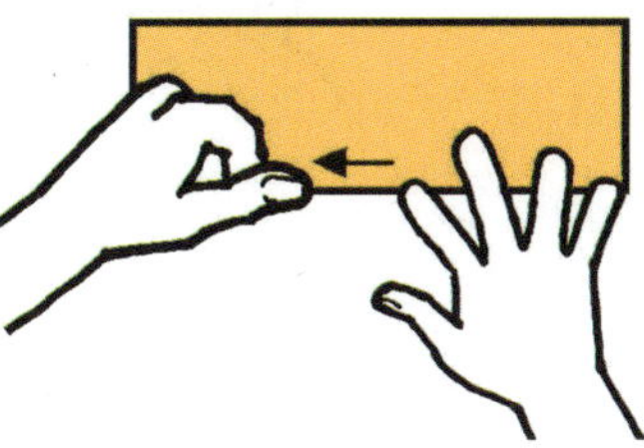

Adjust Your Planes Before Flying Them!

Proper adjustment will make your airplane fly better. Remember the following adjustment techniques and the correct way to throw the airplane that suits its design.

1 Correcting Twists in the Airplane

First, look at the airplane from the front to check if the wings have any significant twists. If the wings are twisted or bulging, the airplane won't fly well. For wings with a lot of twist, place them on the edge of a desk and straighten them by "burnishing" from above with a ruler or similar object.

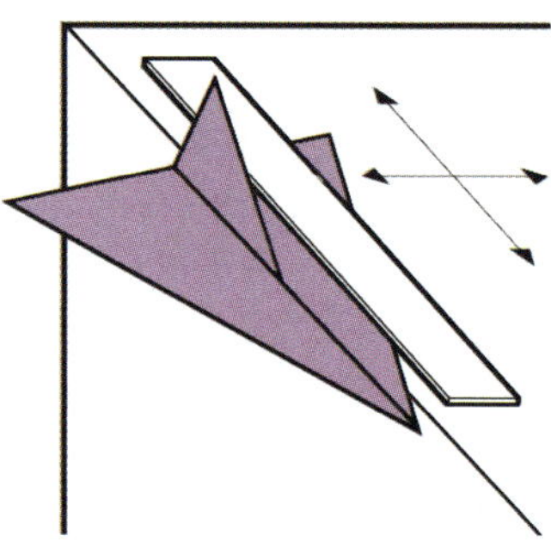

2 Adding Elevators

Elevators are the horizontal control surfaces at the back of the plane that affect lift. To emulate them on your paper airplane, twist the rear of the wings slightly upward by a little less than ¼ inch (6 mm), lifting them with your fingertips. Having elevators will significantly improve the airplane's performance, and the dimples tend to help the wing layers stay together.

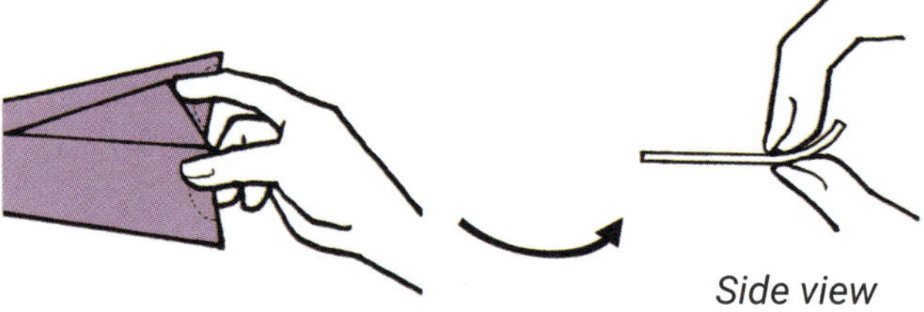

Side view

3 Test the Effect of the Elevators

Gently throw the airplane with a motion that pushes it straight out away from you, aiming about 5 degrees downward. Don't snap your wrist, but throw it almost like you would throw a dart.

It's best to hold the airplane at a point that's one-third of the distance from the nose of the plane.

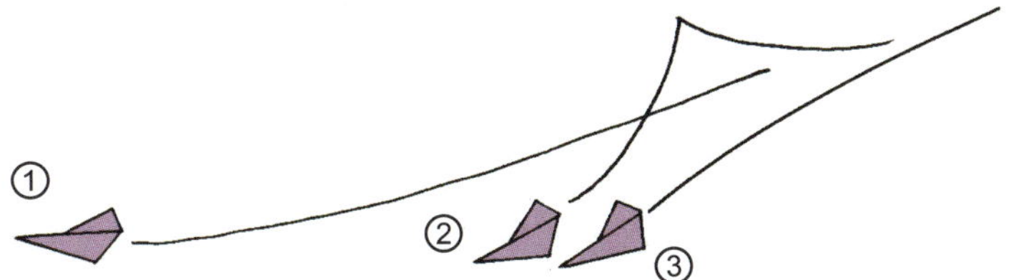

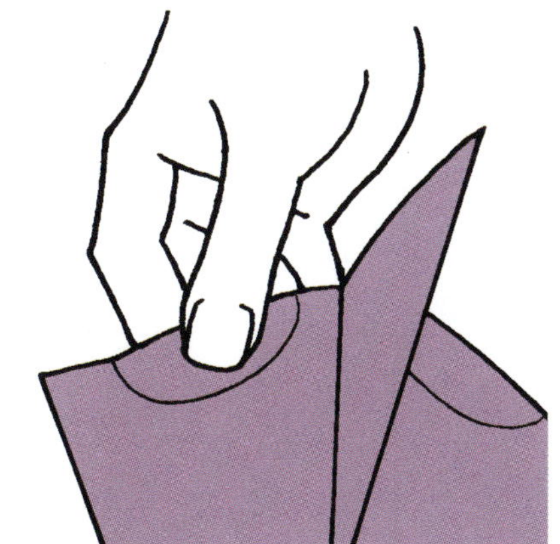

① If it flies straight and smoothly like in trajectory 1 above, it's ready—the elevators are angled correctly.

② If it quickly ascends and then dives like in trajectory 2, the angle of the elevators is too steep. Adjust by slightly lowering them.

③ If it drops steeply down like in trajectory 3, the angle of the elevators is too shallow. Adjust by slightly raising them.

Adjustments for Left or Right Turns

If the airplane tends to curve left or right, adjust by tweaking only one of the elevators. Twisting the right elevator upward will make the airplane curve to the right (Figure 1). Twisting the left elevator upward will make it curve to the left.

Also, looking at the vertical tail (rudder) from above, twisting it to the right will make the airplane turn right (Figure 2), and twisting it to the left will make it turn left.

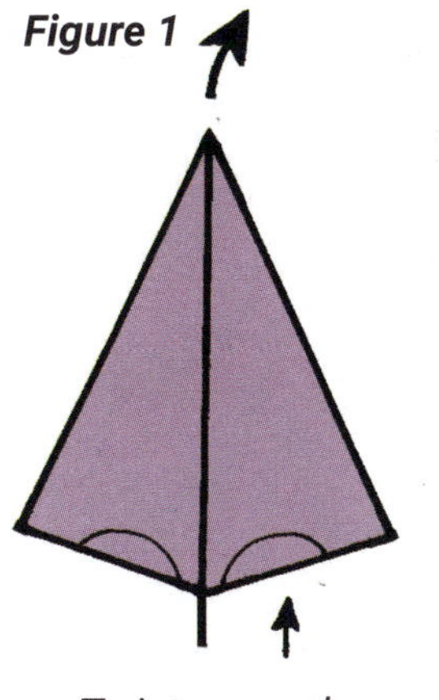

Figure 1

Twist upward

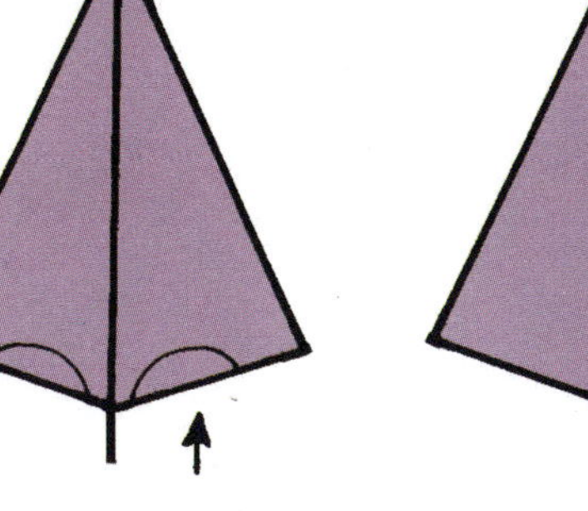

Figure 2

Twist to the right

Avoid adjusting the rudder if possible

Adjusting the rudder first can balance the flight, but it makes the airplane more vulnerable to destabilization from air current turbulence. It's better to adjust the direction by tweaking the elevators on the main wings whenever possible.

How to Throw a Paper Airplane for Super Long Flights

Try throwing your plane straight up as shown in the diagram. If it transitions smoothly to horizontal flight between 30–65 feet (10–20 m) in the air, like in example ① below, it's a successful launch. If it turns sharply and rapidly descends from the zenith of its trajectory like in example ②, it is a failure. In that case, reduce the twist of the rudder.

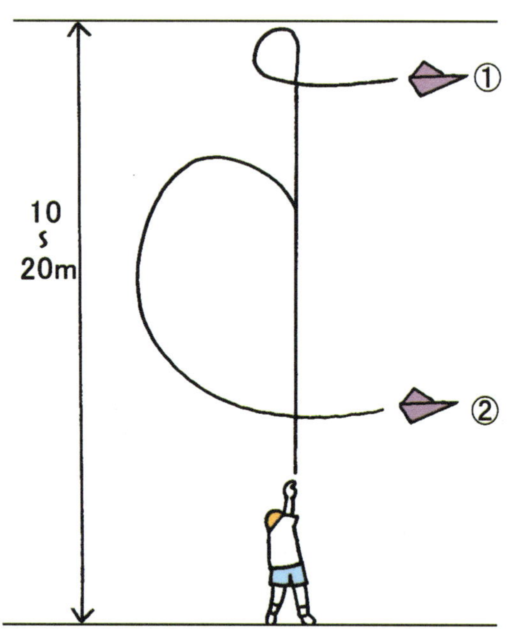

Slightly lower your body into a crouch, aim almost straight up, and throw—with your whole body acting like a spring. Do not use a wrist-snap follow-though—throw it as if you are pushing it upward.

A More Gentle Method (for Test Flights, Etc.)

This is a method of throwing suitable for when you are adjusting the paper airplane and confirming the effects of the adjustments with gentle test flights. Push the airplane straight out from beside your face. It's a gentle throw that's also suitable for young children, the elderly or anyone not able to execute the hard throw described above.

Selecting Suitable Paper by Plane Type

• For the ***glider*** types (planes that stay aloft for a long time—the subject of this book), and paper airplanes with complex folds: use smooth, lightweight/thin A4 size (8.27 in × 11.69 in / 21 cm × 29.7 cm) copy paper.

• For ***distance*** types (planes that fly a long distance from their launch points in relatively direct paths): use slightly heavier-weight/thicker A4 size (8.27 in × 11.69 in / 21 cm × 29.7 cm) copy paper.

Paper with a shiny surface is not suitable for paper airplanes because it is thin and heavy. Furthermore, for paper airplanes that require complex folds, thin and slightly stiff paper is preferable. Stiff paper doesn't bulge at the creases due to the paper's elasticity when folded, and it has the strength to withstand the stress of strong throws.

The stiffness of the paper can be determined by how steeply it droops when the unsupported edge is extended horizontally off the edge of a table, as shown in Figure 1.

The more you handle paper, the more it absorbs oils and moisture from your hands, making the paper lose its crispness. When folding paper airplanes, try to fold with your fingertips instead of pressing with the palm of your hand to reduce the transfer of moisture.

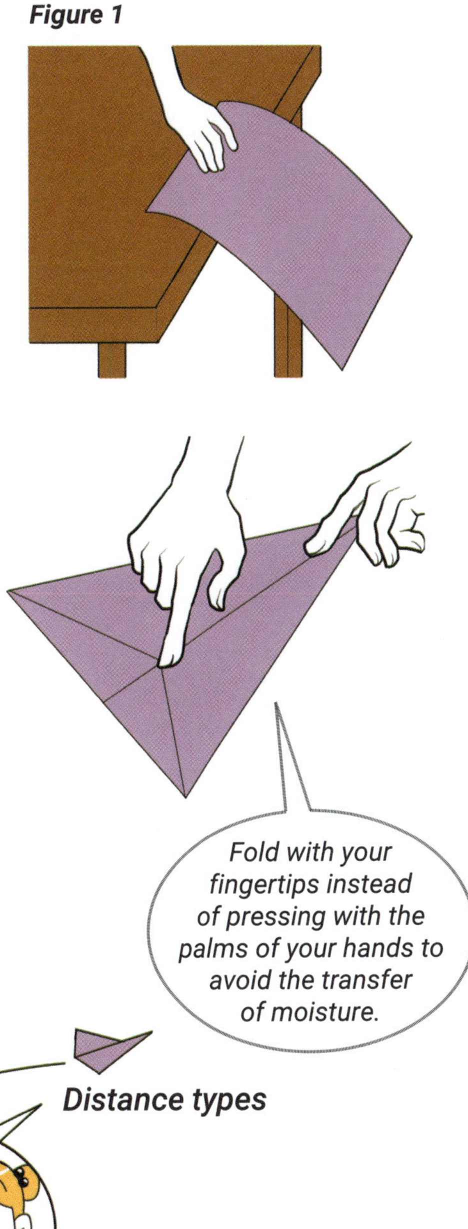

Figure 1

A4
Thin, light-weight paper

Glider types

Distance types

A4
Medium-weight paper

WING ACE

Like a belly-button airplane, this glider is very simple to fold and flies well. Without a rudder to fiddle with, fine-tuning is a snap.

Paper Shape .. Rectangular
Difficulty .... ★

① Fold in half, and then unfold.

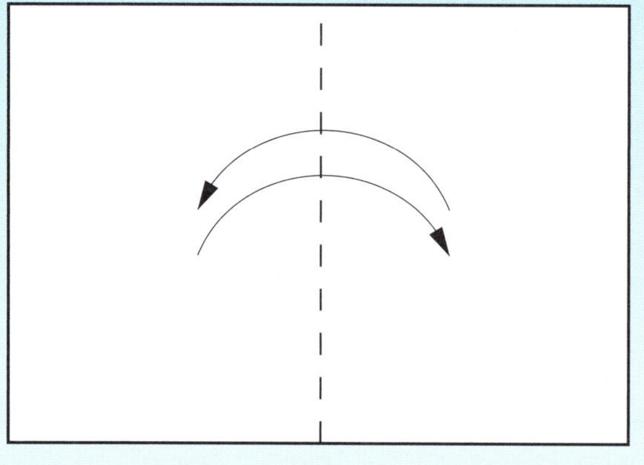

② Fold the bottom corner flaps to the center vertical crease.

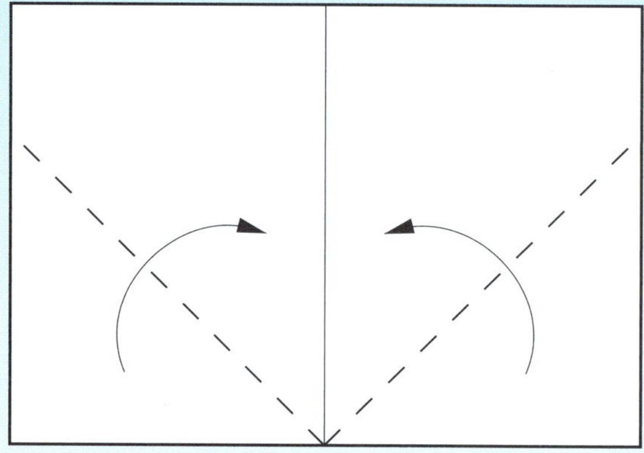

③ Fold the bottom corner to the top.

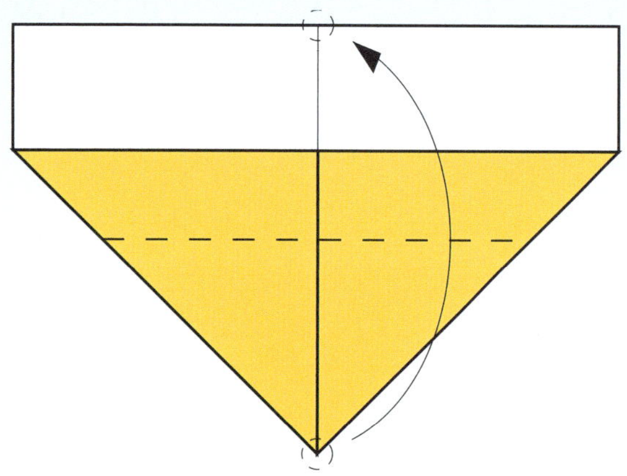

④ Fold, leaving a gap of about 1/16 in (2 mm) in the center.

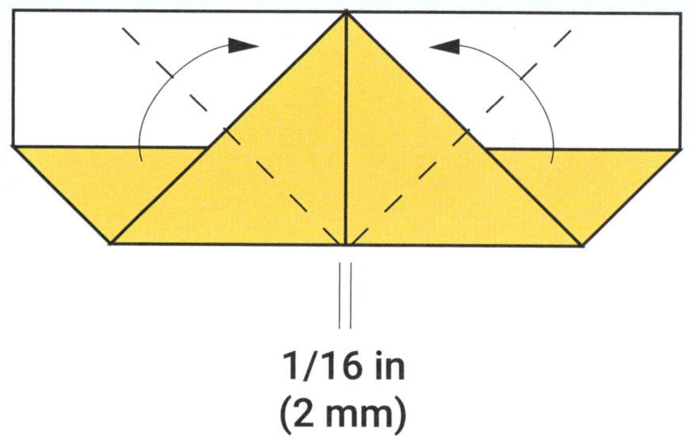

⑤ Fold in half.

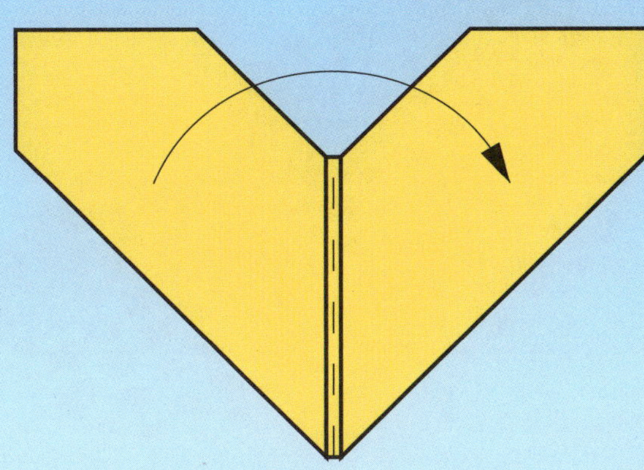

⑥ Fold the top layer to the width of "a."

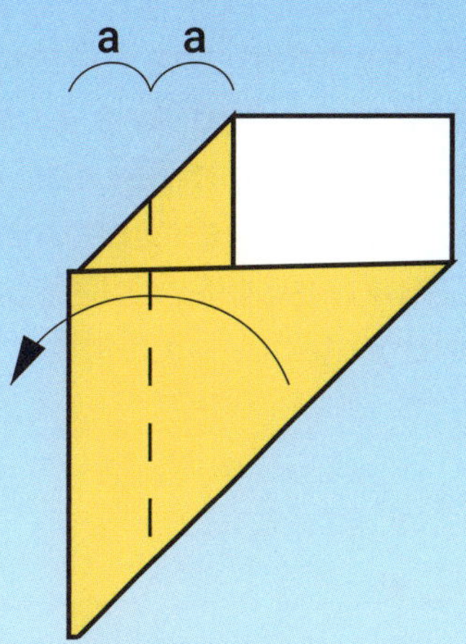

⑦ Turn the paper over.

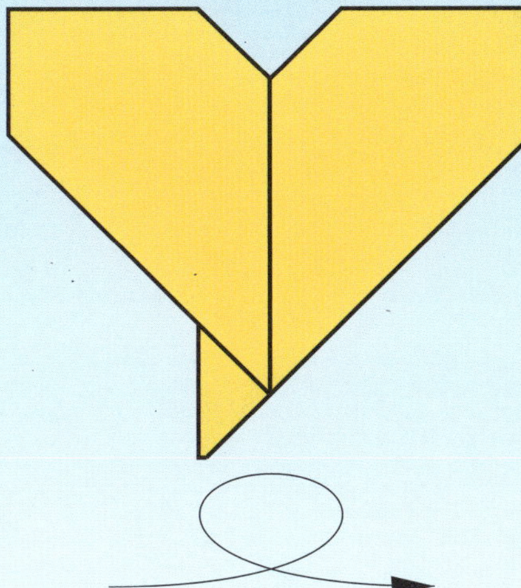

⑧ Fold the left flap to match the one on the right.

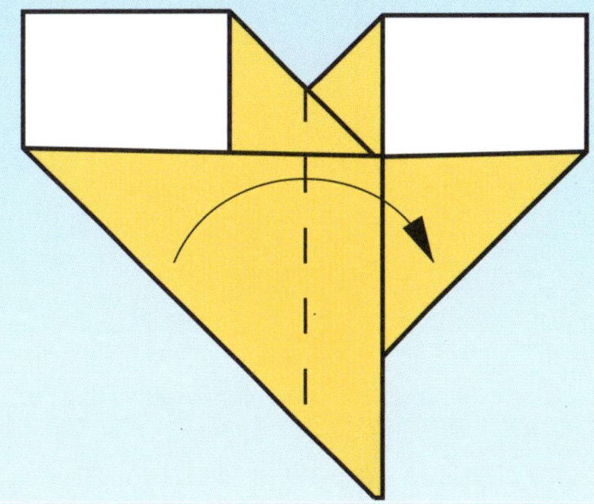

⑨ Fold the top layer to the width of "a."
Fold the opposite side in the same way.

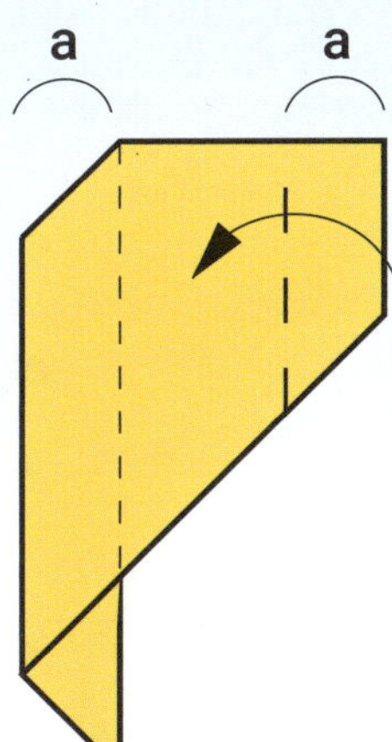

Open out the wings as shown in the 3D diagrams to the right. Completed.

Check after folding ▶ Wing Ace 3D Views

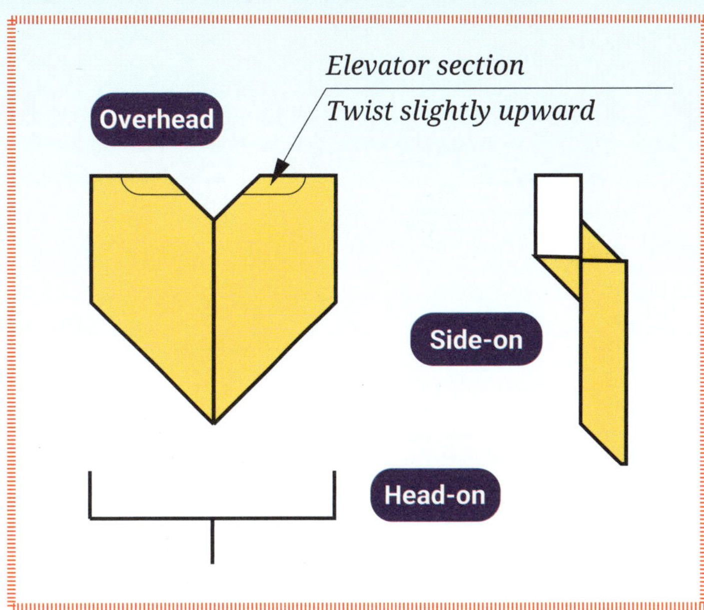

FLYING HEART

Up to the halfway point, the folding method matches that of the Wing Ace. Like that plane, this one is also simple and easy to fold. The finished overhead profile forms a heart shape, making this design particularly popular around Valentine's Day!

Paper Shape .. Rectangular

Difficulty .... ★

① Fold in half, and then unfold.

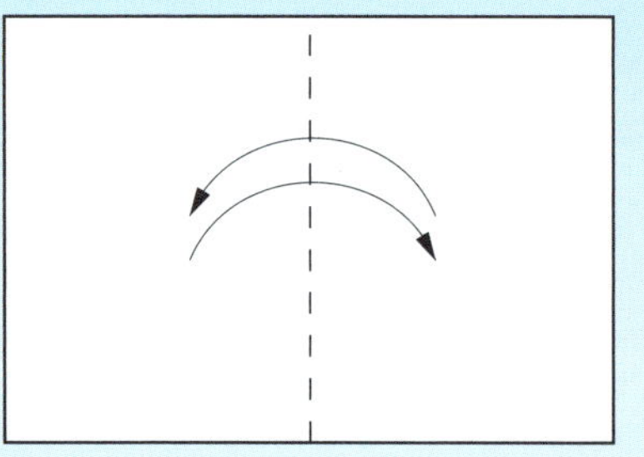

② Fold the bottom corner flaps to the center vertical crease.

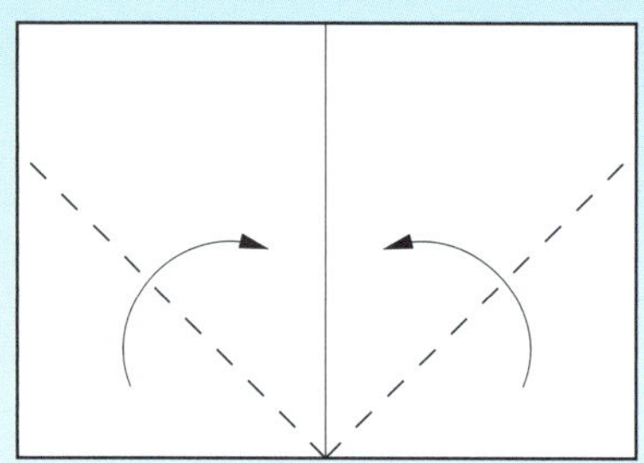

③ Fold the bottom corner to the top.

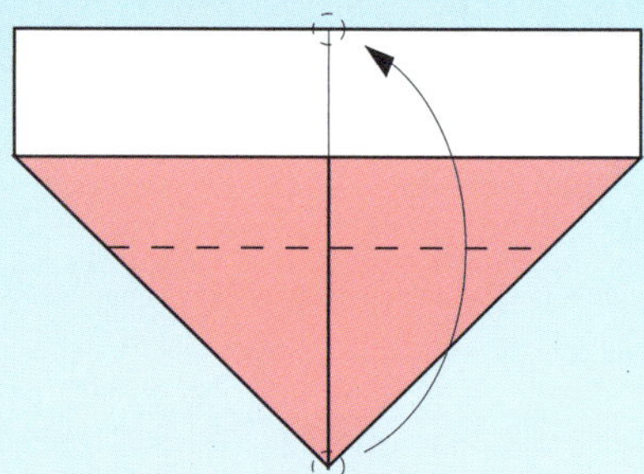

④ Fold, leaving a gap of about 1/16 in (2 mm) in the center.

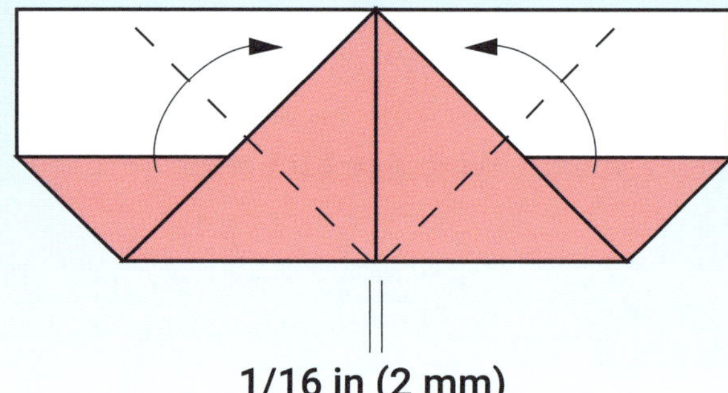

⑤ Turn the paper over.

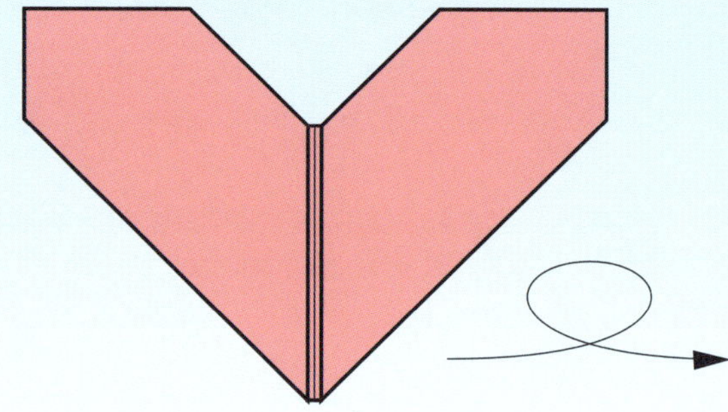

⑥ Fold the bottom point into a triangular flap at the indicated position.

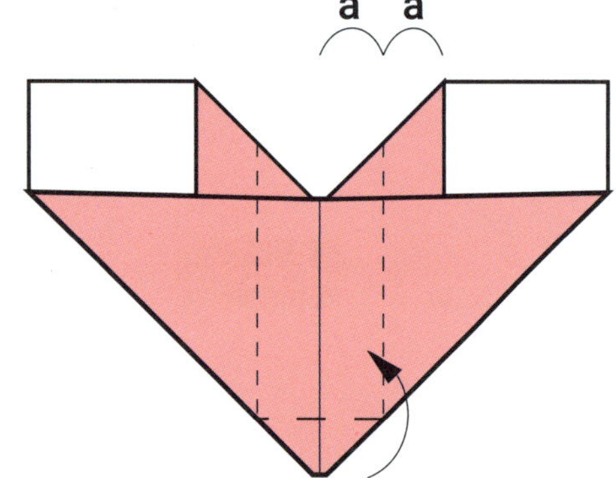

⑦ Fold and unfold triangular flaps at the top left and right corners as indicated.

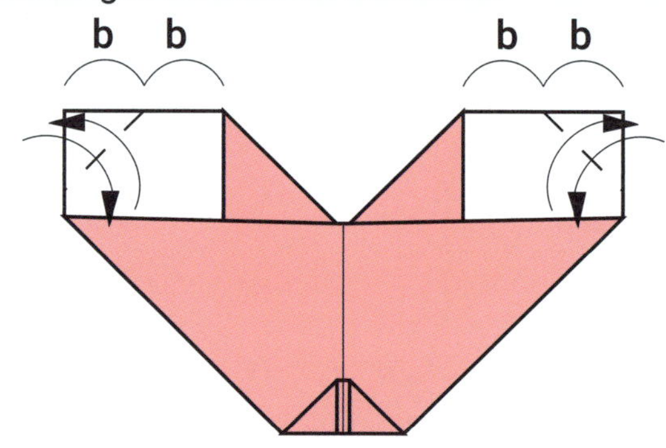

⑧ Fold the corners into triangular flaps that meet the creases from step 7, and then refold step 7.

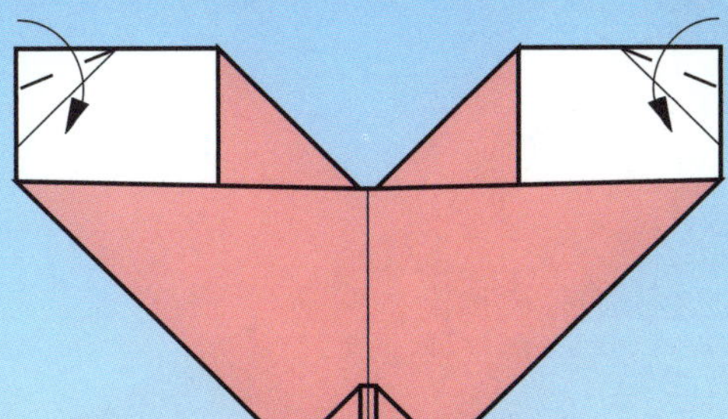

⑨ Turn the paper over.

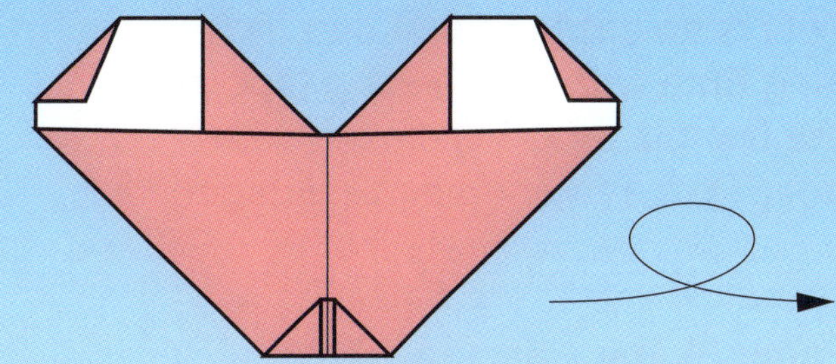

⑩ Fold in half.

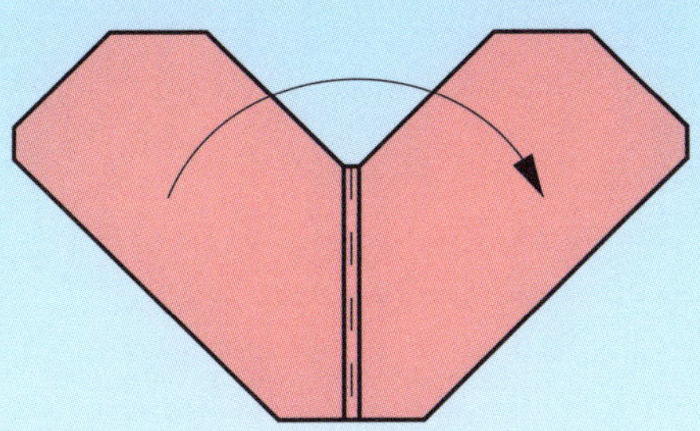

⑪ Fold the top layer to the width of "a."

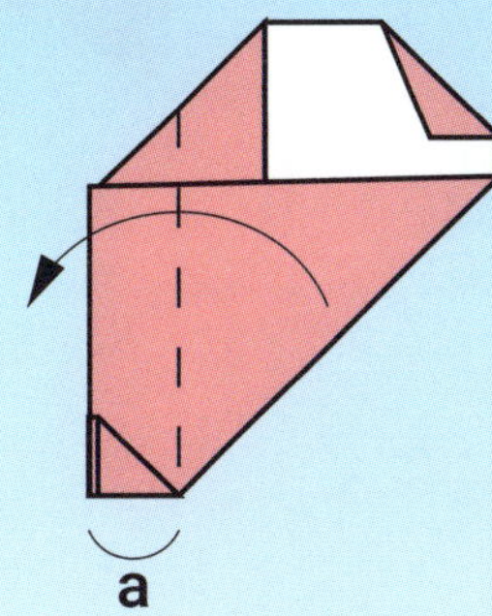
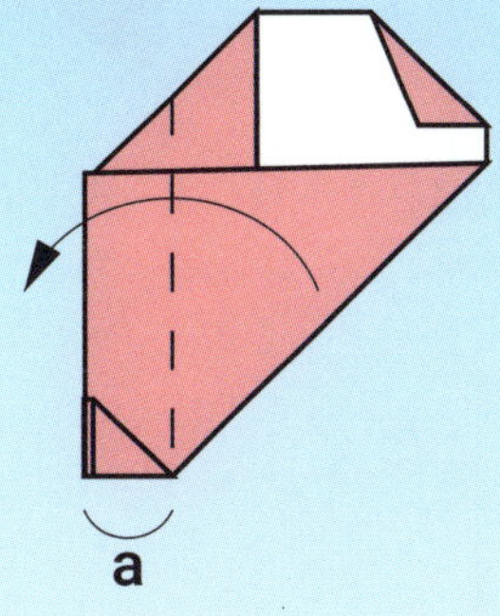

⑫ Turn the paper over.

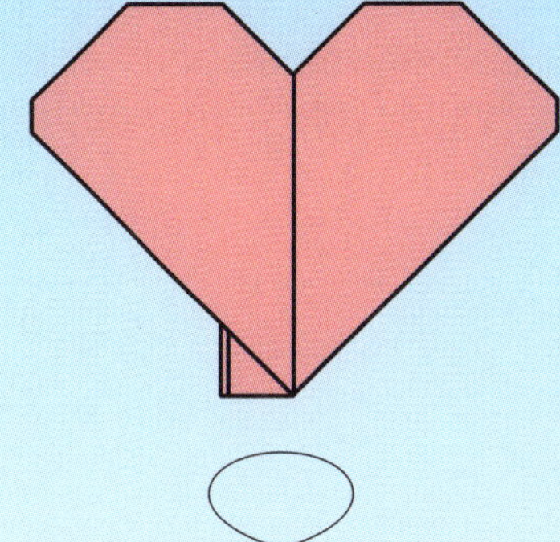

⑬ Fold the top layer to the width of "a."

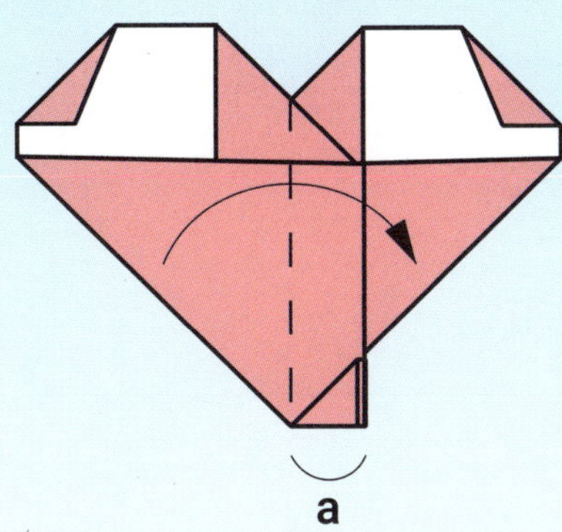

⑭ Fold the uppermost flap to the width of "c." Fold the opposite side in the same way.

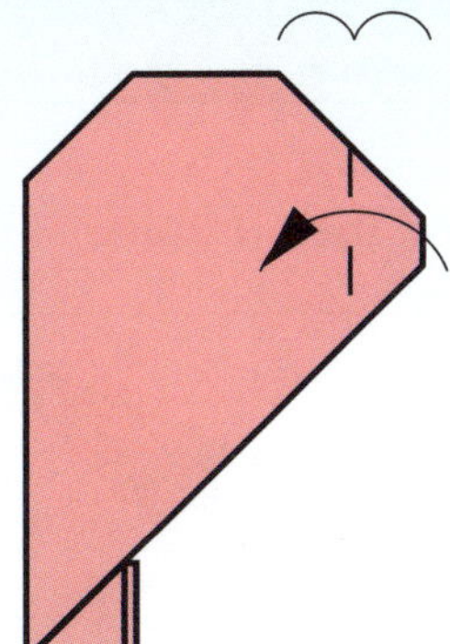

Open out the wings as shown in the 3D diagrams to the right. Completed.

Check after folding ▶ Flying Heart 3D Views

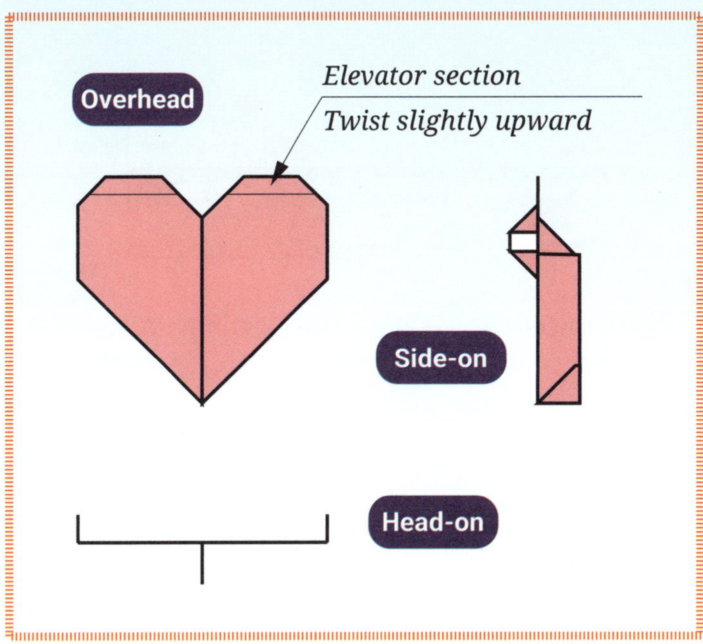

FLYER-GO

This is an airplane that can fly for a long time without needing tape, as the front is properly closed with a nose lock, reducing air resistance.

Paper Shape .. **Rectangular**

Difficulty .... ★★

① Mountain fold in half left to right, and then unfold. Valley fold in half bottom to top, and then unfold.

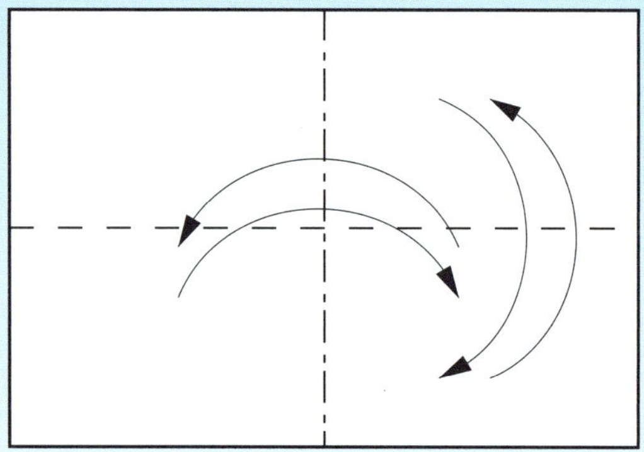

② Fold as indicated.

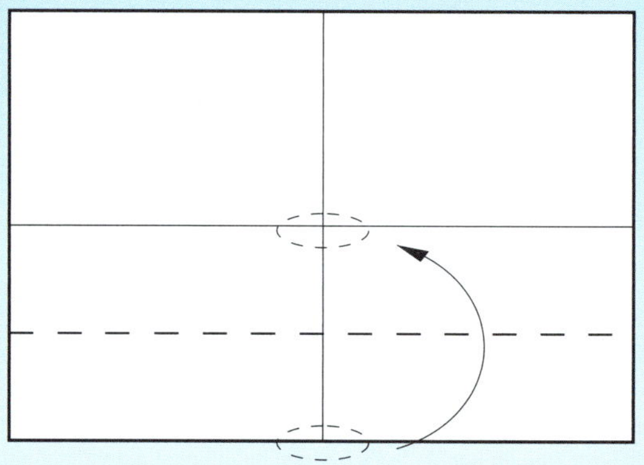

③ Fold the bottom corners to the center. Unfold.

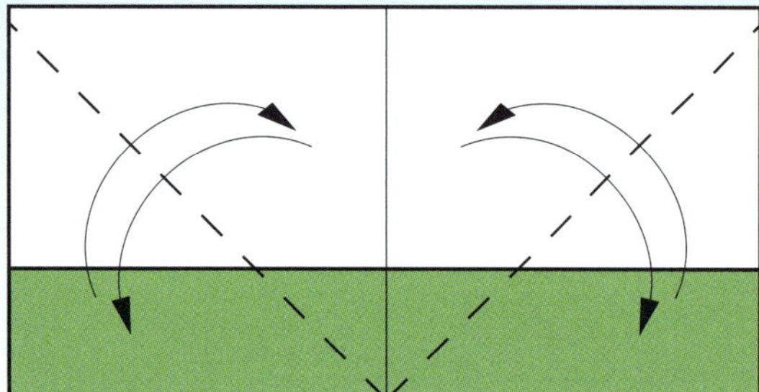

④ Fold as indicated.

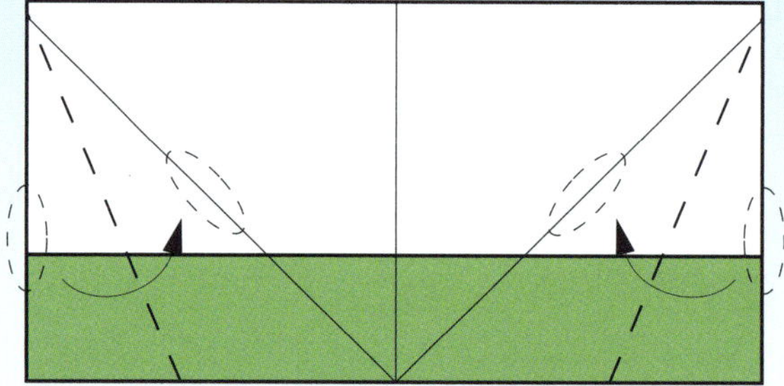

⑤ Fold inward again along the existing creases.

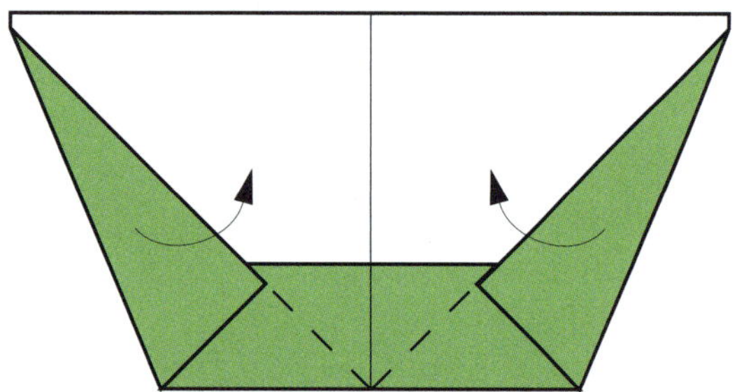

⑥ Fold as indicated, and then unfold.

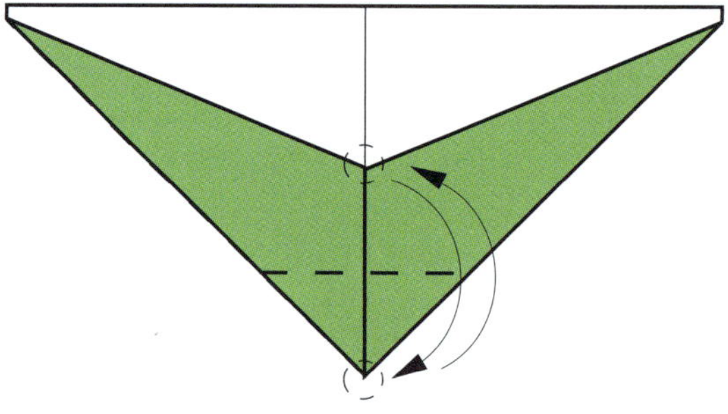

⑦ Fold in half to the back. Rotate 90° clockwise.

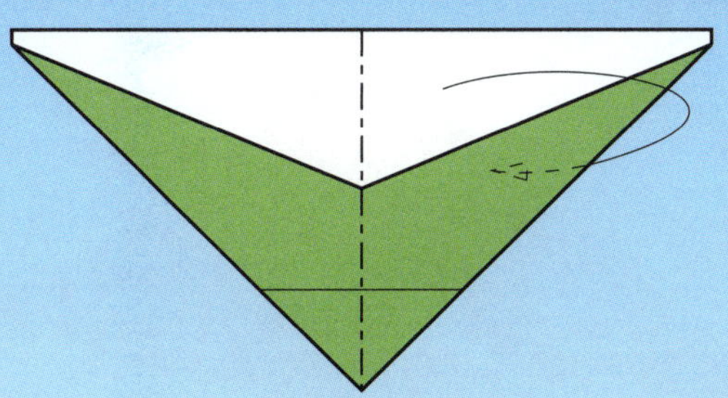

⑧ Fold the nose. Refer to the enlarged diagrams below.

Zoomed-in Diagrams: How to Fold the Nose

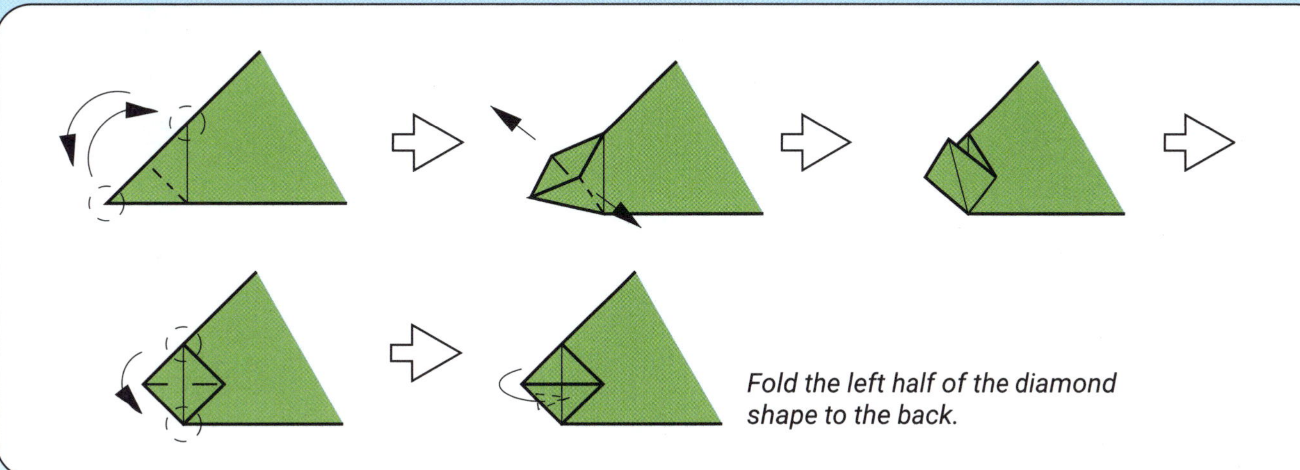

Fold the left half of the diamond shape to the back.

⑨ Fold the top layer to the width of "a." Fold the opposite side in the same way.

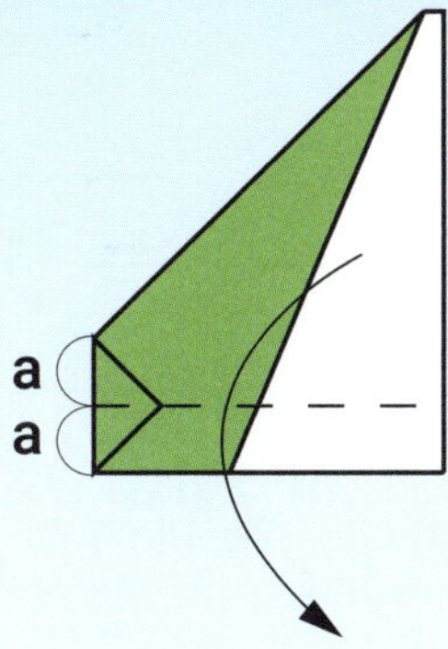

⑩ Fold the top layer to the width of "a." Fold the opposite side in the same way.

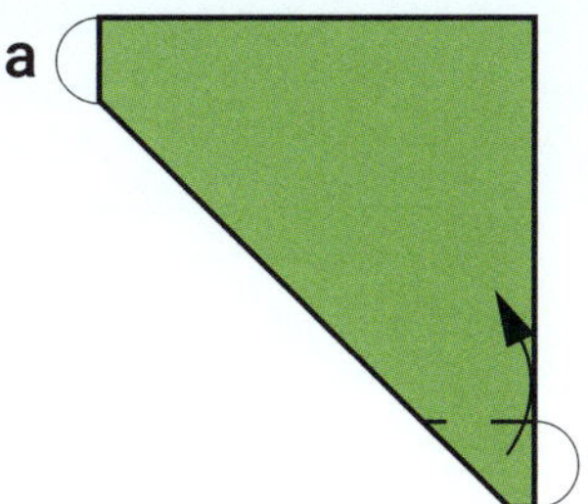

Open out the wings as shown in the 3D diagrams to the right. Completed.

Check after folding ▶ **Flyer-Go 3D Views**

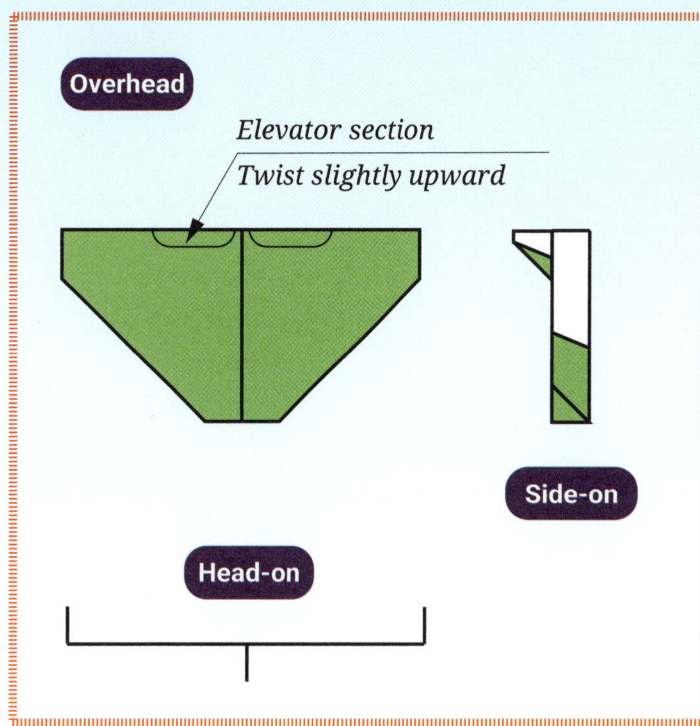

AIR SHOOTER

This plane is nose-locked to prevent the front end from opening up. The lock also serves as ballast, making it able to withstand strong upward launches and suitable for hang-time competitions.

Paper Shape .. **Rectangular**

Difficulty .... ★★

① Mountain fold in half left to right. Unfold. Valley fold in half bottom to top. Unfold.

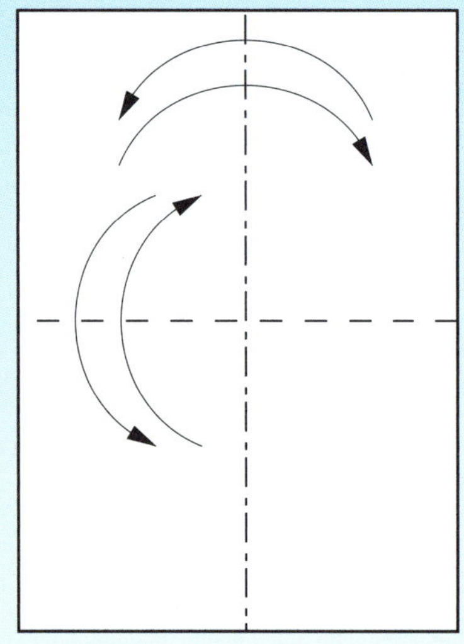

② Fold as indicated, and then unfold.

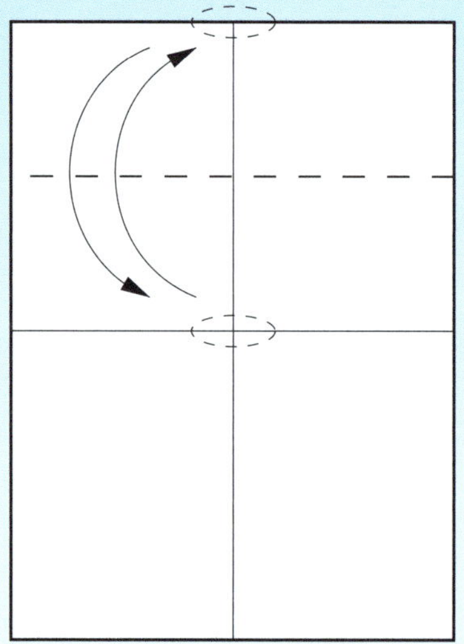

③ Fold as indicated.

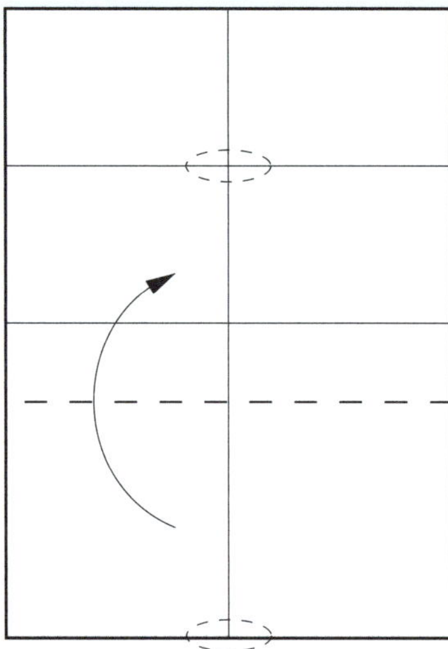

④ Fold the bottom corners to the crease. Unfold.

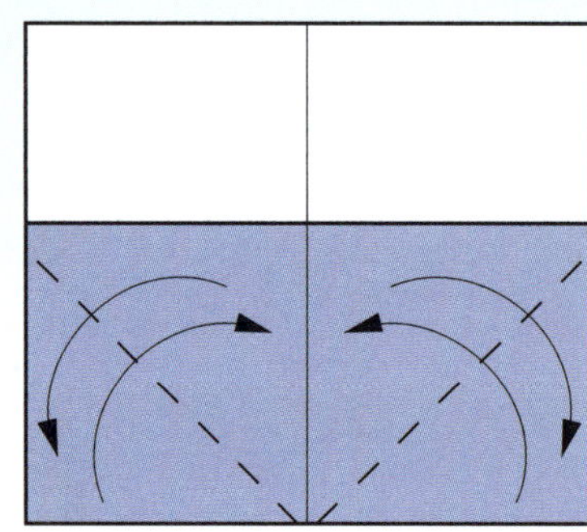

⑤ Fold as indicated.

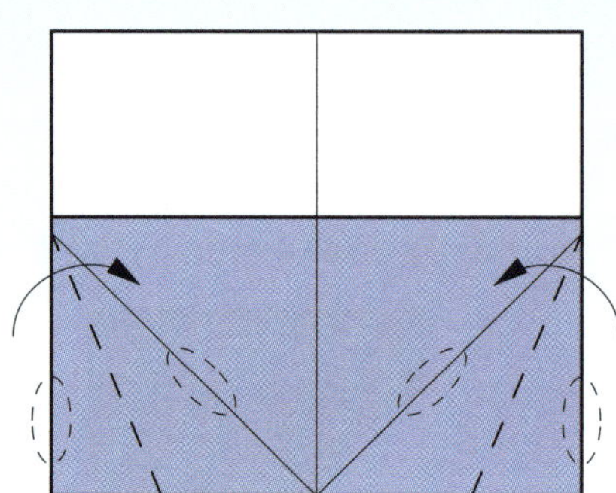

⑥ Fold inward again along the existing creases.

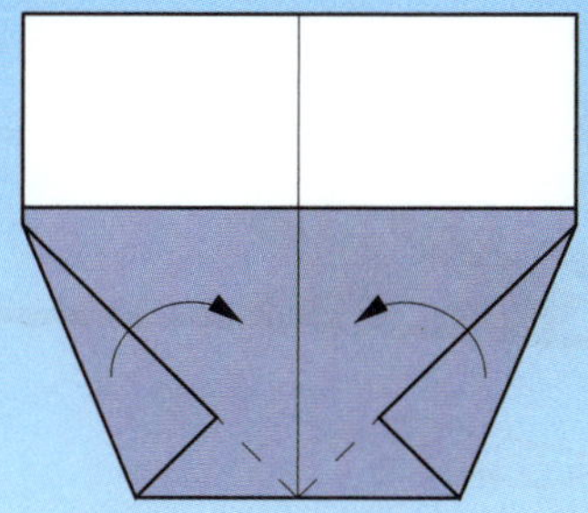

⑦ Fold the bottom point up as indicated, and then unfold. Then, fold in half to the back.

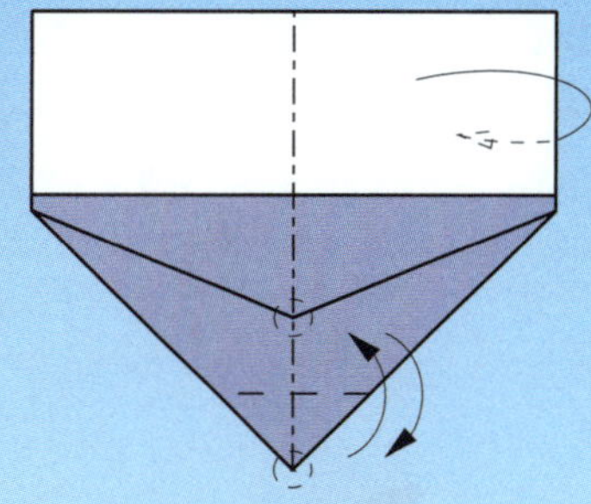

⑧ Fold the nose. Refer to the enlarged diagrams below.

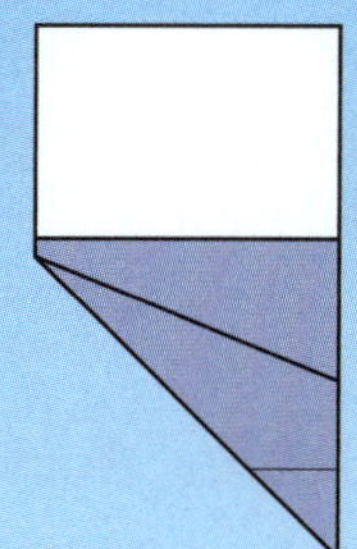

Zoomed-in Diagrams (Rotated View): How to Fold the Nose

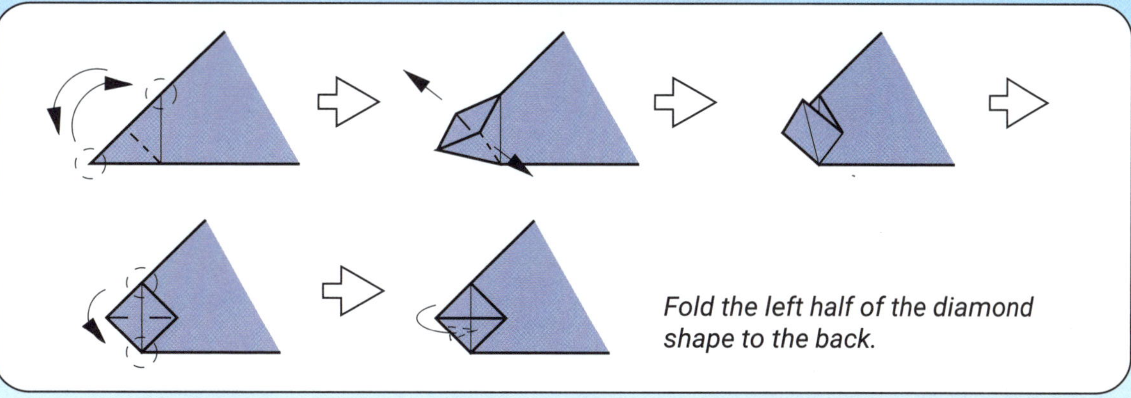

Fold the left half of the diamond shape to the back.

⑨ Fold as indicated, and then unfold.

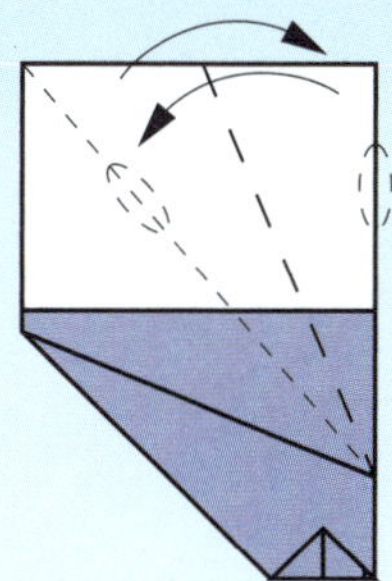

⑩ Inside reverse fold. Refer to page 6.

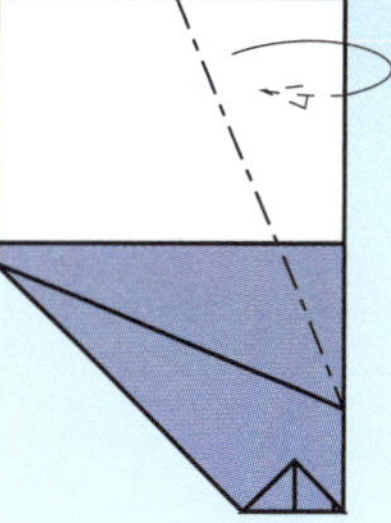

⑪ Fold the top layer at the indicated position. Fold the opposite side in the same way.

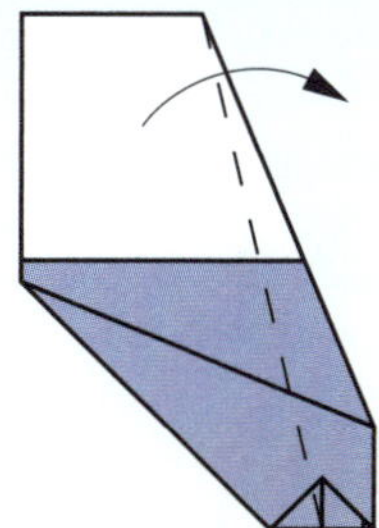

Open out the wings as shown in the 3D diagrams to the right. Completed.

Check after folding ▶ **Air Shooter 3D Views**

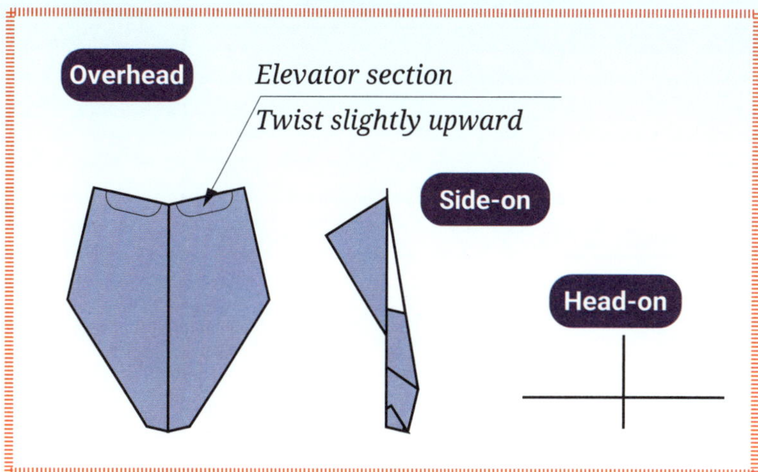

SLIDER

This paper airplane was named "Slider" because it smoothly glides. With its large wings and high stability, it's a well-designed model.

Paper Shape .. **Rectangular**

Difficulty .... ★★

① Valley fold in half left to right, and then unfold. Valley fold in half bottom to top, and then unfold. Turn the paper over.

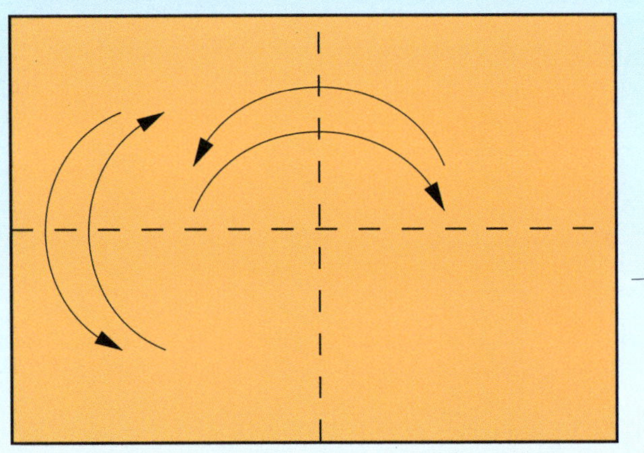

② Fold as indicated, and then unfold.

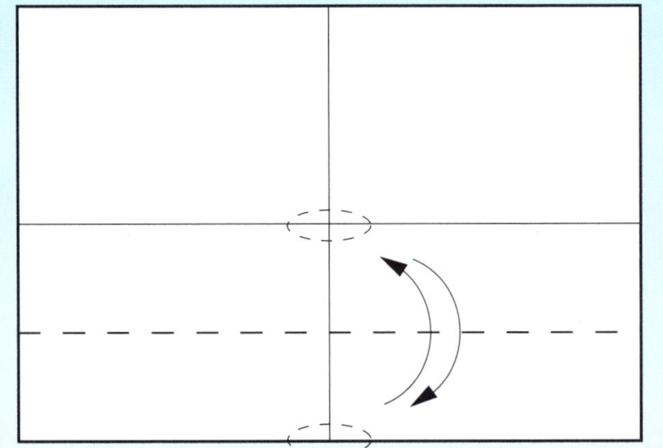

③ Fold as indicated.

④ Fold the bottom corners as indicated, and then unfold.

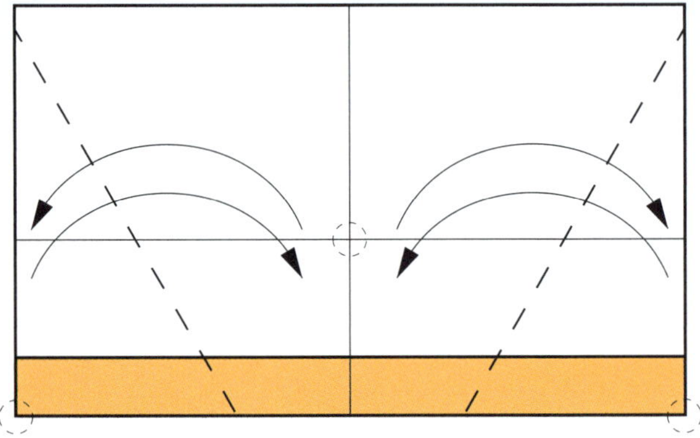

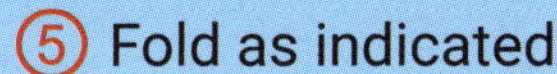

⑤ Fold as indicated.

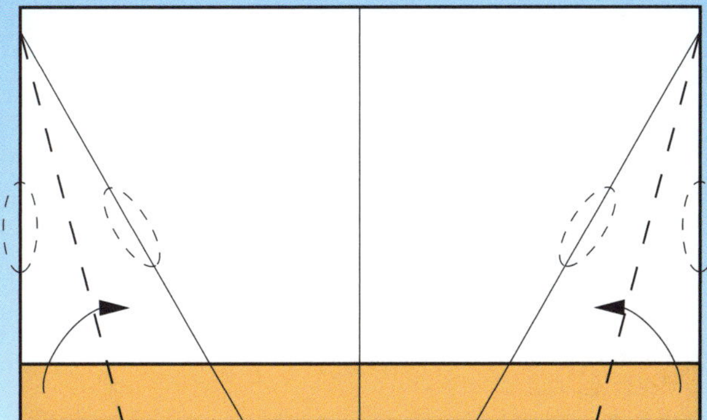

⑥ Fold inward again along the existing creases.

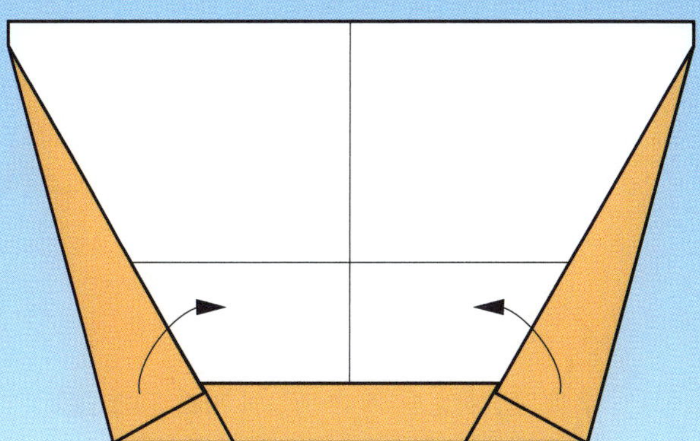

⑦ Fold as indicated.

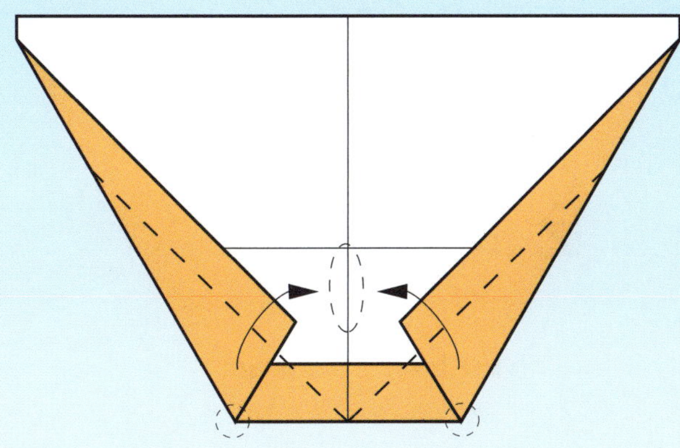

⑧ Fold the bottom point up as indicated, and then unfold.

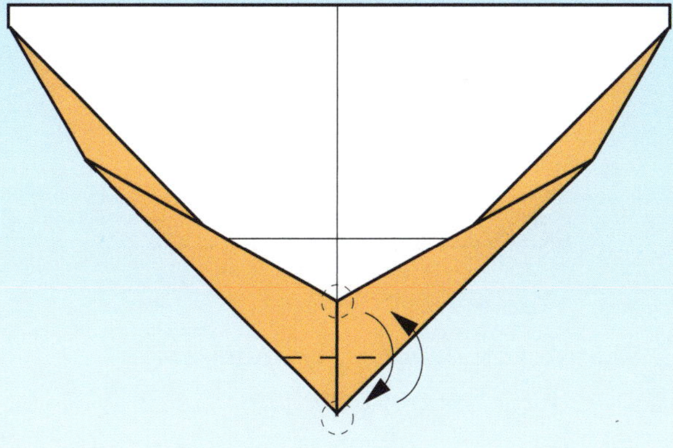

⑨ Fold in half to the back. Rotate 90° clockwise.

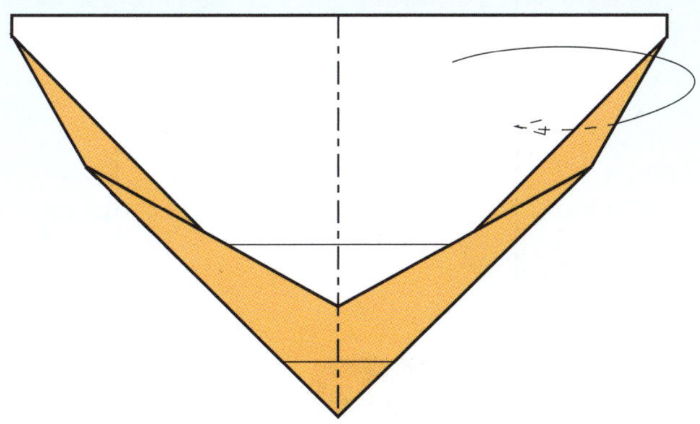

⑩ Fold the nose. Refer to the enlarged diagrams on page 22.

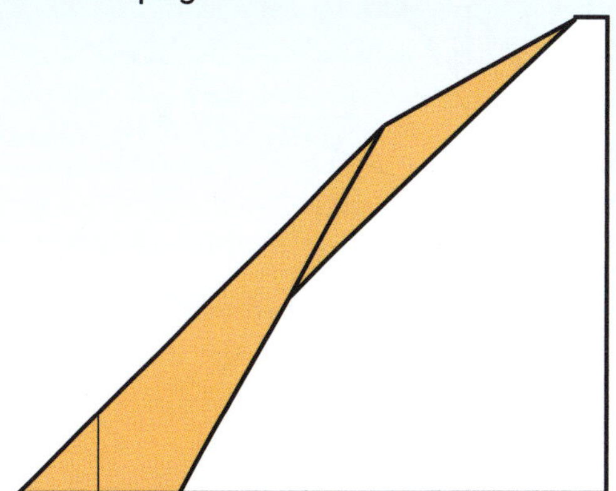

Zoomed-in Diagrams: How to Fold the Nose

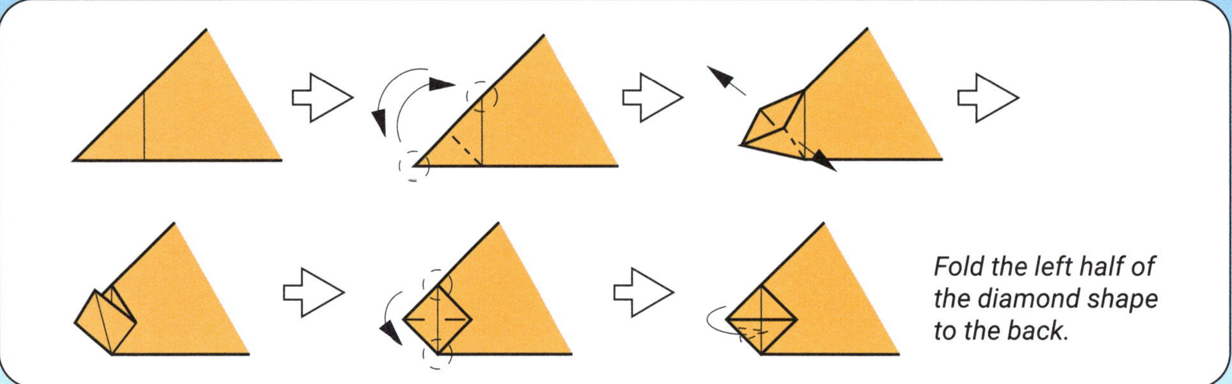

⑪ Fold as indicated, and then unfold.

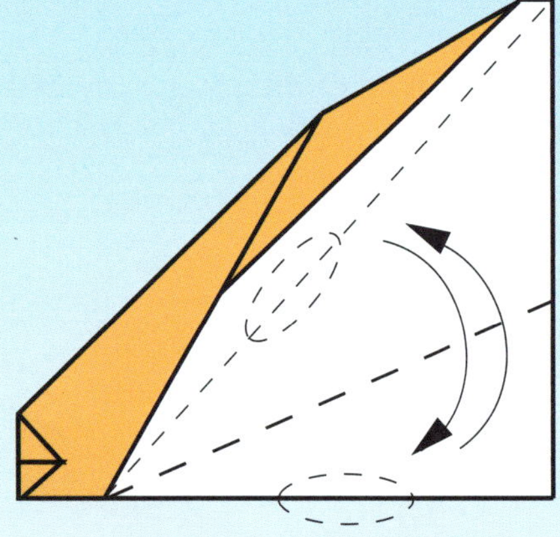

⑫ Inside reverse fold. Refer to page 6.

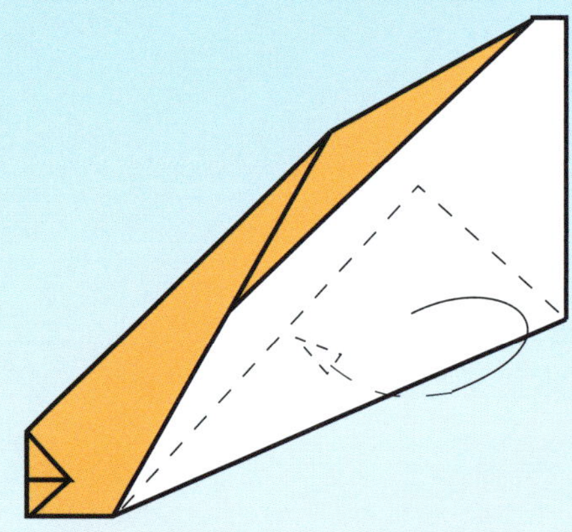

⑬ Fold the top layer at the indicated position. Fold the opposite side in the same way.

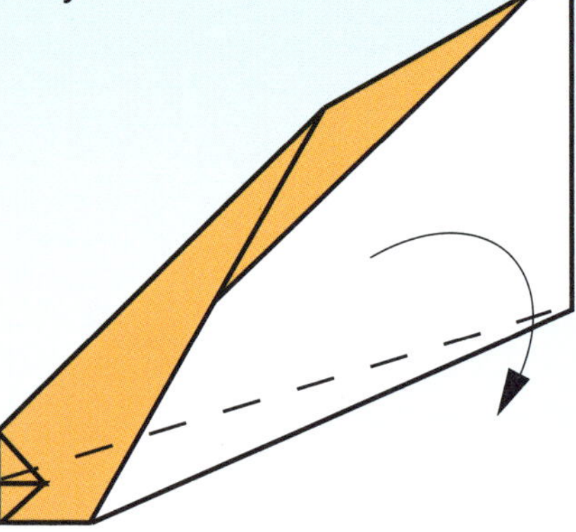

Open out the wings as shown in the 3D diagrams to the right. Completed.

Check after folding ▶ Slider 3D Views

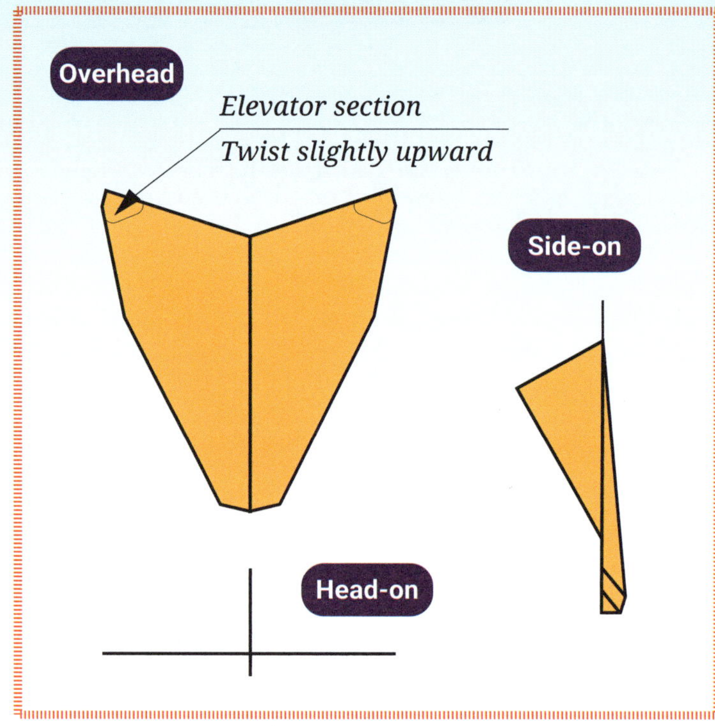

ICARUS

This plane has clean fold lines, making it easy to fold while maintaining a well-balanced shape. The design has been improved by removing the vertical stabilizer, allowing it to withstand vigorous vertical launches. When launched from a high place and carried by the wind, it glides for a long time.

Paper Shape .. **Rectangular**

Difficulty .... ★★★

① Fold in half, unfold, and then flip it over.

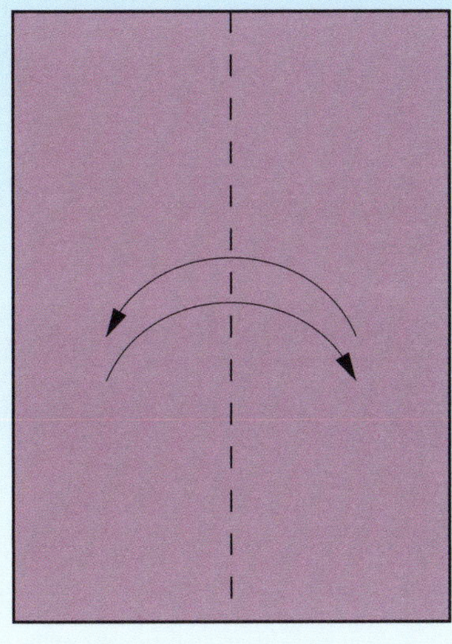

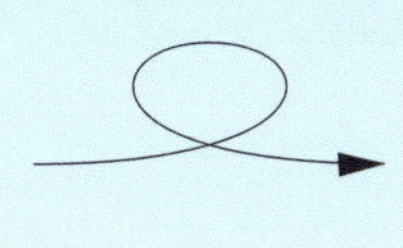

② Fold the corner flaps to the center crease.

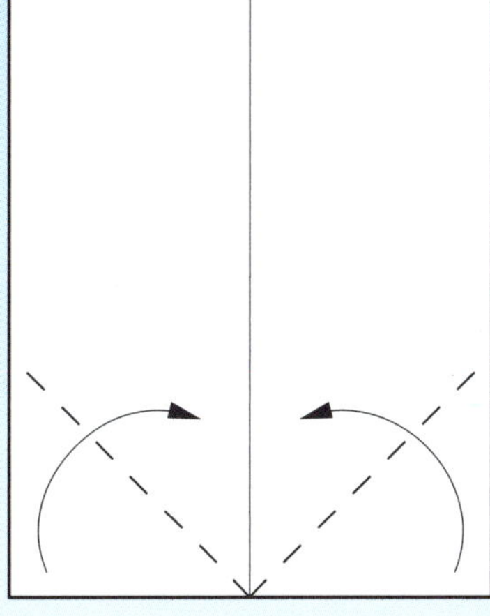

③ Fold as indicated.

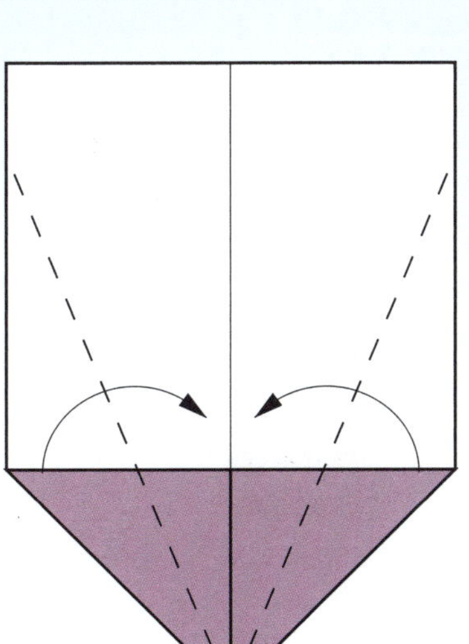

④ Fold bottom to top.

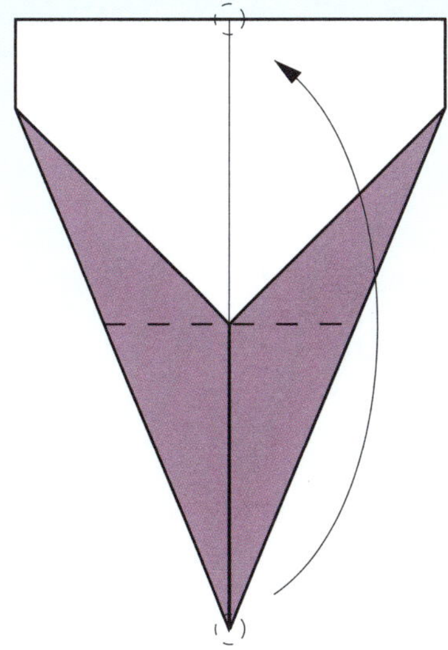

⑤ Fold as indicated.

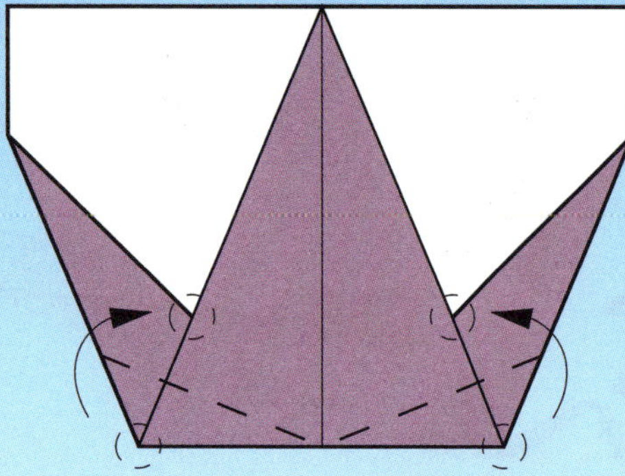

⑥ Fold the flap down along the indicated span.

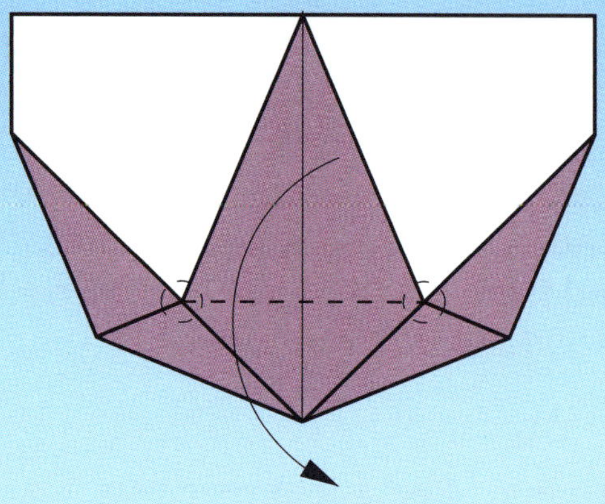

⑦ Fold the triangular tip using width "a" as a guide.

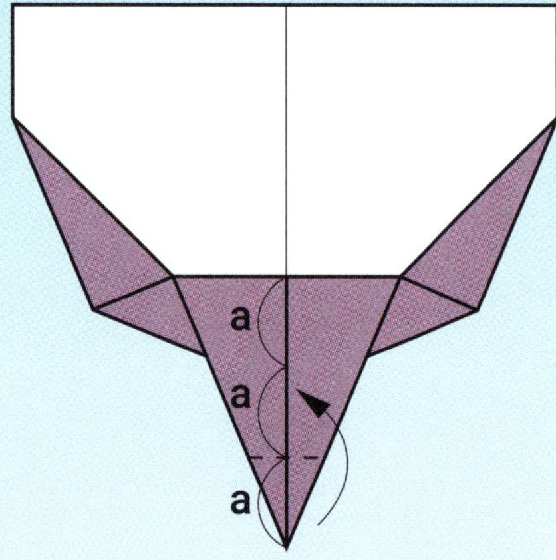

⑧ Fold in half to the back.

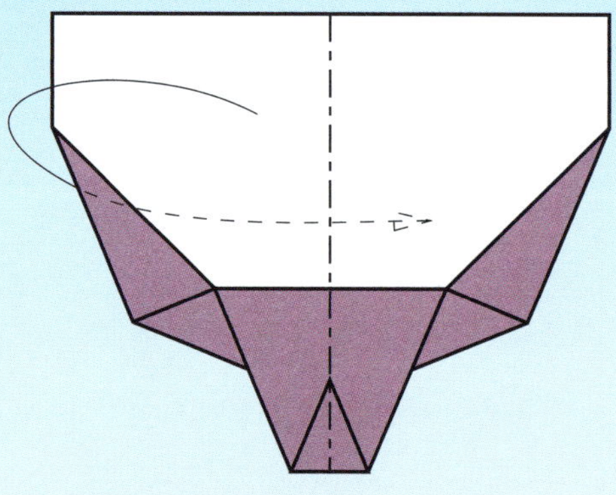

⑨ Fold the top layer as indicated. Fold the opposite side in the same way.

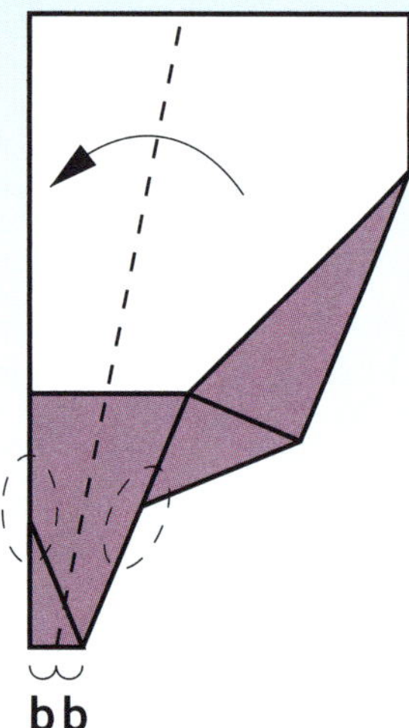

Open out the wings as shown in the 3D diagrams to the right. Completed.

Check after folding ▶ Icarus 3D Views

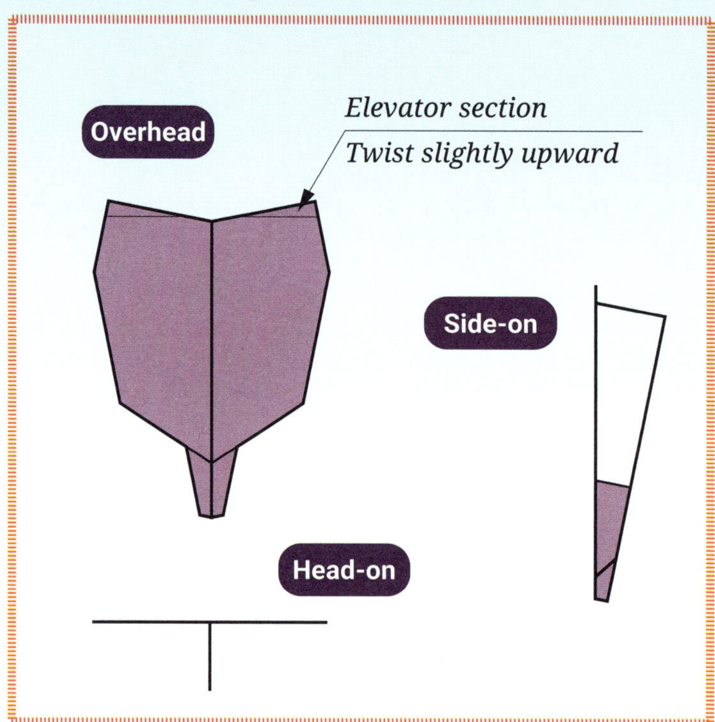

SIREN

By reversing the initial fold of the Icarus (page 23), the shape of the nose changes.

Paper Shape .. Rectangular

Difficulty .... ★★★

① Fold in half, and then unfold.

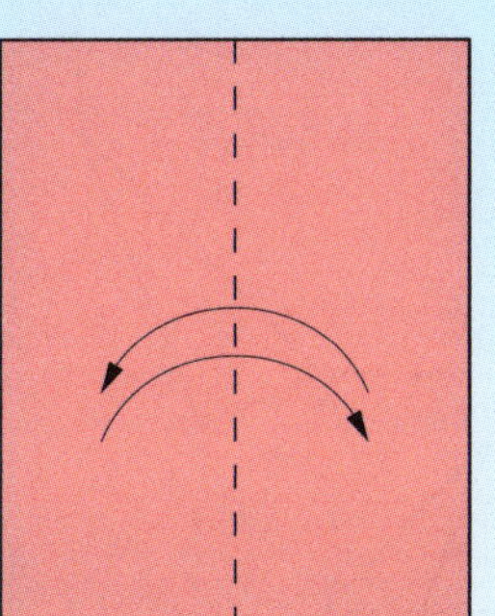

② Fold the corner flaps to the center crease. Then, turn it over.

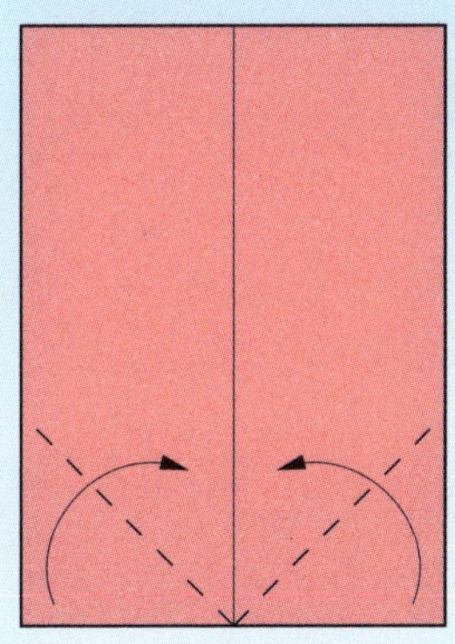

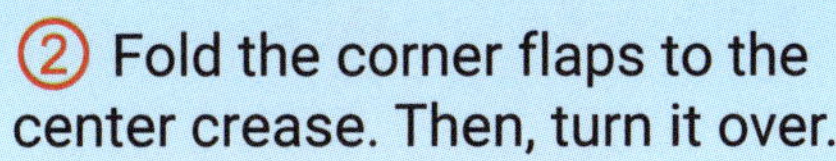

③ Fold as indicated.

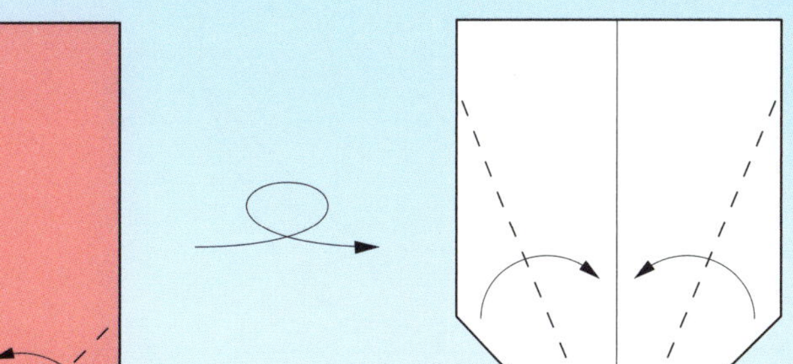

④ Swing the flaps out from behind.

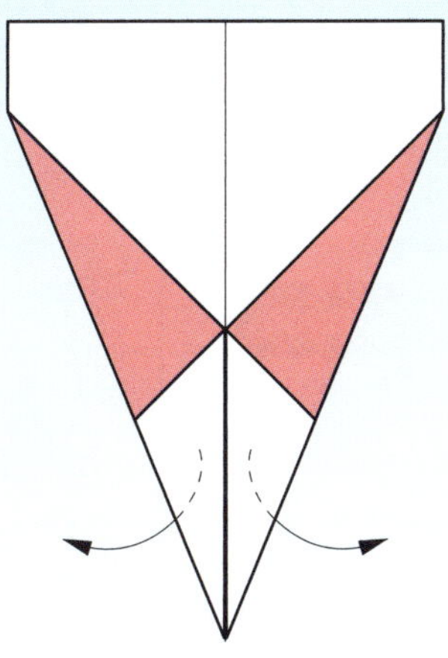

⑤ Fold as indicated.

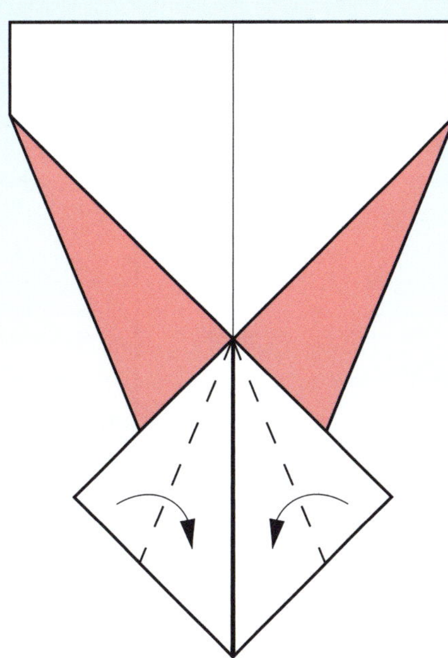

⑥ Fold bottom to top.

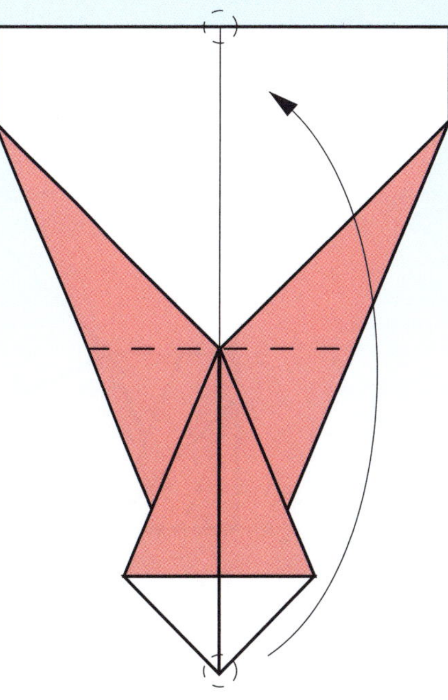

⑦ Fold as indicated.

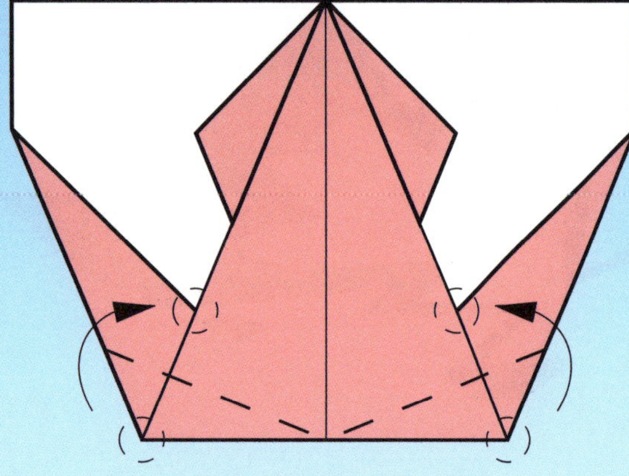

⑧ Fold the flap down along the indicated span.

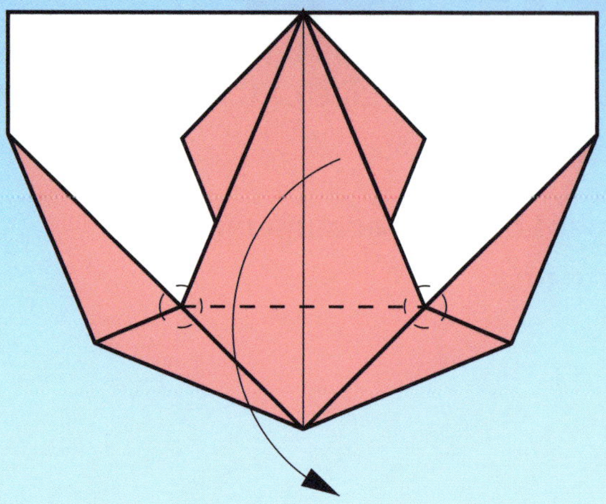

⑨ Fold as indicated.

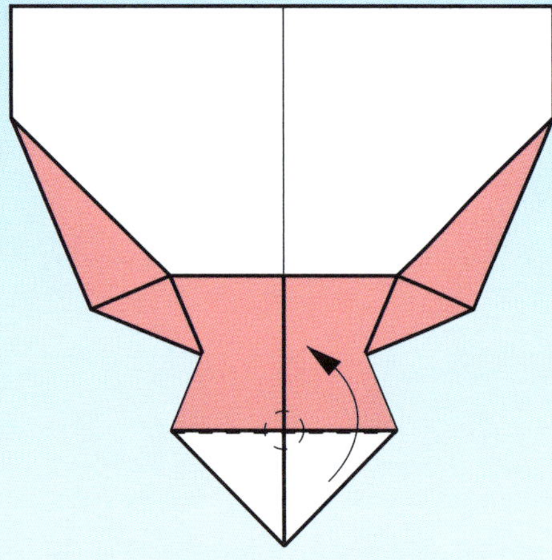

⑩ Fold in half to the back.

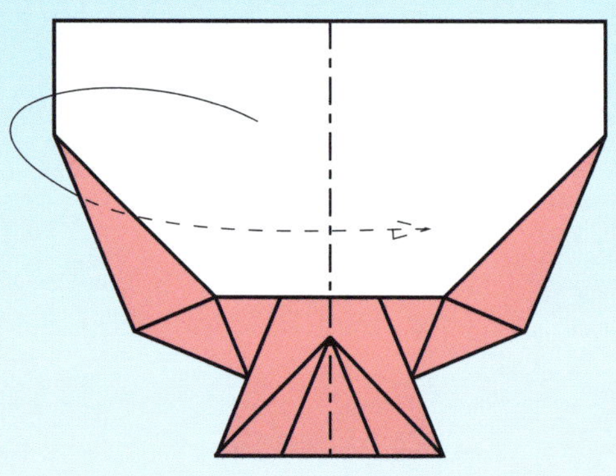

⑪ Fold the top layer to the width of "a." Fold the opposite side in the same way.

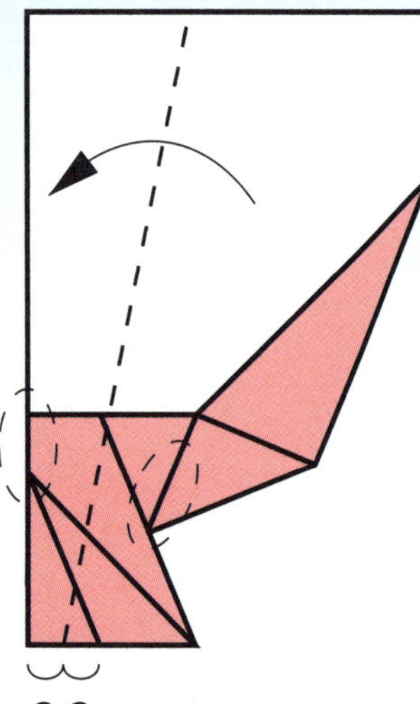

Open out the wings as shown in the 3D diagrams to the right. Completed.

Check after folding ▶ Siren 3D Views

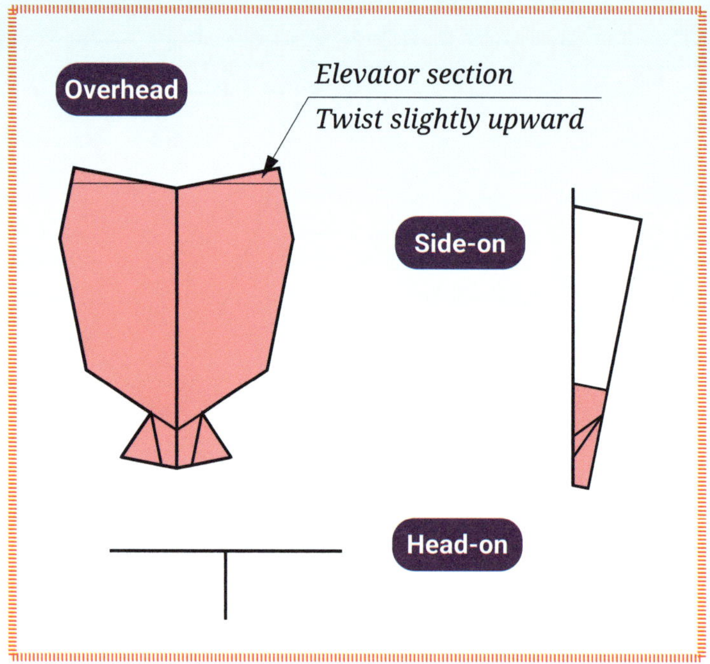

POSEIDON I

The folding process is similar to the Siren (page 25) up to a certain point. By adding "ears" to the nose section, this design is not only fun to fly but also visually unique and enjoyable.

Paper Shape .. **Rectangular**

Difficulty .... ★★★★

① Fold in half, and then unfold.

② Fold the corner flaps to the center crease. Then, turn it over.

③ Fold as indicated.

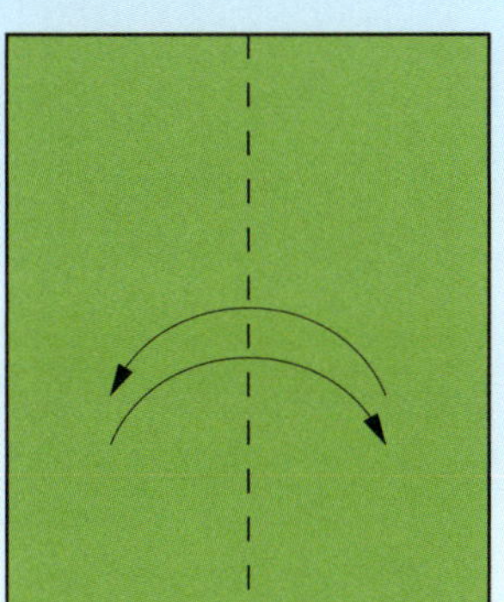

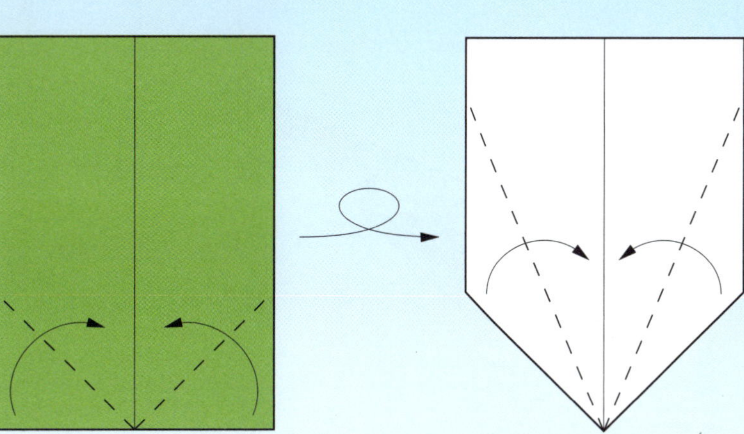

④ Turn the paper over.

⑤ Open up the triangular flaps.

⑥ Fold bottom to top.

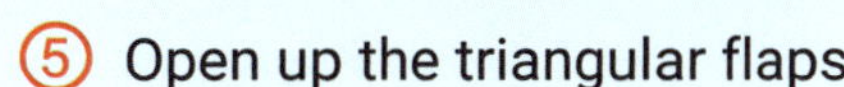

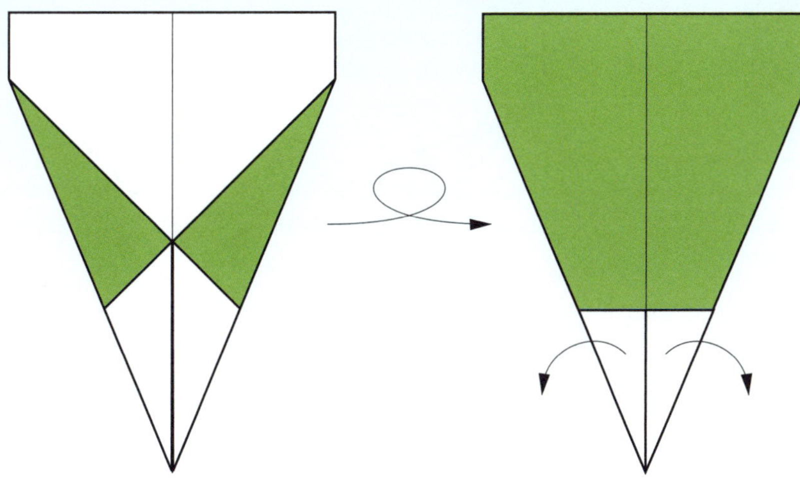

⑦ Turn the paper over.

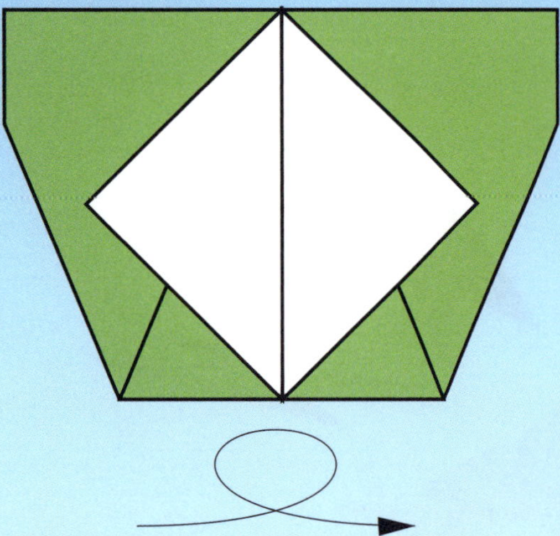

⑧ Fold up the bottom corners along the edges.

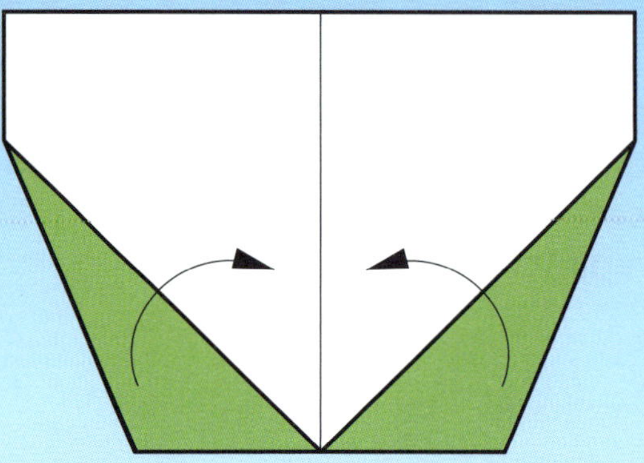

⑨ Fold along the indicated span. Turn over.

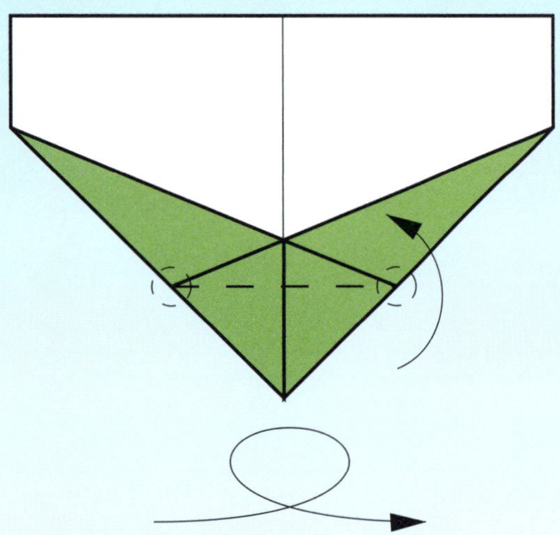

⑩ Swing open the flap at the indicated hinge.

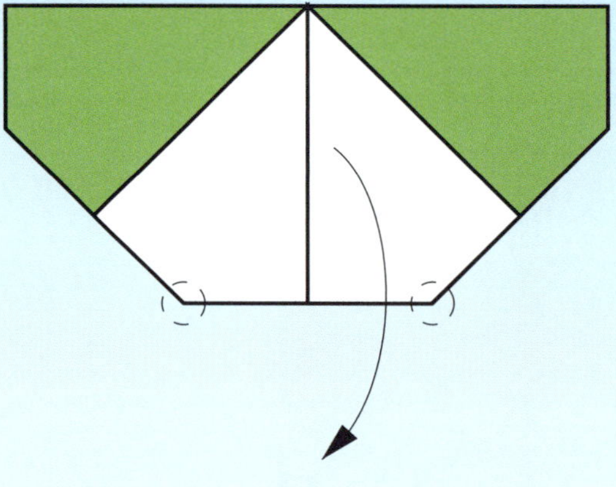

⑪ Turn the paper over.

⑫ Fold the diamond shape in half.

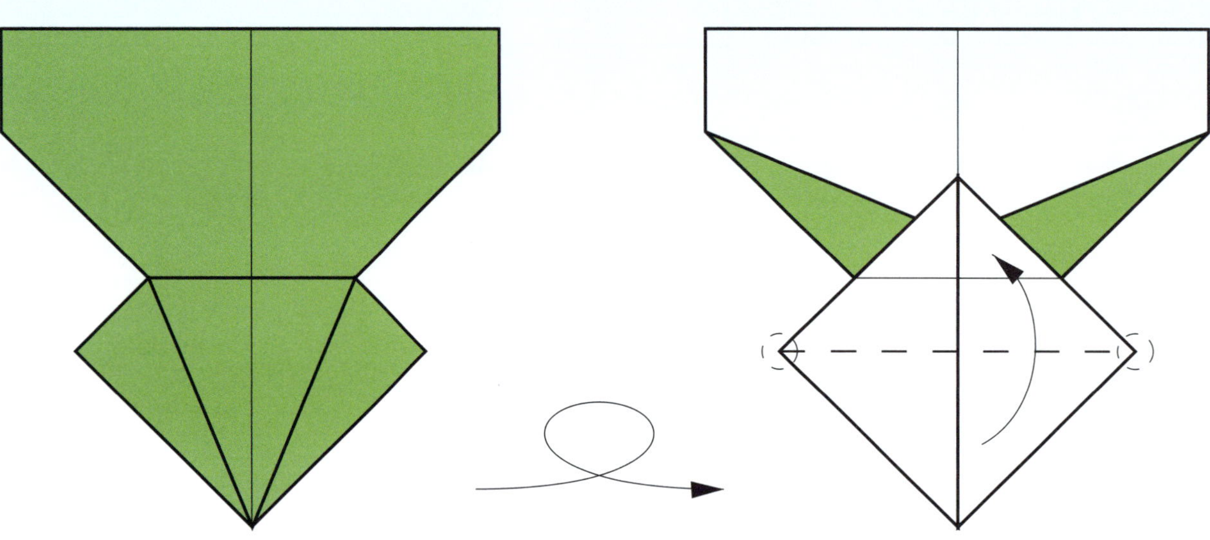

⑬ Fold triangular flaps as indicated.

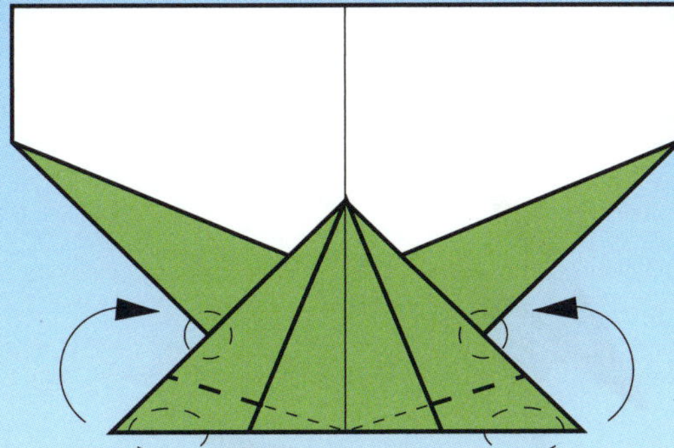

⑭ Fold in half to the back.

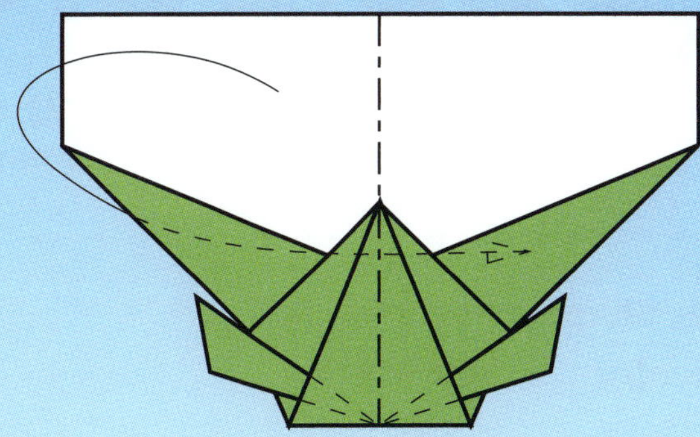

⑮ Fold the top layer to the width of "a." Fold the opposite side in the same way.

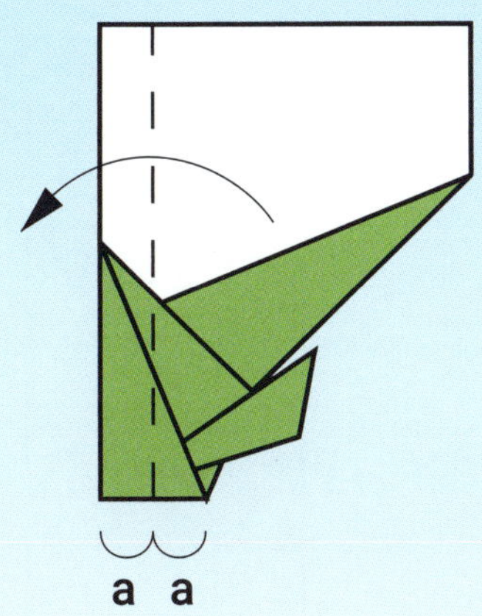

⑯ Fold the top layer to the width of "a." Fold the opposite side in the same way.

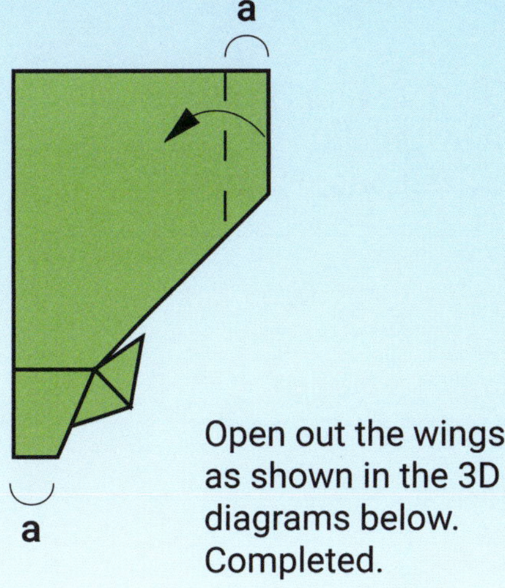

Open out the wings as shown in the 3D diagrams below. Completed.

Check after folding ▶ **Poseidon I 3D Views**

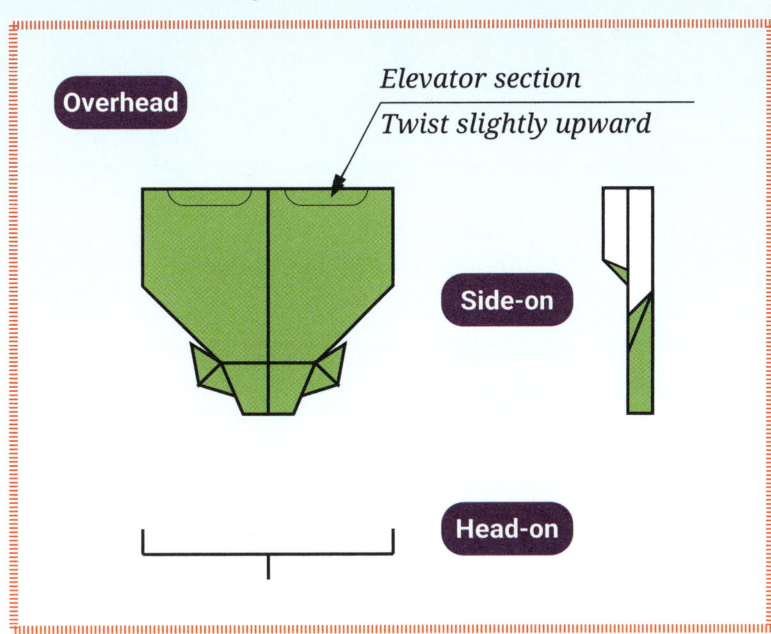

POSEIDON II

The shape and flight performance are similar to those of Poseidon I (page 27), but the folding method is completely different.

Paper Shape .. Rectangular

Difficulty .... ★★★★★

① Valley fold in half left to right. Unfold. Then, valley fold in half bottom to top.

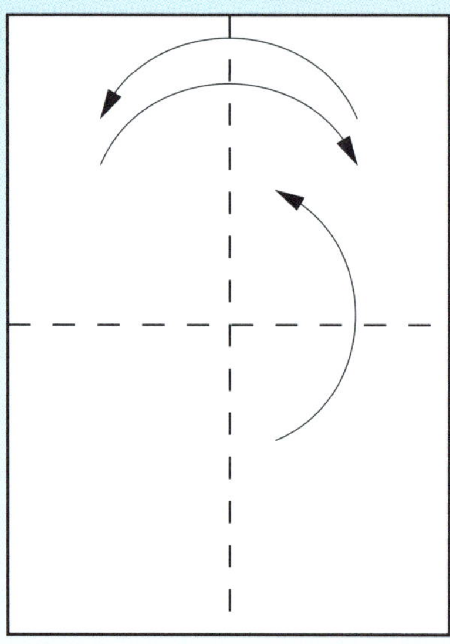

② Fold in half again.

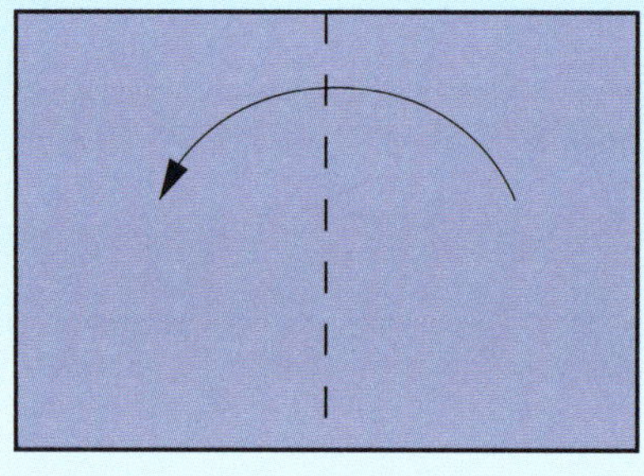

③ Open the top layer while folding the lower side into a triangle.

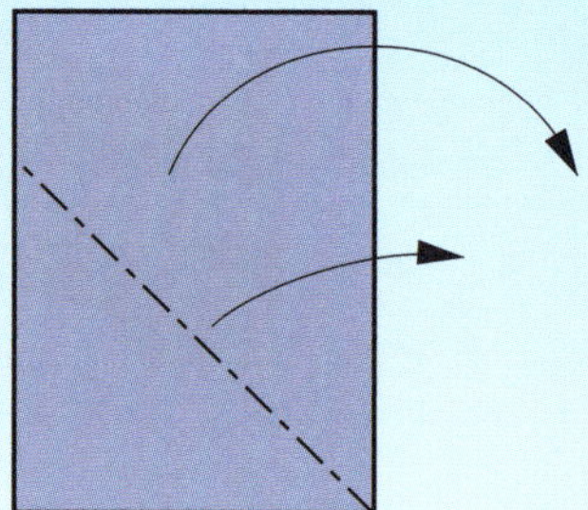

④ Swing the uppermost left flap to the right.

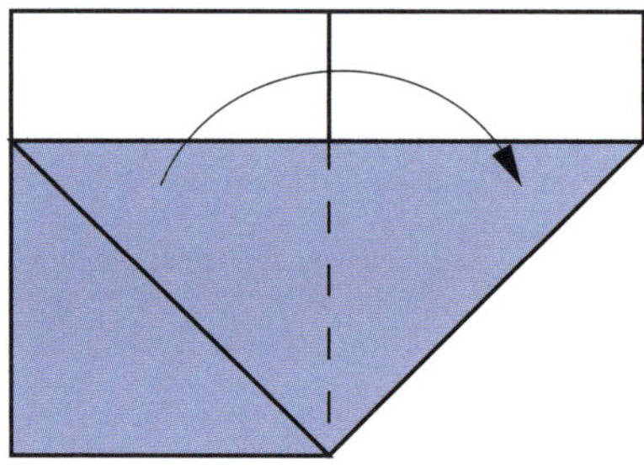

⑤ Repeat step 3, opening the top layer while folding the lower side into a triangle.

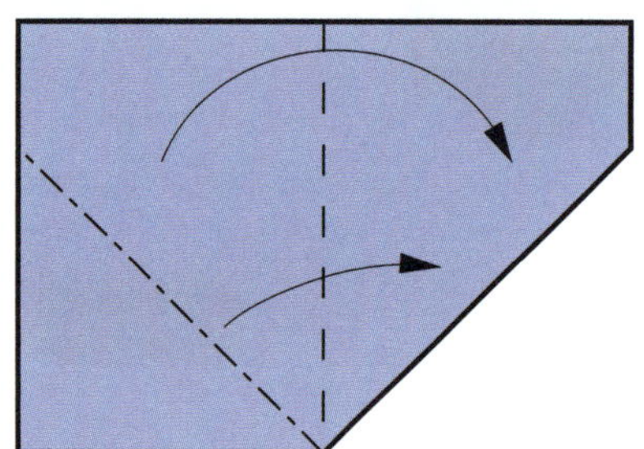

⑥ Swing the uppermost right flap to the left.

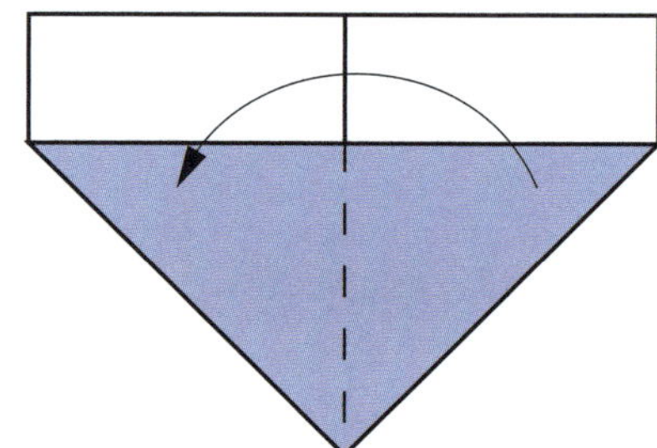

⑦ Fold the top corners of the uppermost flaps to the center crease, and then unfold.

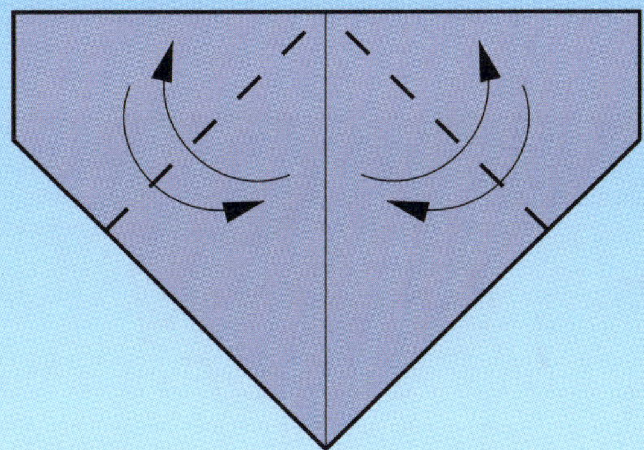

⑧ Fold the right-side top edge to the left-side crease made in step 7, and then unfold. Repeat on the other side.

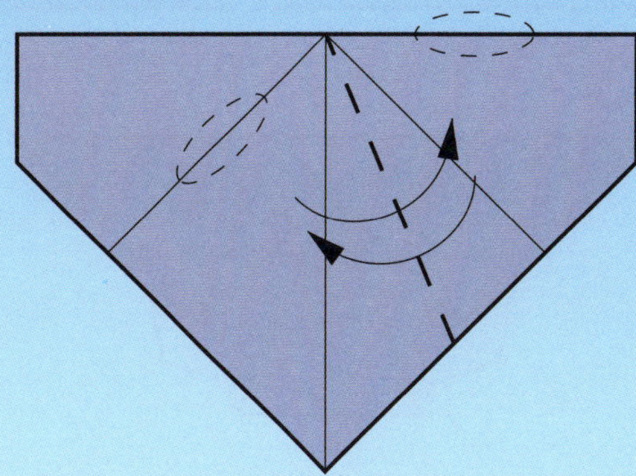

⑨ Fold the bottom point up along the indicated span, and then unfold.

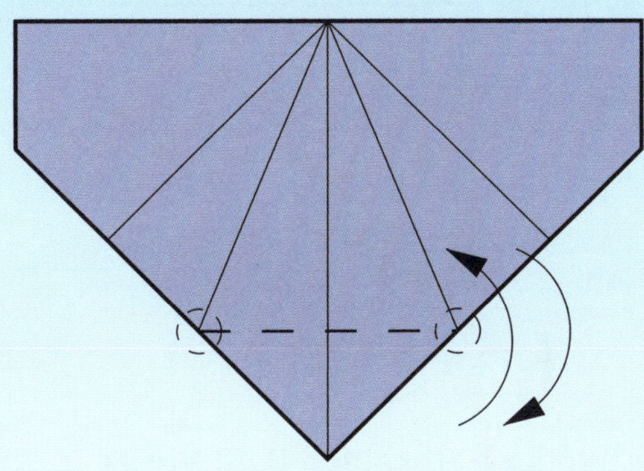

⑩ Open the top layer along the crease made in step 9, and collapse the paper by inverting the step-8 creases into mountain folds and refolding along the step-7 valley folds.

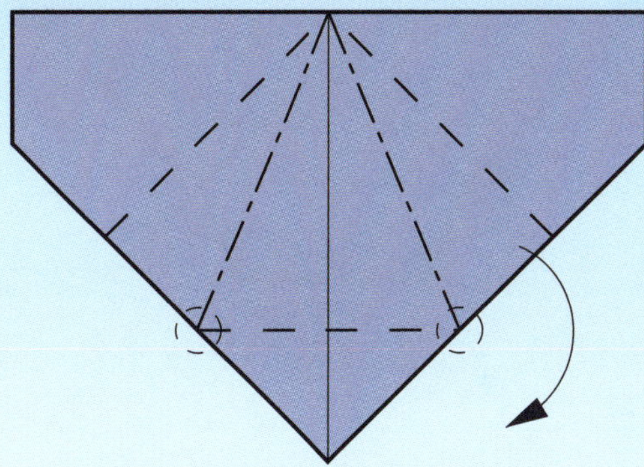

⑪ Fold the diamond shape in half along the indicated span.

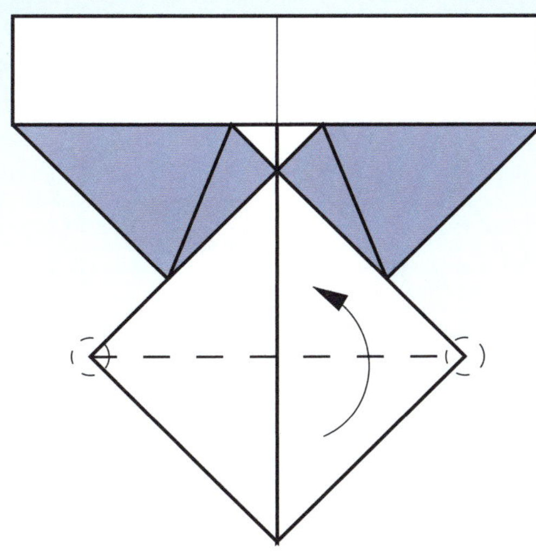

⑫ Fold triangular flaps as indicated.

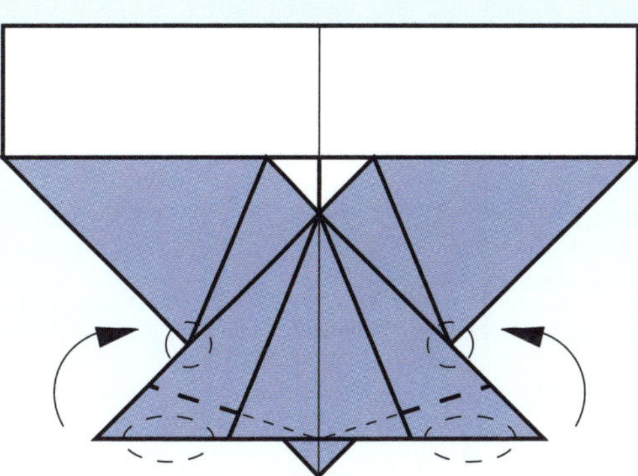

⑬ Turn the paper over.

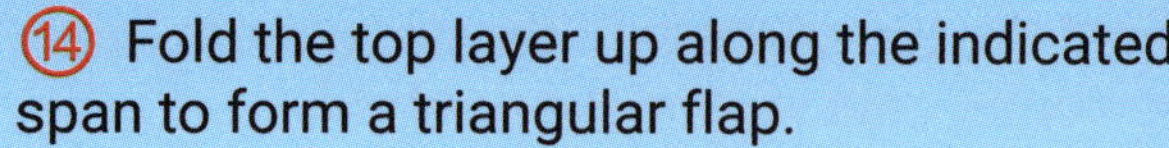

⑭ Fold the top layer up along the indicated span to form a triangular flap.

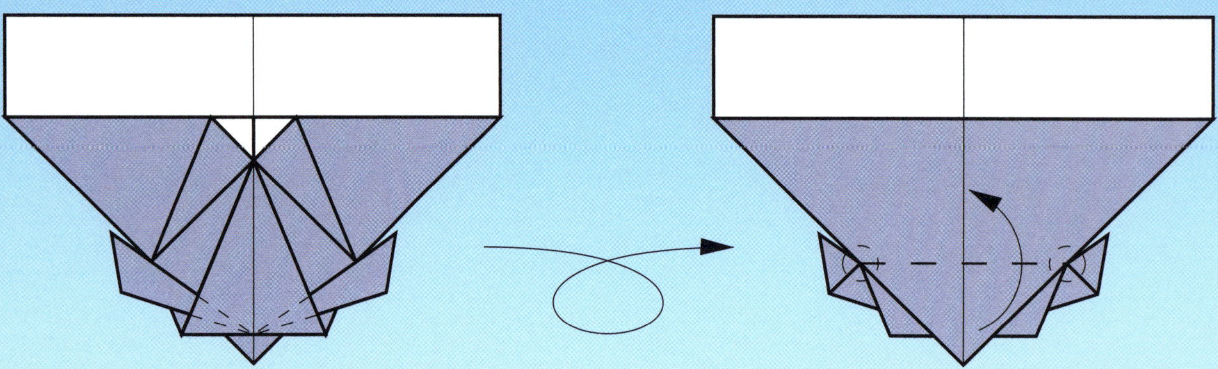

⑮ Fold in half.

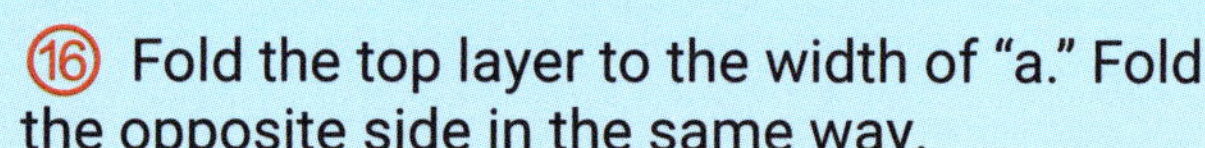

⑯ Fold the top layer to the width of "a." Fold the opposite side in the same way.

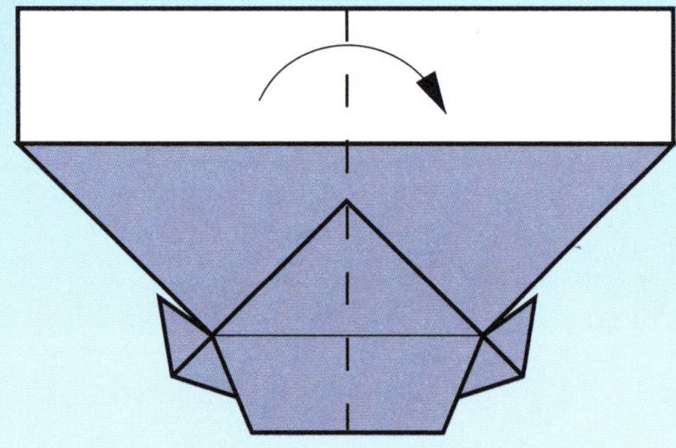

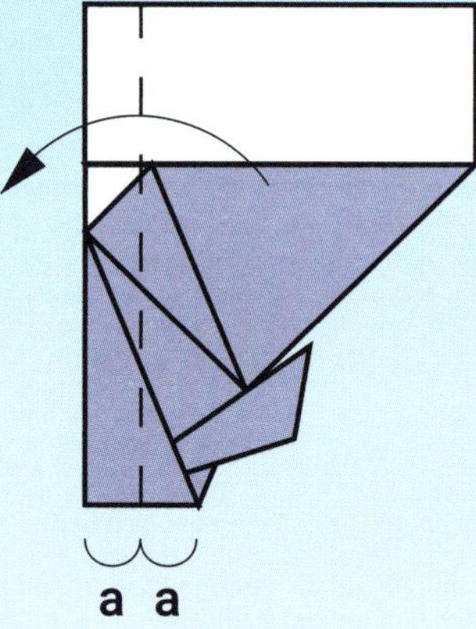

⑰ Fold the top layer to the width of "a." Fold the opposite side in the same way.

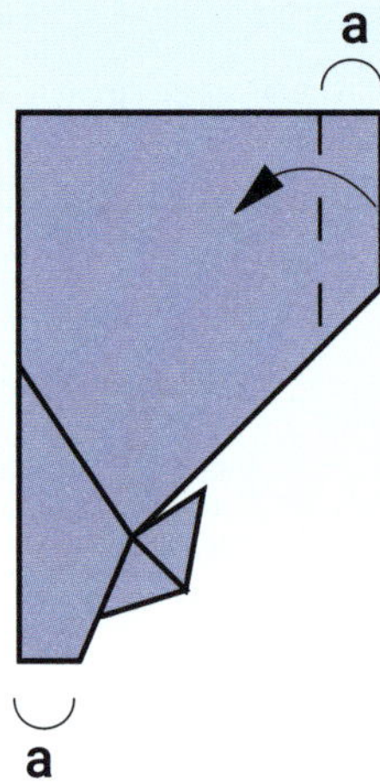

Open out the wings as shown in the 3D diagrams to the right. Completed.

Check after folding ▶ Poseidon II 3D Views

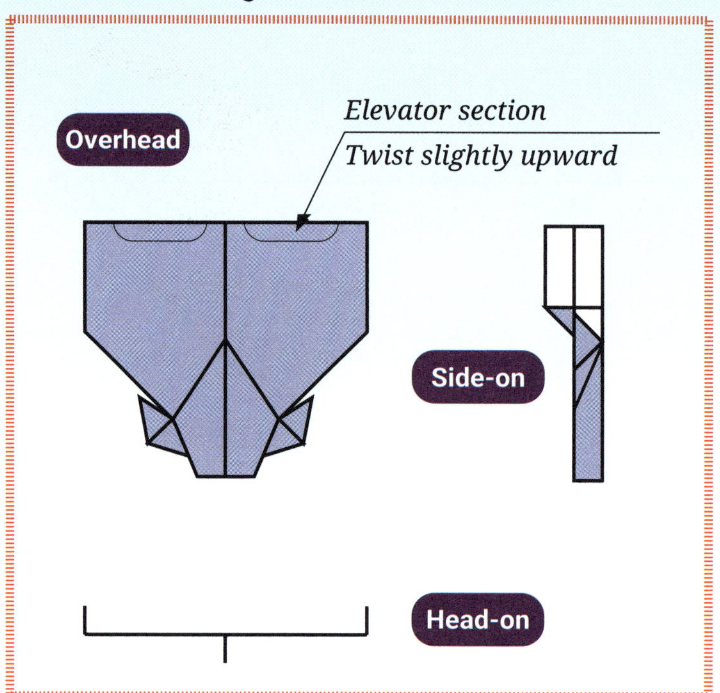

SPEEDER

This plane's center of gravity is slightly forward, but the wings have a large surface area. With properly adjusted elevators, you'll be poised to set flight records!

Paper Shape .. Rectangular

Difficulty .... ★★★★

① Fold in half, unfold, and then turn it over.

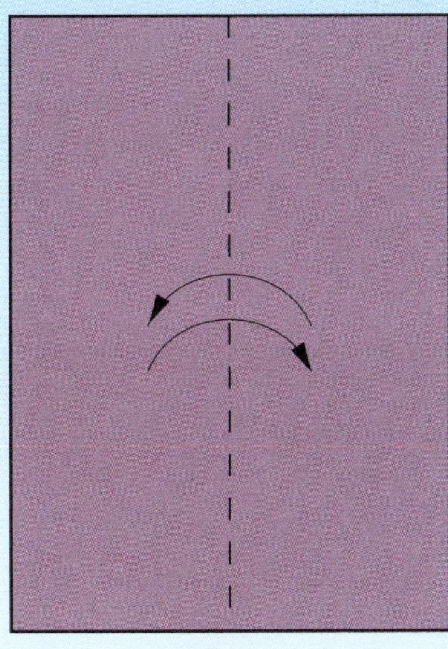

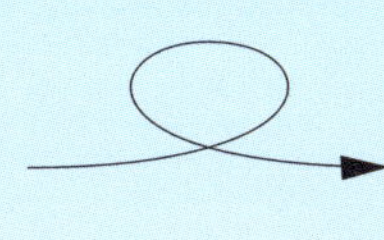

② Fold in half and unfold.

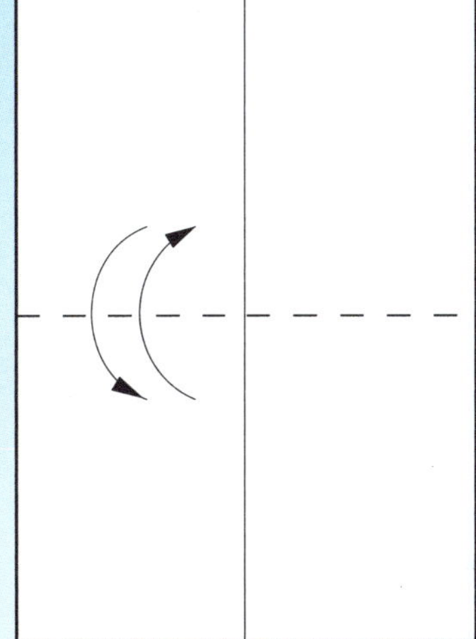

③ Fold the top and bottom edges to the center. Unfold after each.

④ Fold as indicated.

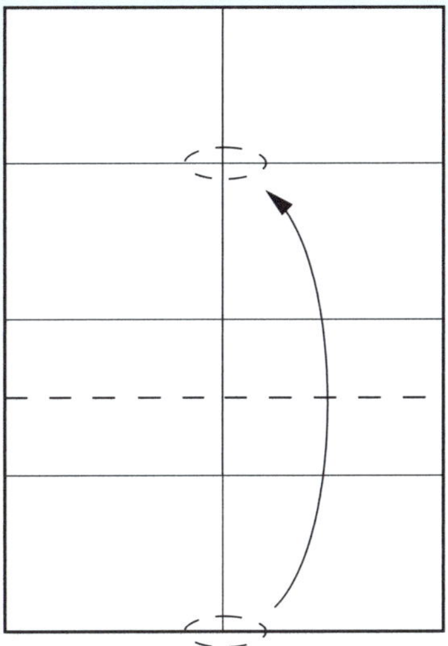

⑤ Fold the bottom corners to the indicated point.

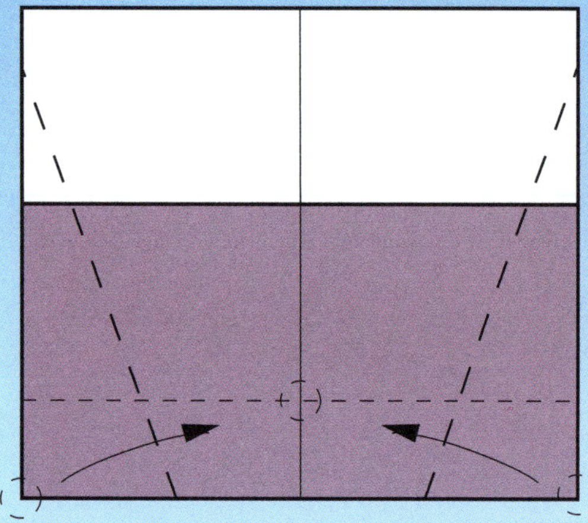

⑥ Fold the bottom corners to the indicated point.

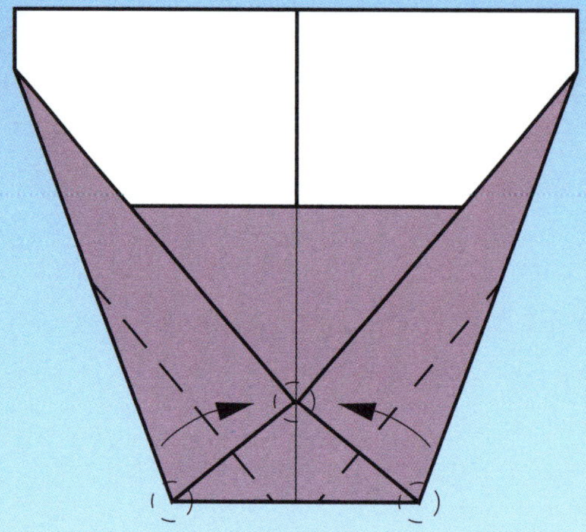

⑦ Fold the bottom edge to the indicated point, and then unfold.

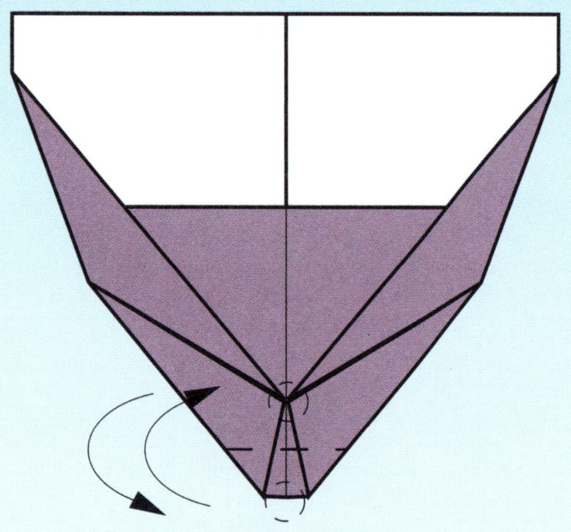

⑧ Fold in half to the back. Rotate 90° clockwise.

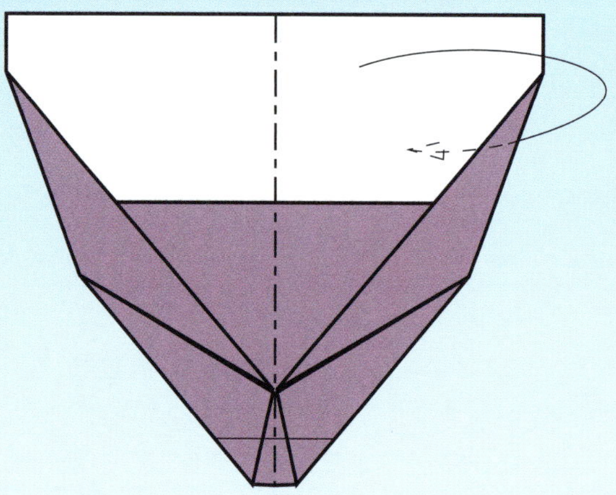

⑨ Fold the nose. Refer to the enlarged diagrams at the top of the opposite page.

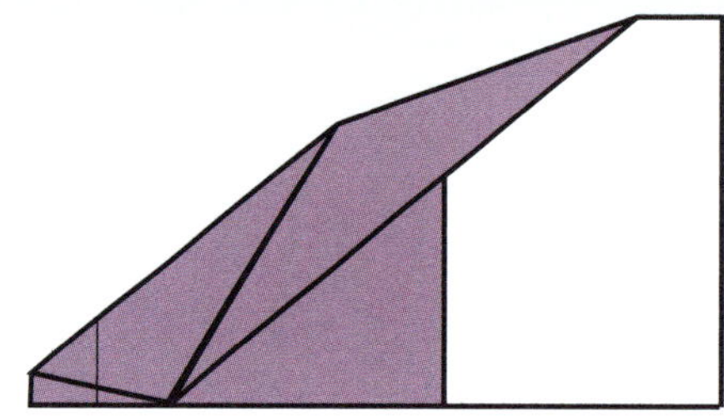

Zoomed-in Diagrams: How to Fold the Nose

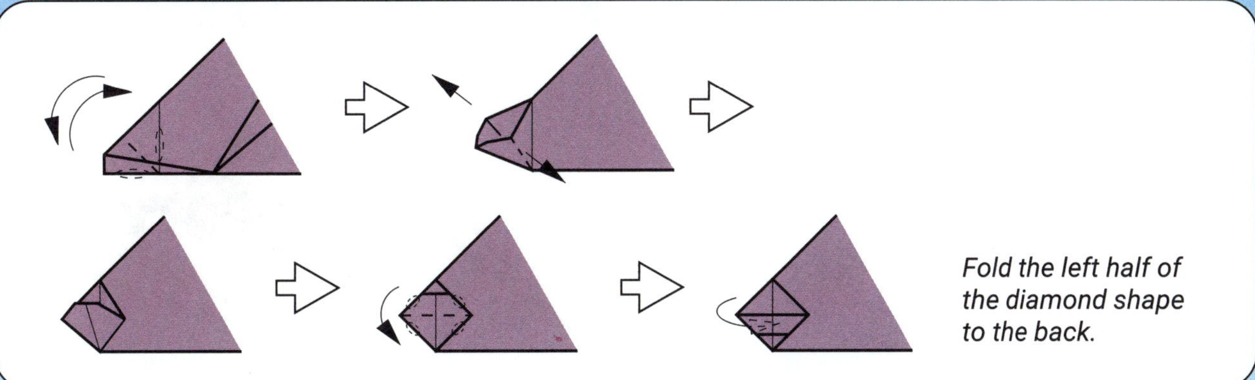

⑩ Fold the top layer to the width of "a." Fold the opposite side in the same way.

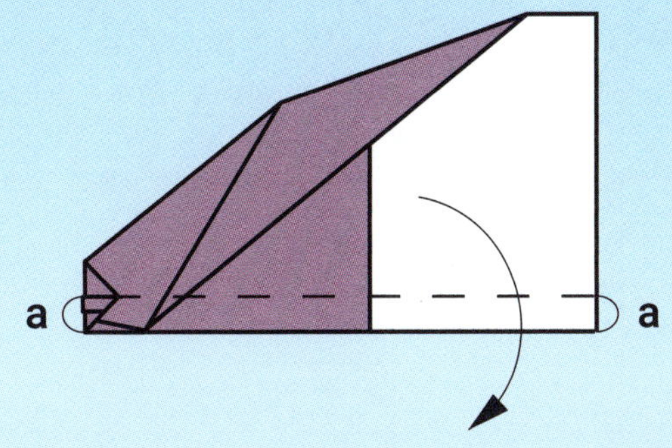

⑪ Fold the top layer to the width of "a." Fold the opposite side in the same way.

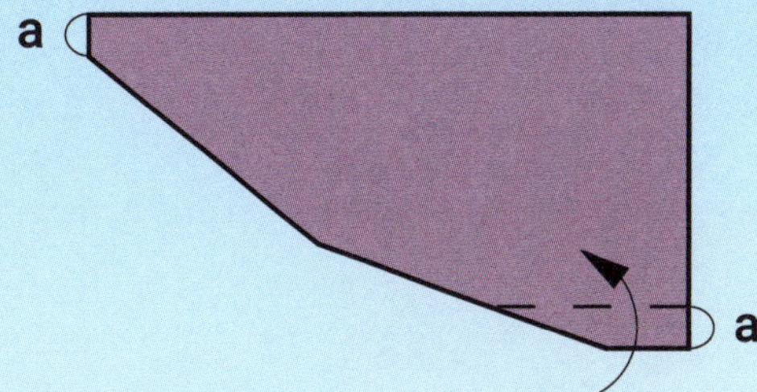

Open out the wings as shown in the 3D diagrams below. Completed.

Check after folding ▶ **Speeder 3D Views**

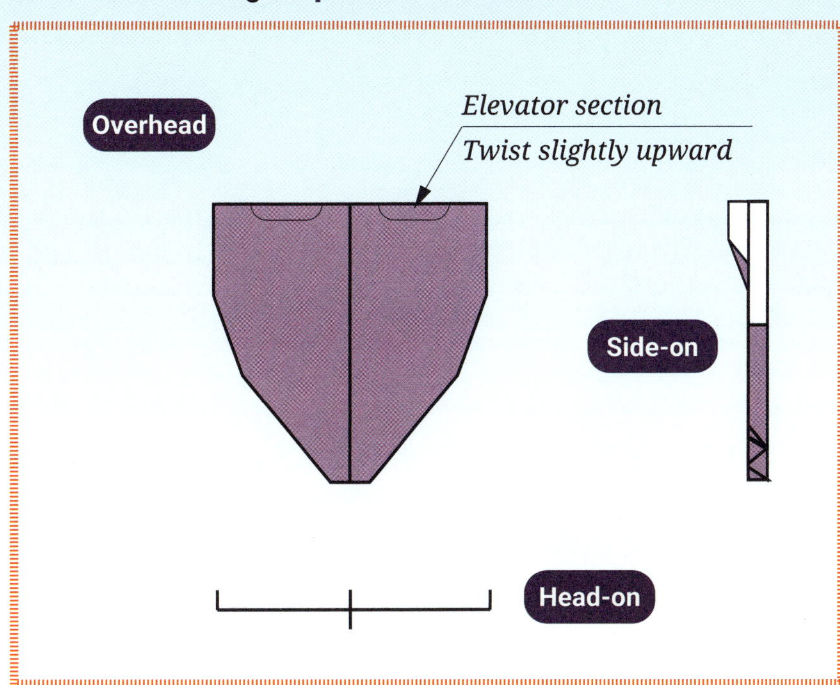

BELLY-BUTTON KING

This is a new design that builds on the basic "belly-button" paper airplane by using the Toda fold for the nose, enhancing stability and maximizing airtime performance.

Paper Shape .. Rectangular
Difficulty ....★★

① Fold in half, unfold, and then turn it over.

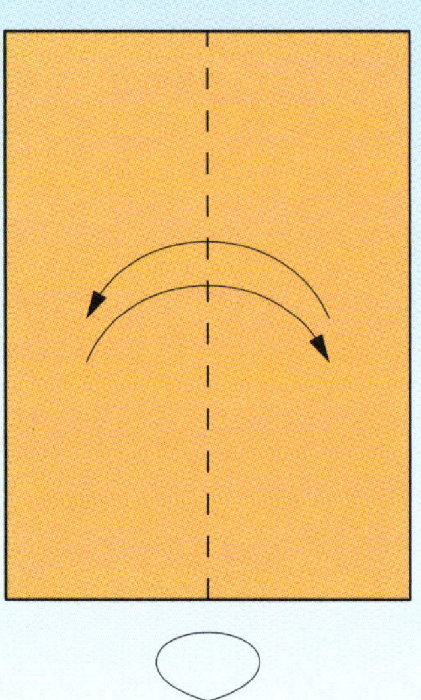

② Fold the corner flaps to the center crease.

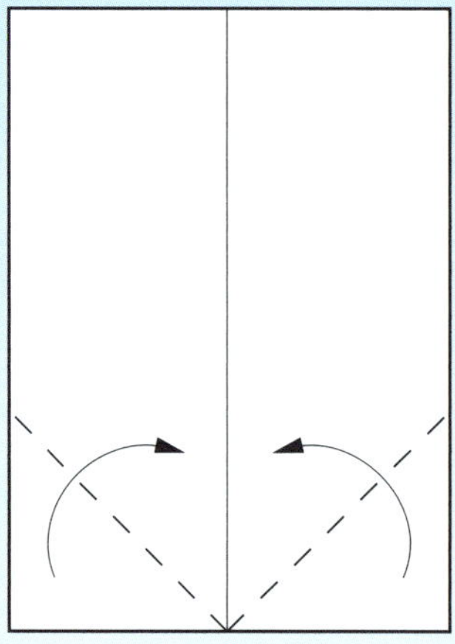

③ Fold so that the spans identified as "a" are equal.

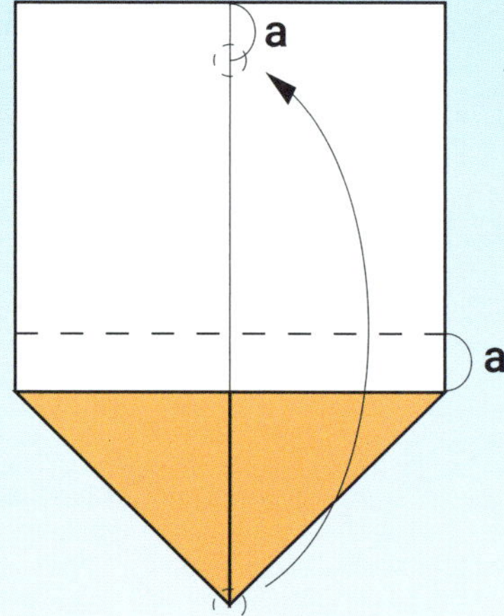

④ Fold the bottom corners to the center crease.

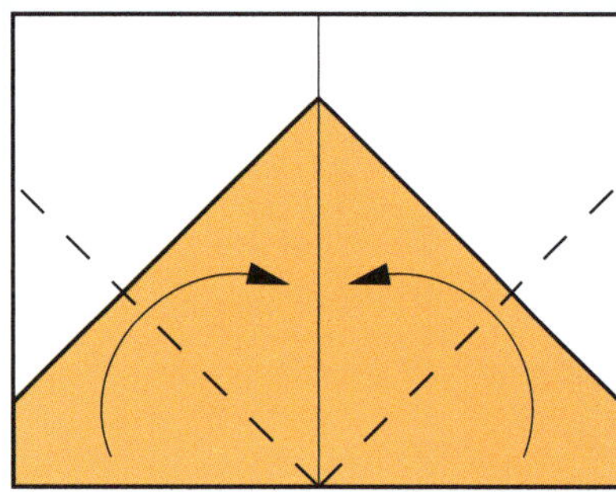

⑤ Fold down the triangular flap labeled "b," and then fold the tip in at half the width of "b" and unfold.

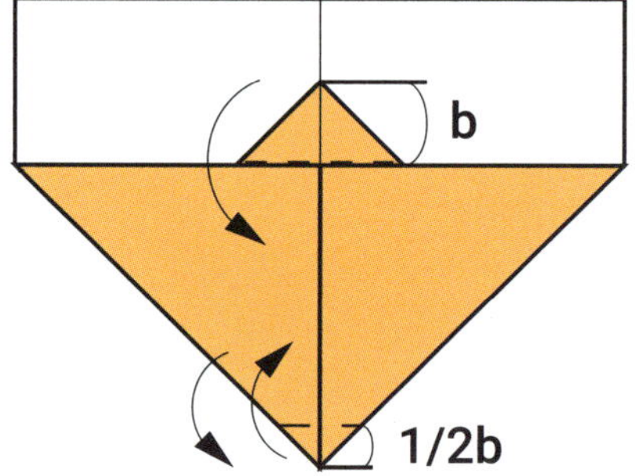

⑥ Fold in half to the back. Rotate 90° clockwise.

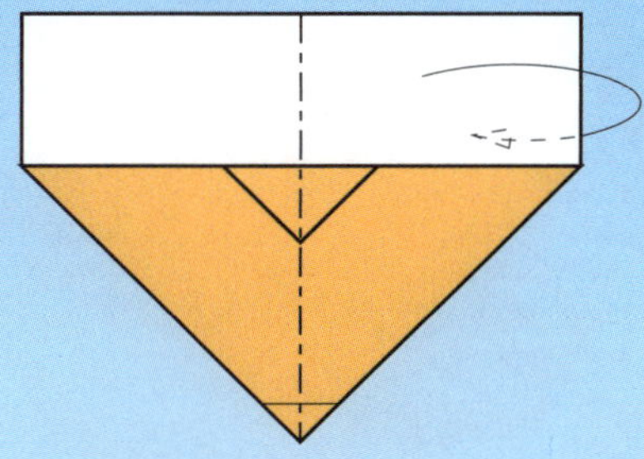

⑦ Fold the nose. Refer to the enlarged diagrams below.

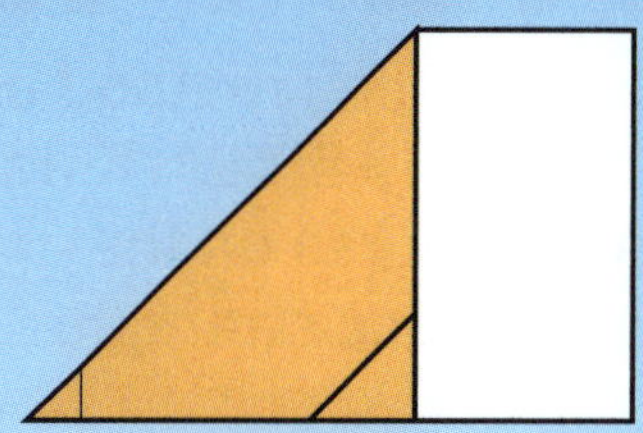

Zoomed-in Diagrams: How to Fold the Nose

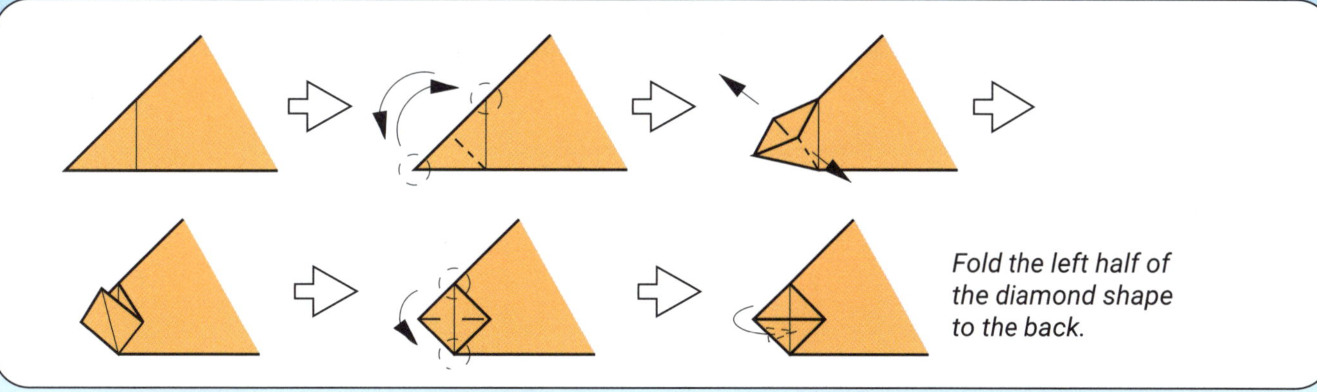

⑧ Fold the top edge of the top layer to meet the indicated point at the bottom right. Fold the opposite side in the same way.

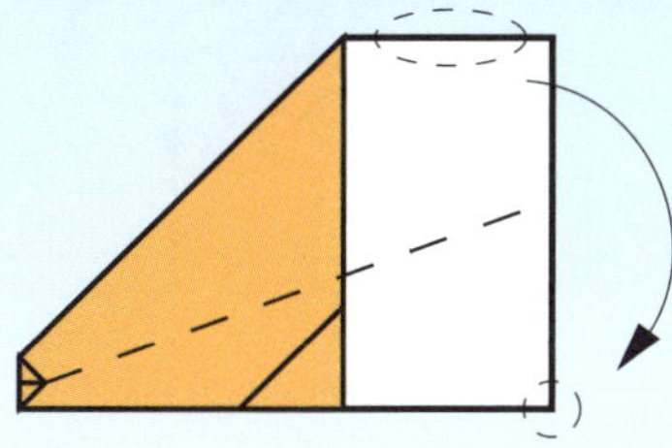

⑨ Open out the wings as shown in the 3D diagrams to the right. Completed.

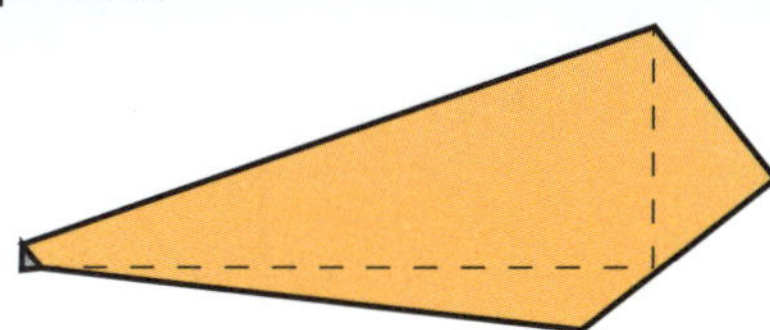

Check after folding ▶ **Belly-Button King 3D Views**

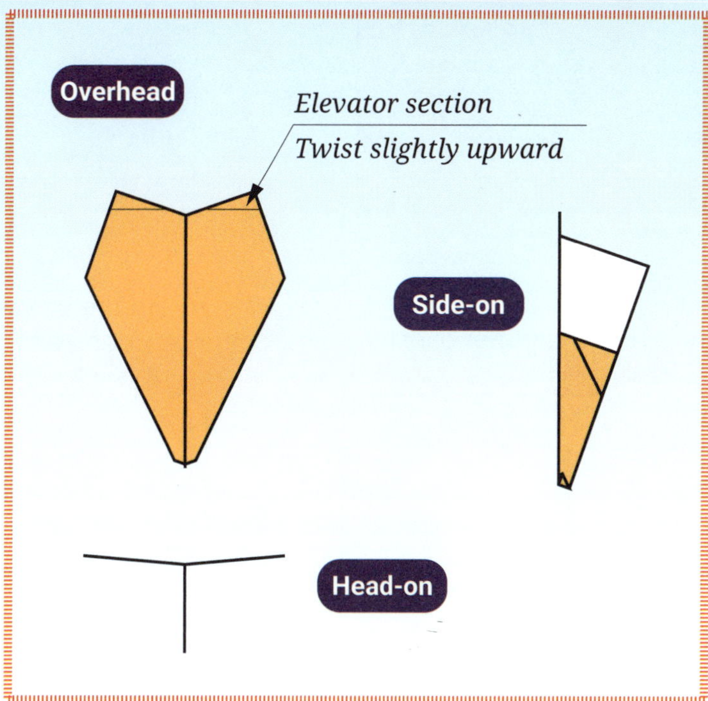

WING MASTER

The shape and folding method are similar to those of the Belly-Button King, but the overlapping structures on the upper and lower wings increase strength.

Paper Shape .. Rectangular

Difficulty ....★

① Fold in half, unfold, and then turn it over.

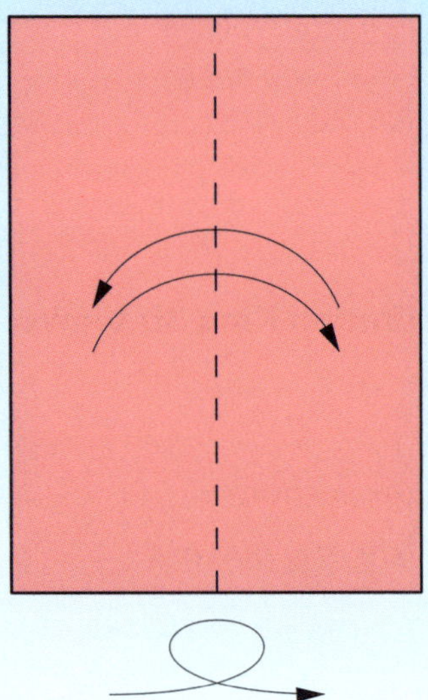

② Fold the corner flaps to the center crease.

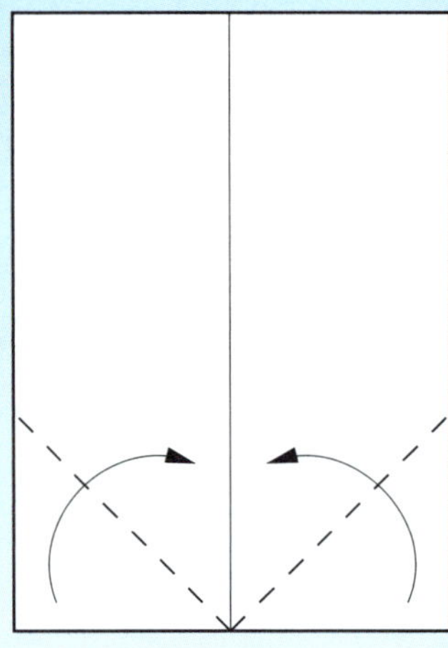

③ Fold along the indicated span.

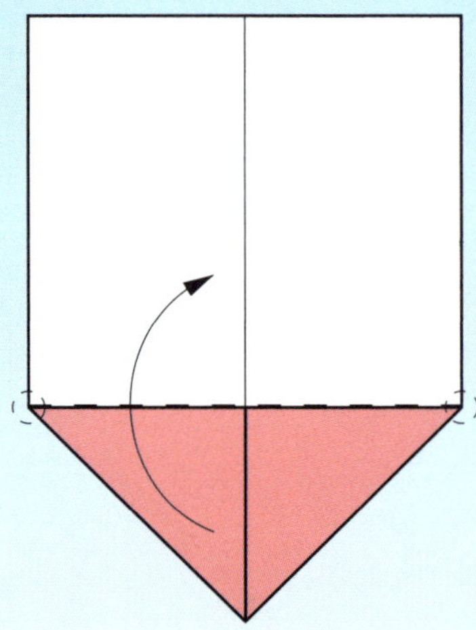

④ Turn the paper over.

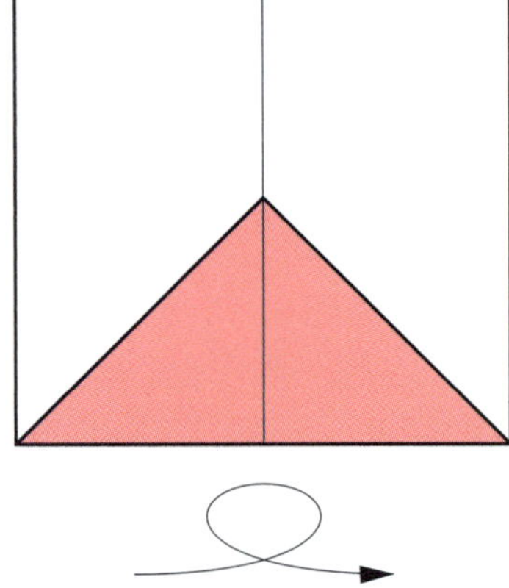

⑤ Fold the corner flaps to the center crease.

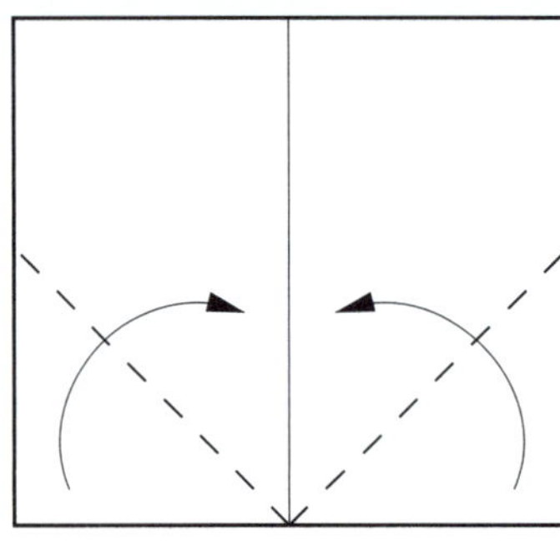

⑥ Turn it over again.

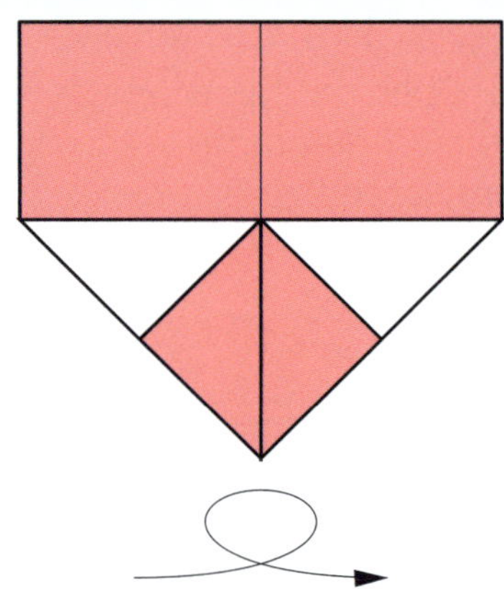

⑦ Fold the top of the diamond shape down as indicated. Unfold.

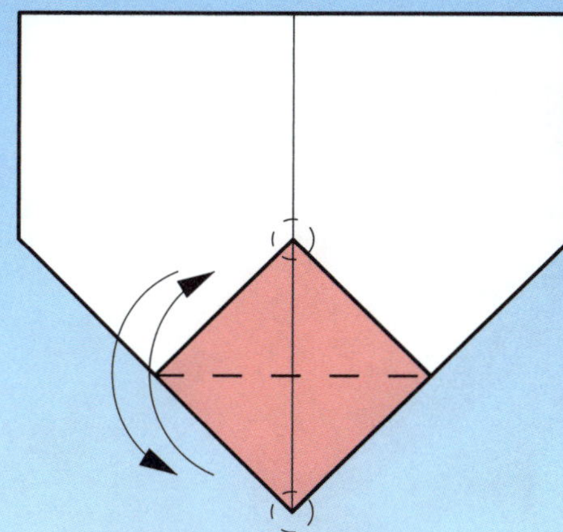

⑧ Fold the bottom point to the indicated intersection.

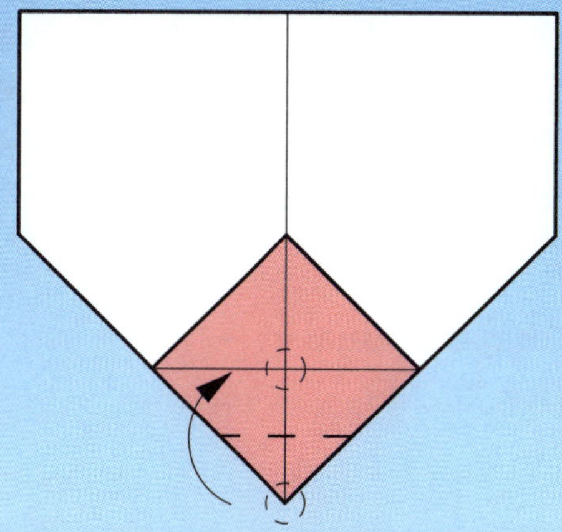

⑨ Fold in half to the back.

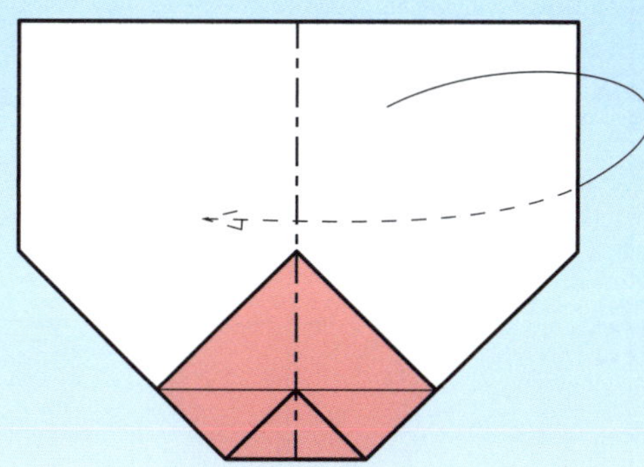

⑩ Fold the left edge of the top layer to meet the indicated point at the top right. Fold the opposite side in the same way.

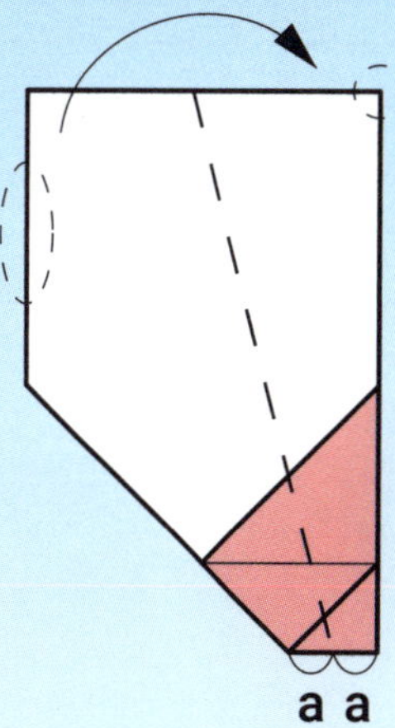

⑪ Open out the wings as shown in the 3D diagrams to the right. Completed.

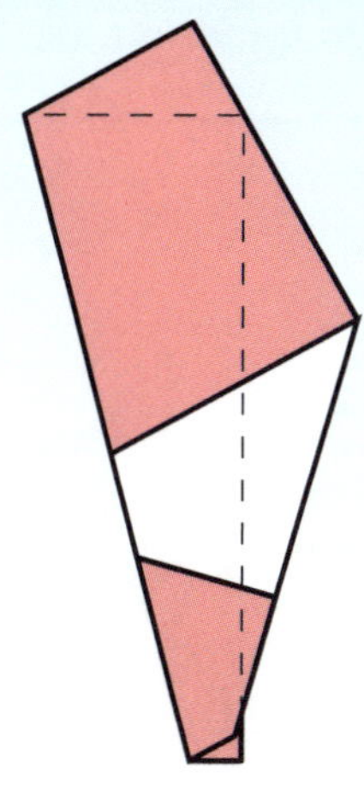

Check after folding ▶ Wing Master 3D Views

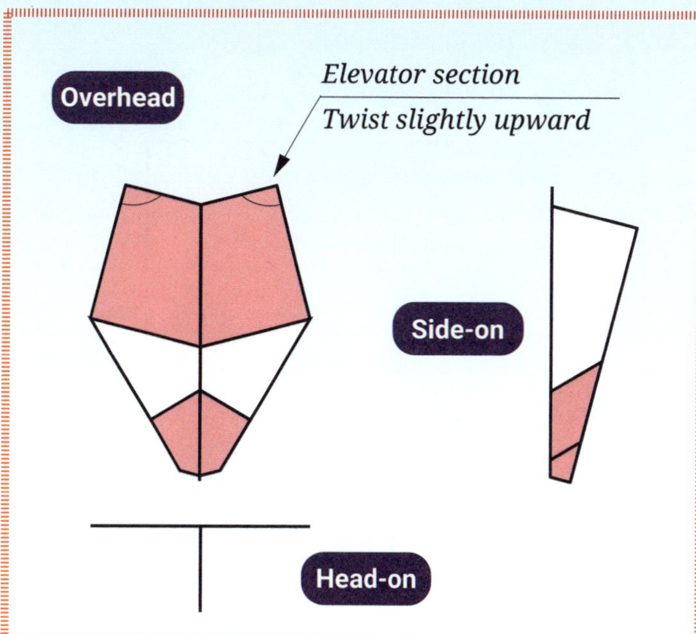

MAGIC CARPET

This is a paper airplane folded from a square sheet. When viewed from directly above, it looks just like a magic carpet soaring through the air.

Paper Shape .. Square
Difficulty .... ★

① Fold in half left to right, and then unfold.

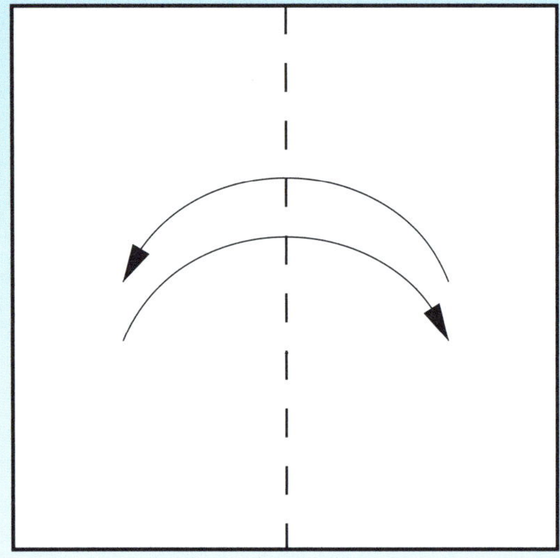

② Fold in half bottom to top, and then unfold.

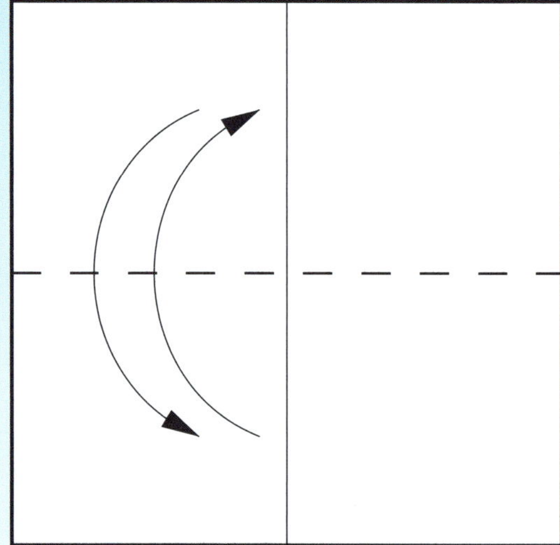

③ Fold the bottom edge to the step-2 crease.

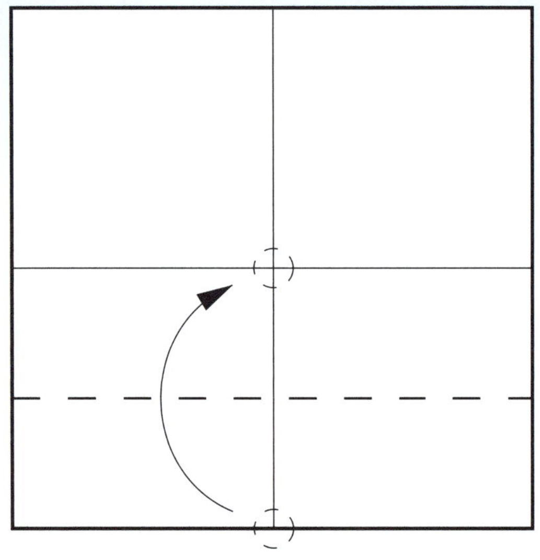

④ Refold along the crease made in step 2.

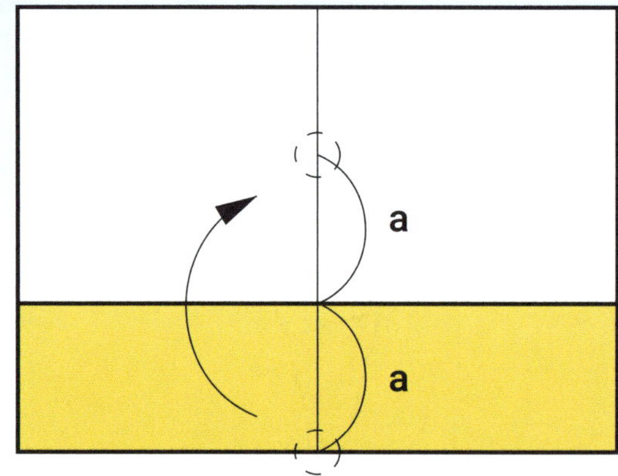

⑤ Fold the bottom corners as indicated.

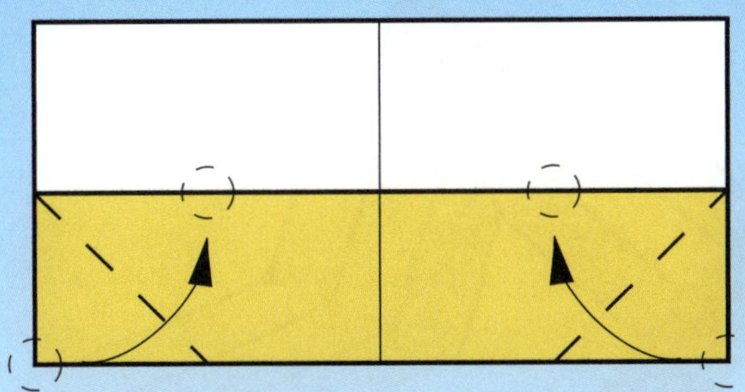

⑥ Fold up the bottom edge at the width of "b."

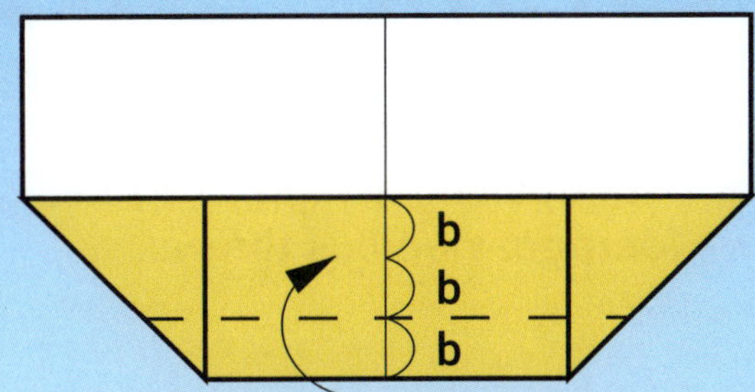

⑦ Fold in half to the back.

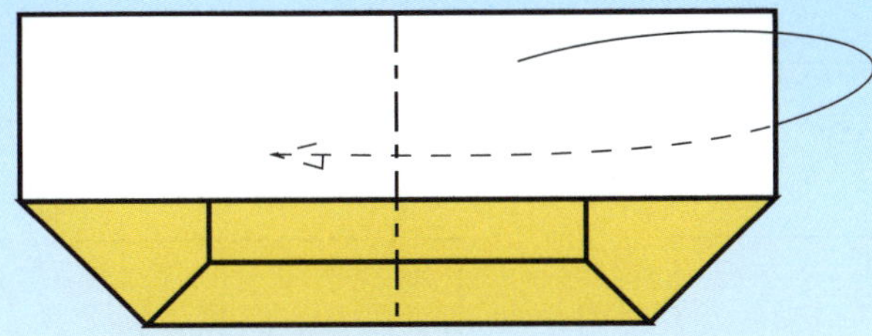

⑧ Fold the top layer as indicated. Fold the opposite side in the same way.

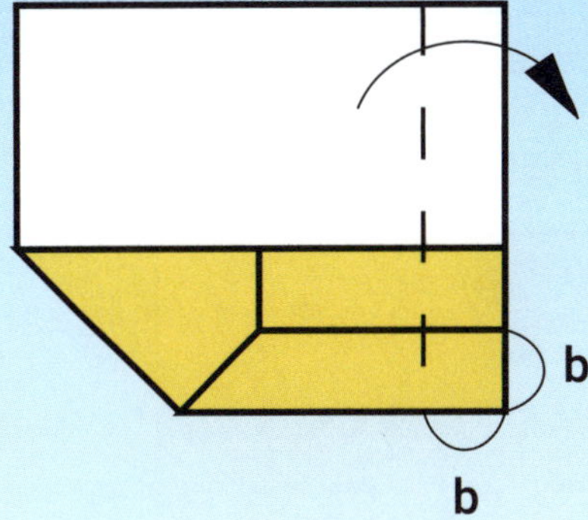

⑨ Fold the top layer to the width of "b." Fold the opposite side in the same way.

⑩ Open out the wings as shown in the 3D diagrams to the right. Completed.

Check after folding ▶ **Magic Carpet 3D Views**

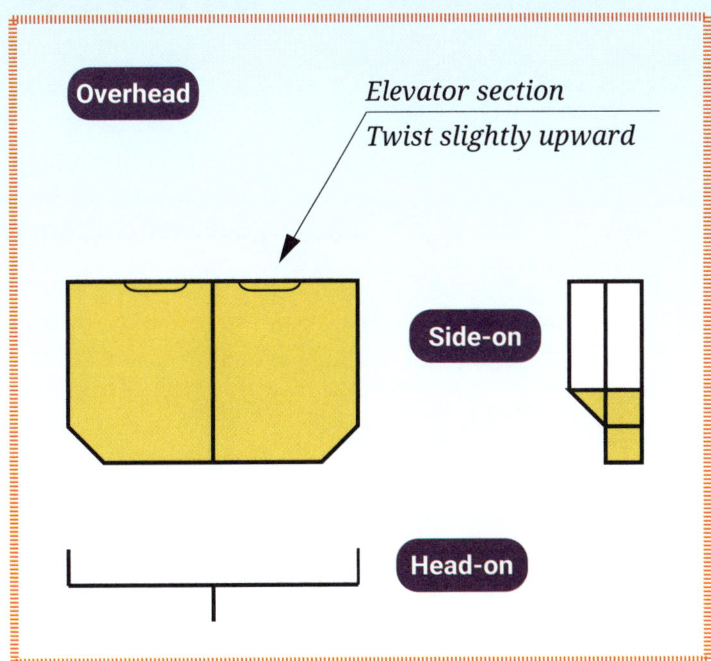

FOUR-SIDER

This model features folded layers in the front section, preventing the layers of paper from opening in flight. This design allows for more vigorous throws.

Paper Shape .. Rectangular

Difficulty .... ★★★★★

① Valley fold in half left to right. Unfold, and then valley fold in half bottom to top. Unfold.

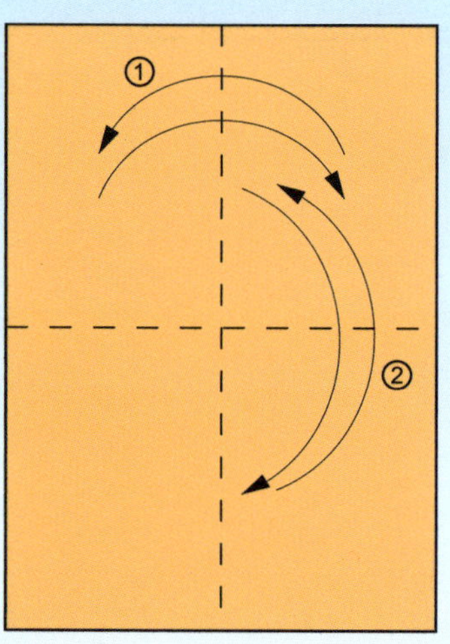

② Fold the bottom edge to the horizontal crease.

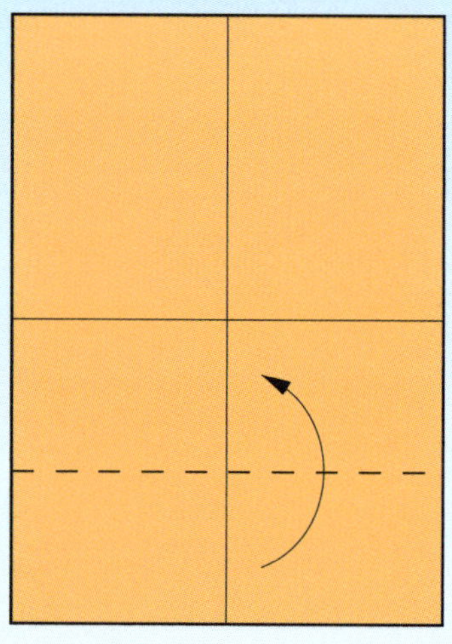

③ Fold the bottom edge to the horizontal crease again. Then, unfold completely.

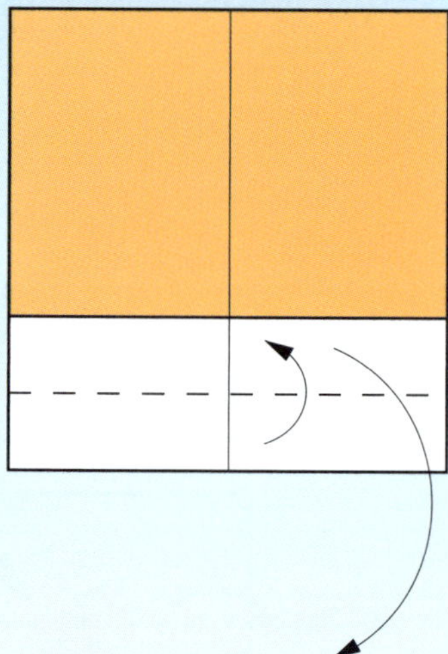

④ Fold in half.

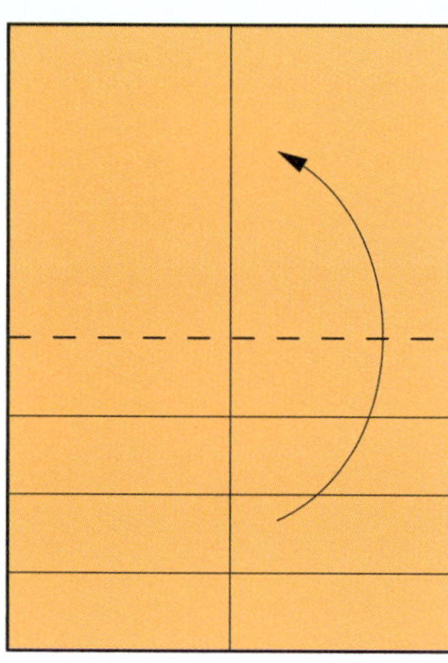

⑤ Fold the bottom edge to the first crease, bringing the indicated points together, and then unfold completely.

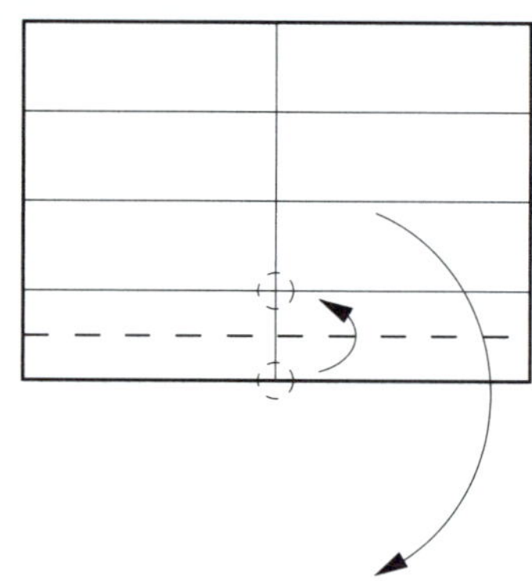

⑥ Fold along the top crease made in step 5.

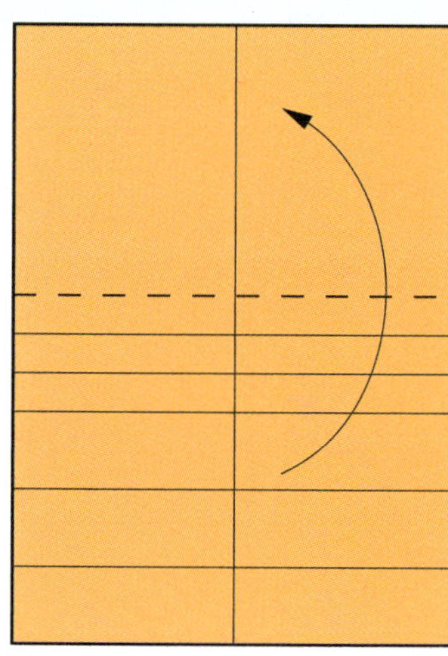

7 Fold the uppermost layer down along the second crease from the top.

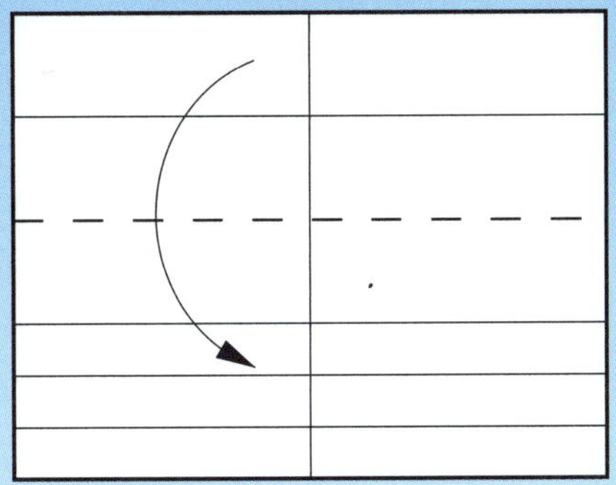

8 Fold the bottom edge up, wrapping around the indicated edge.

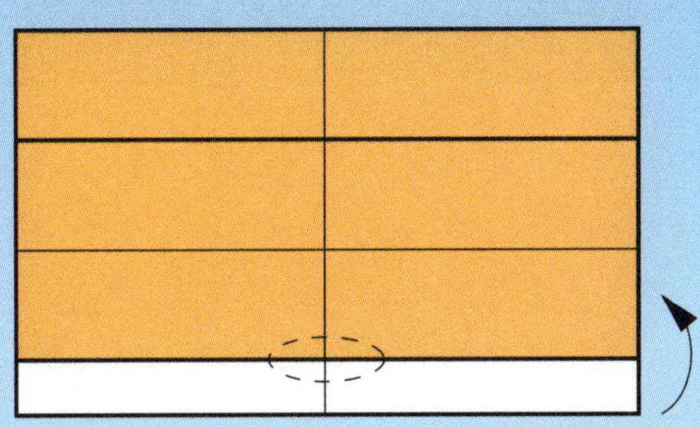

9 Fold the top layer down at the indicated position.

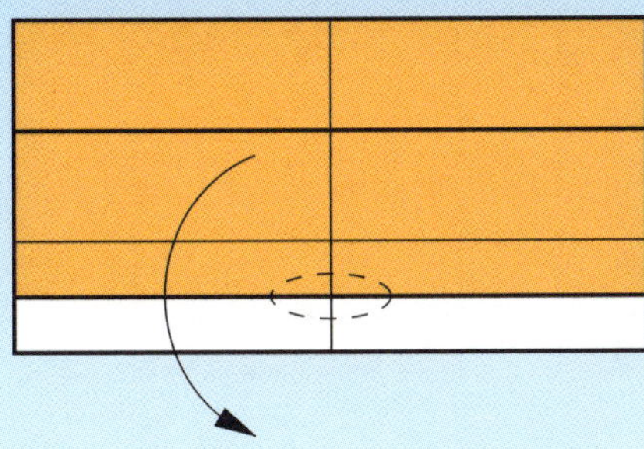

10 Turn the paper over.

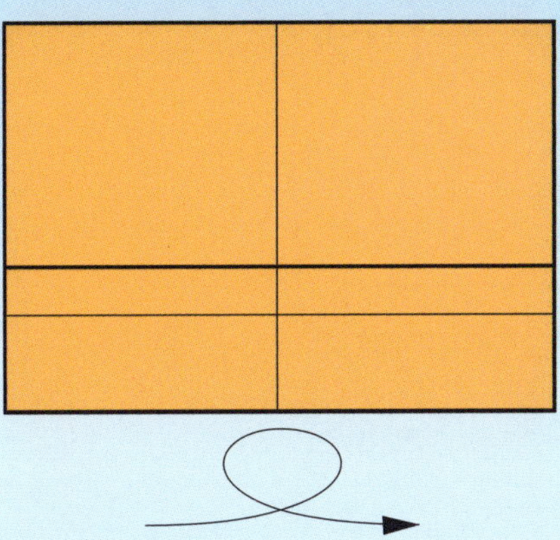

11 Fold the bottom edge to the indicated position.

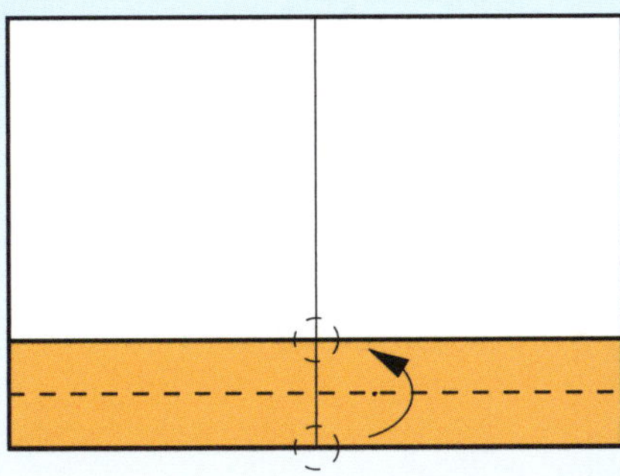

12 Fold in half to the back.

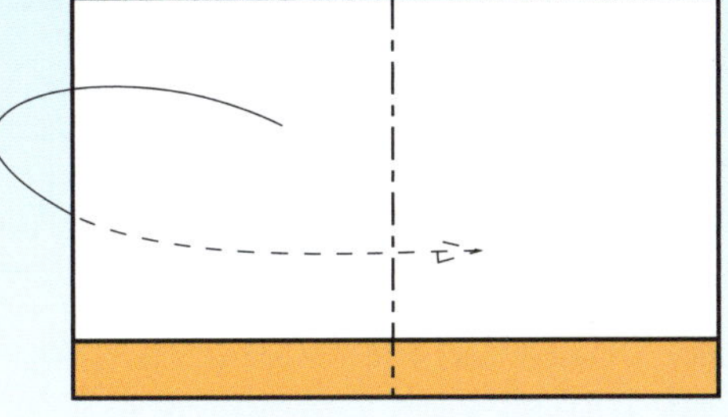

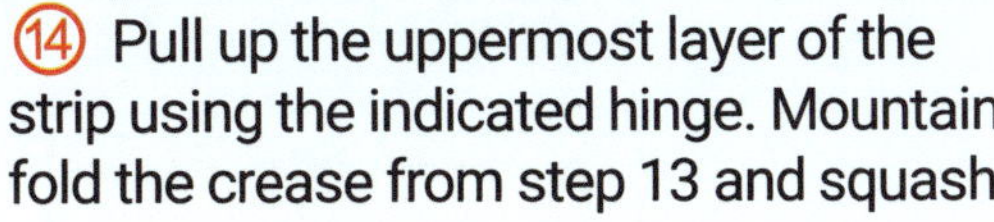

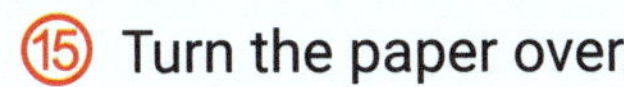

13 Fold the bottom left corner of the strip into a triangular flap, then unfold.

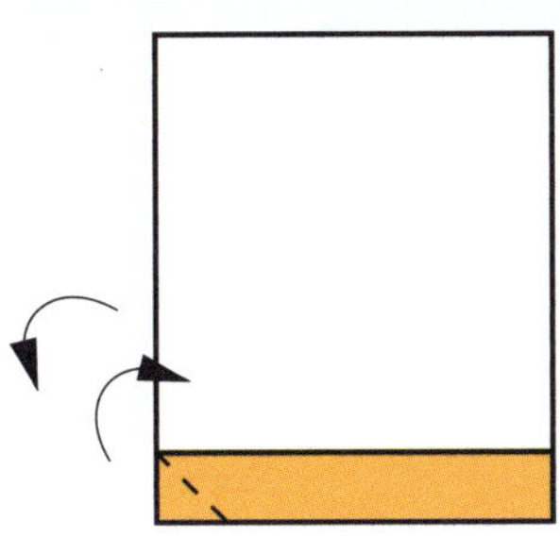

14 Pull up the uppermost layer of the strip using the indicated hinge. Mountain fold the crease from step 13 and squash.

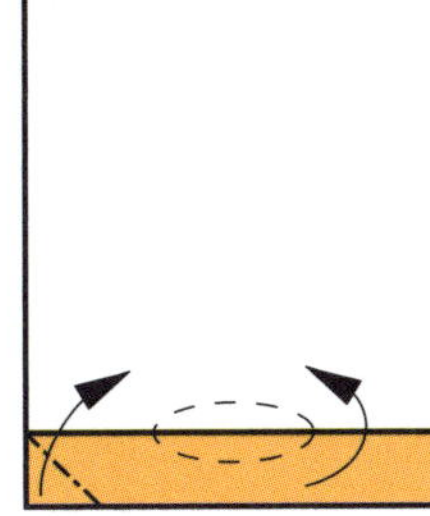

15 Turn the paper over.

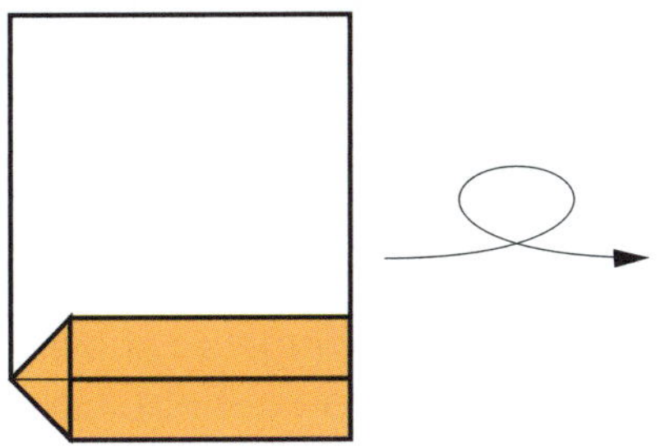

⑯ Fold the bottom edge up, wrapping around the indicated edge.

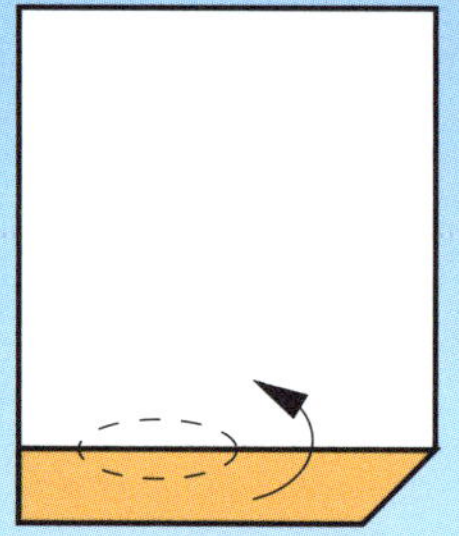

⑰ Fold the top layer as indicated. Fold the opposite side in the same way.

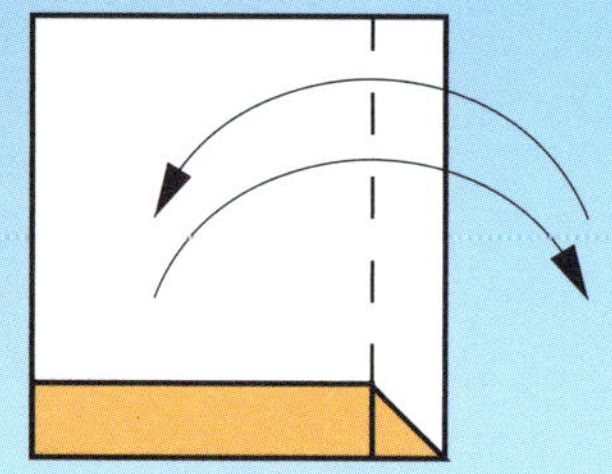

⑱ Fold the top right corner into a triangular flap so that the corner aligns with the indicated crease.

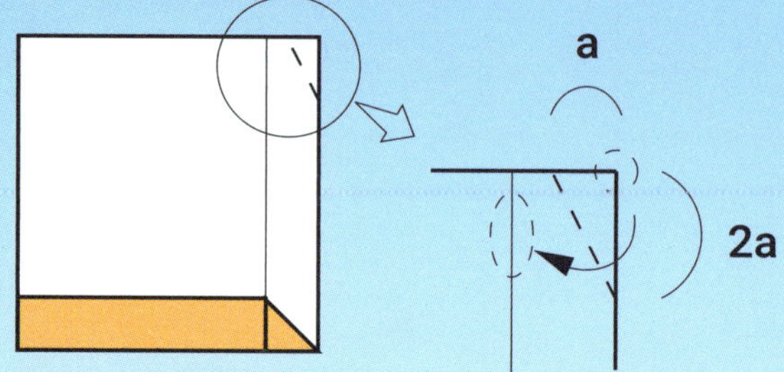

⑲ Wrap the triangular flap inward again, and then unfold.

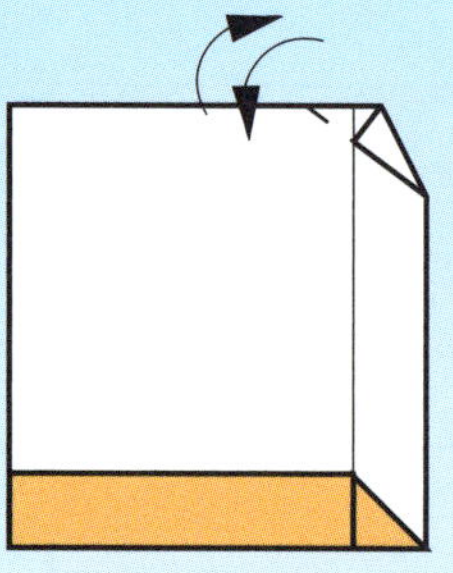

⑳ Open the pocket-like section, making a mountain fold along the crease from step 18 and a valley fold along the crease from step 19.

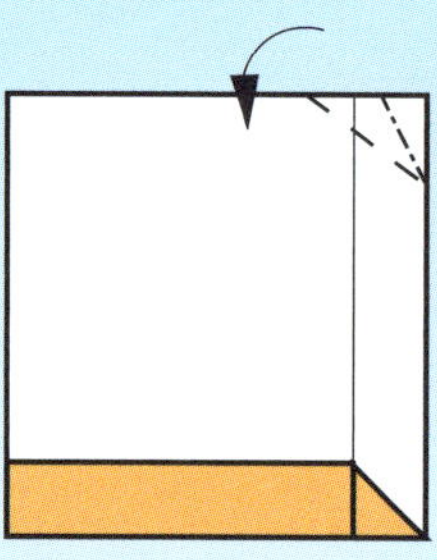

㉑ Turn the paper over.

㉒ Fold along the crease from step 19.

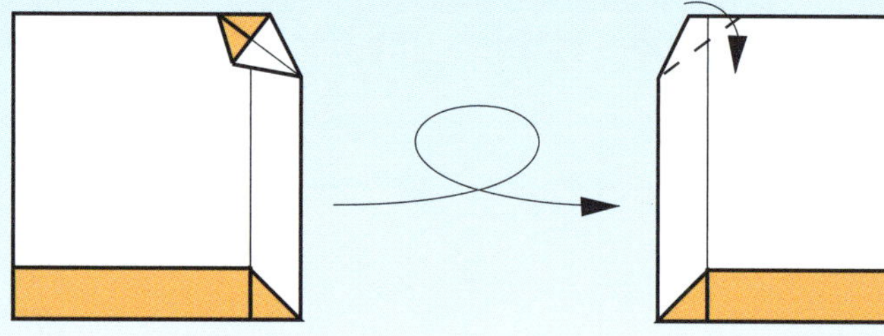

㉓ Fold the top layer along the crease from step 17. Fold the opposite side in the same way.

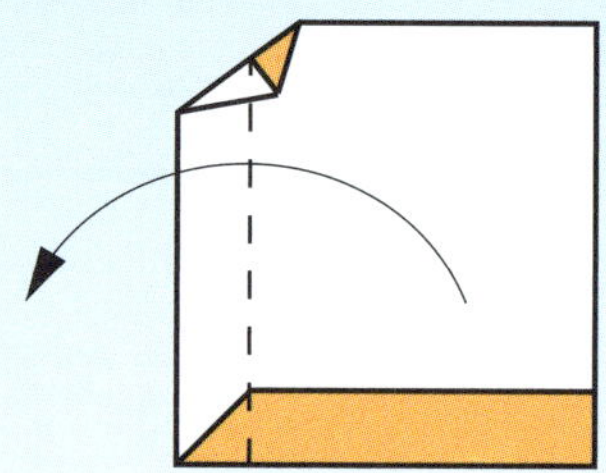

㉔ Fold the top layer to the width of "b." Fold the opposite side in the same way.

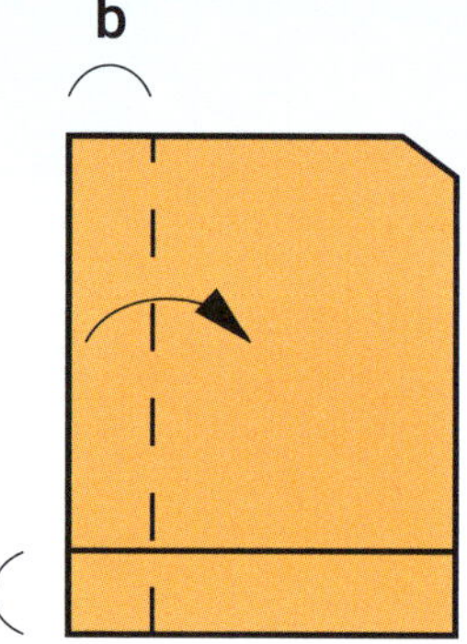

Open out the wings as shown in the 3D diagrams to the right. Completed.

Check after folding ▶ Four-Sider 3D Views

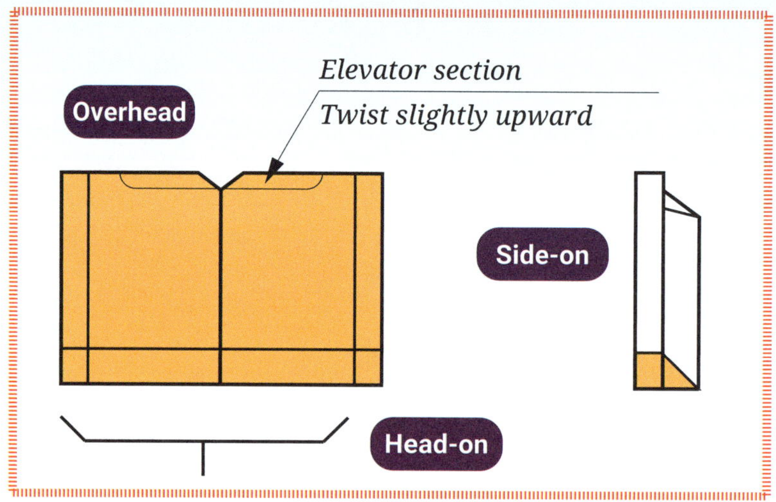

SKY KING

This paper airplane truly is the "King of the Sky." The design helped me set the original world record for longest flight duration. When thrown high, it demonstrates incredibly stable performance.

Paper Shape .. Rectangular

Difficulty .... ★★★

① Fold in half, unfold, and then turn it over.

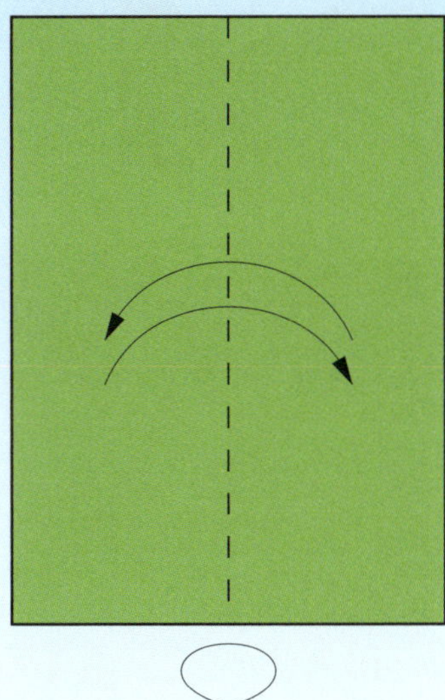

② Fold the corner flaps to the center crease.

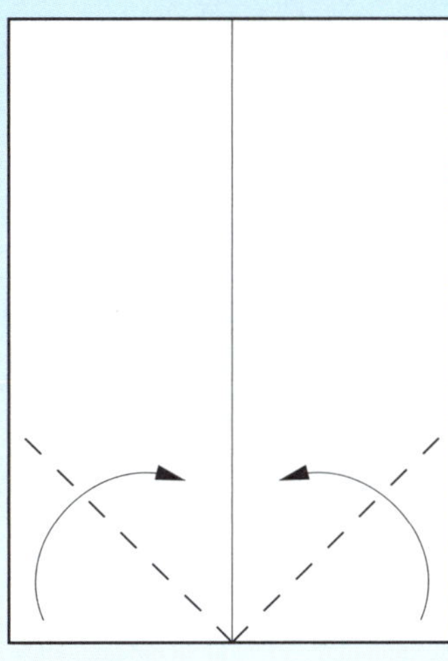

③ Fold and unfold bottom to top ("a"). Then, fold so that the indicated "b" locations meet.

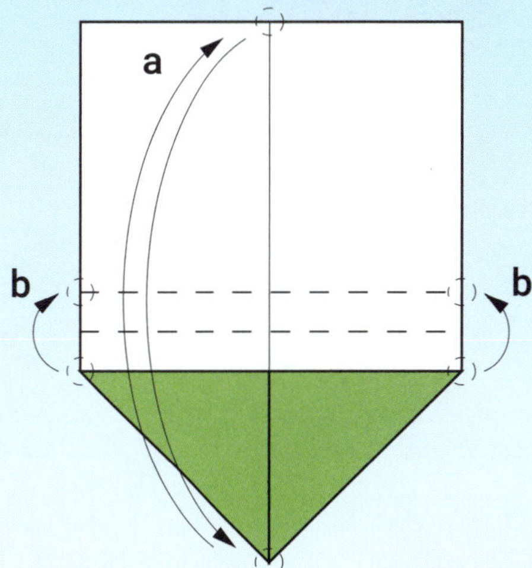

④ Fold the corner flaps to the center crease, then unfold.

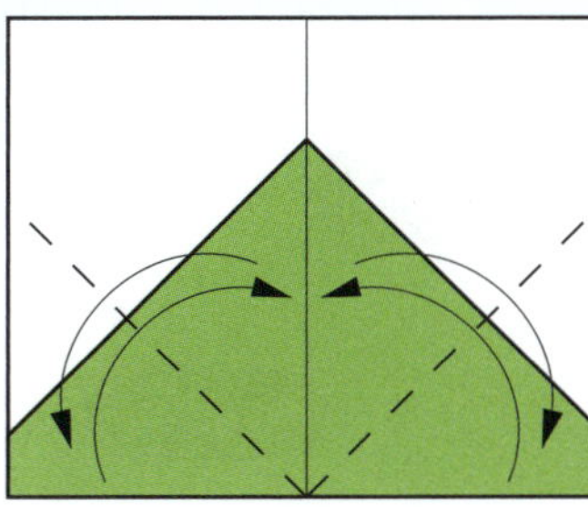

⑤ Fold as indicated.

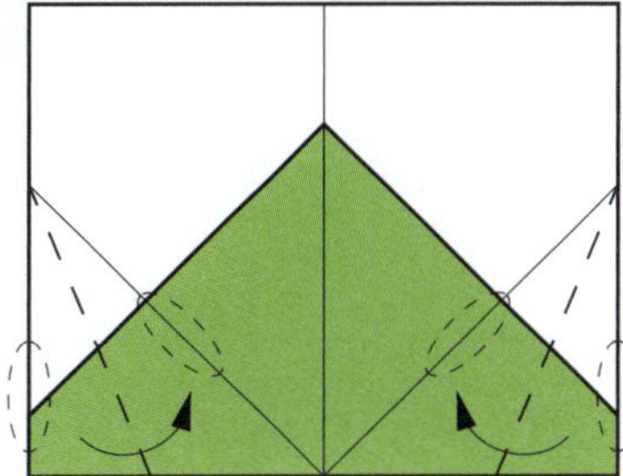

⑥ Fold in along the existing creases, wrapping the edges.

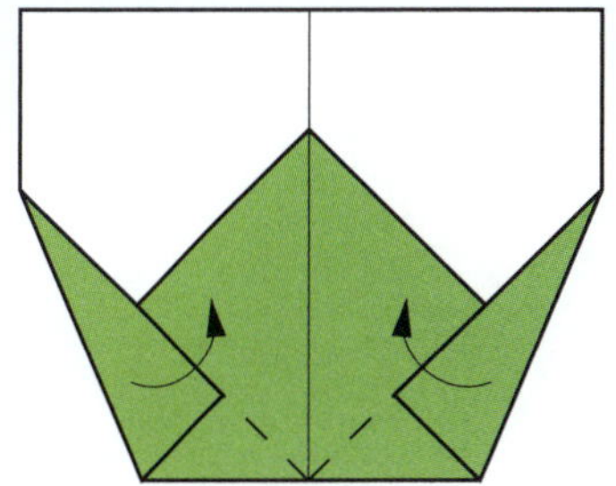

⑦ Bend the tip of the flap to the indicated point, making only a pinch mark in the middle, then unfold.

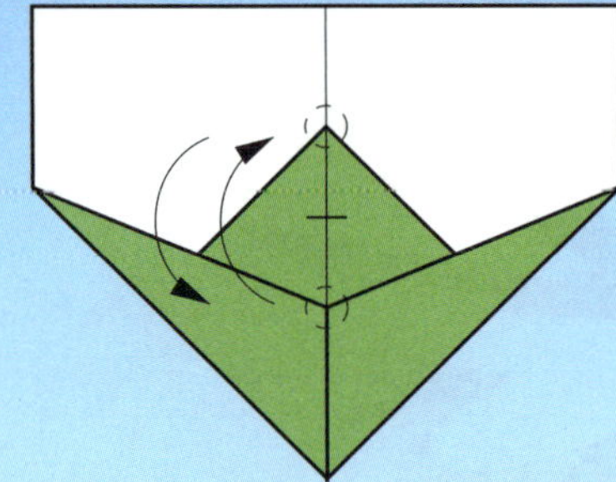

⑧ Fold the tip of the flap to the indicated point, then unfold and fold it to the inside.

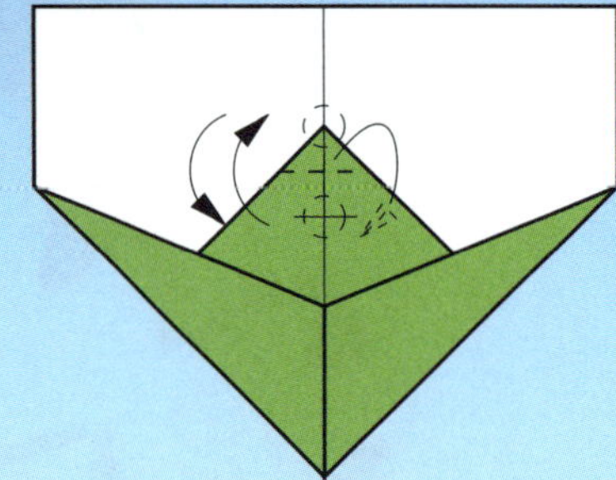

⑨ Fold the bottom point to the indicated location, and then unfold.

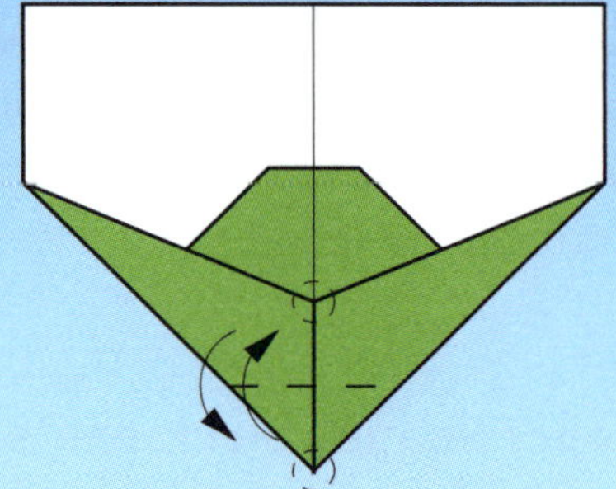

⑩ Fold in half to the back.

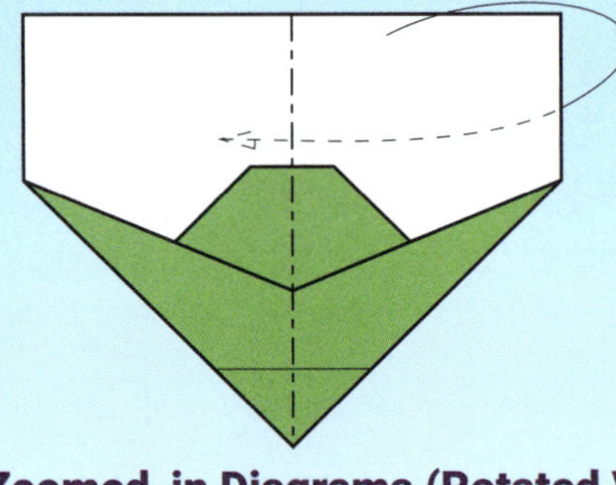

⑪ Fold the nose. Refer to the enlarged diagrams below.

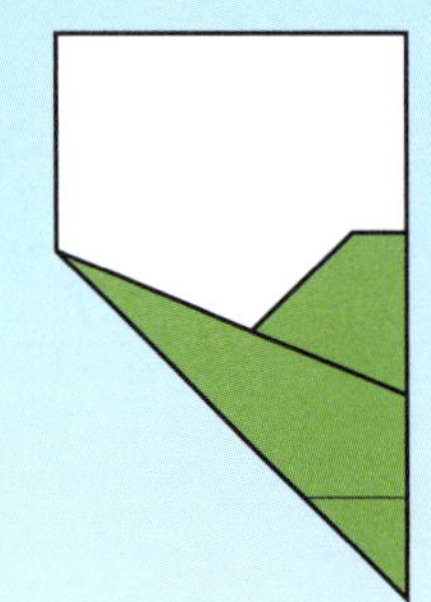

⑫ Fold the top layer to the width of "c." Fold the opposite side in the same way.

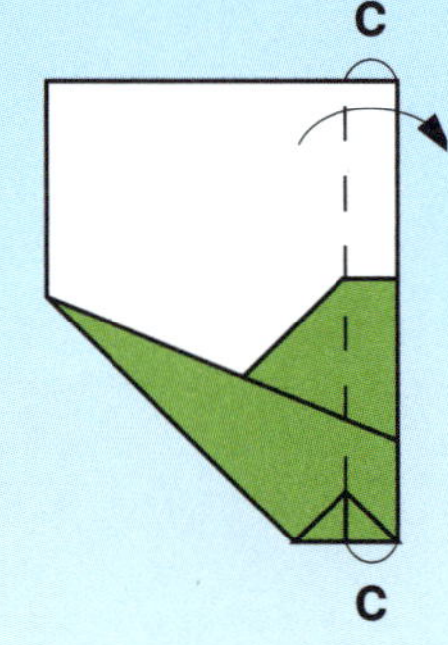

Zoomed-in Diagrams (Rotated View): How to Fold the Nose

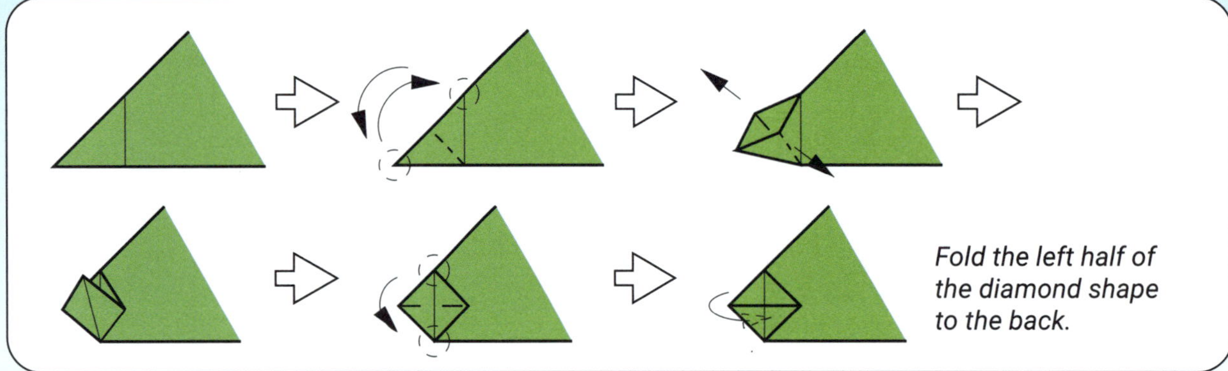

⑬ Fold the top layer to the width of "c." Fold the opposite side in the same way.

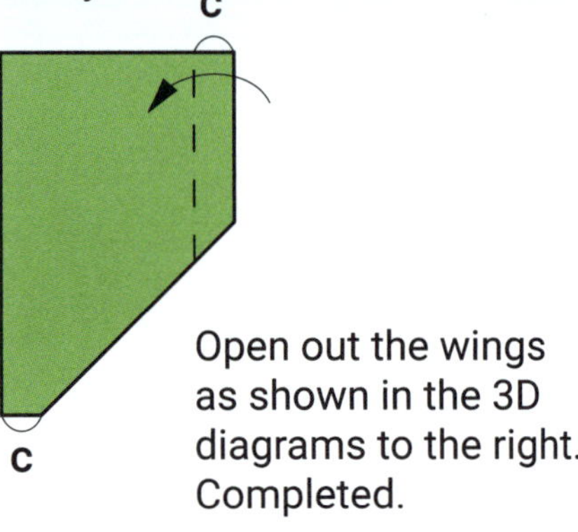

Open out the wings as shown in the 3D diagrams to the right. Completed.

Check after folding ▶ **Sky King 3D Views**

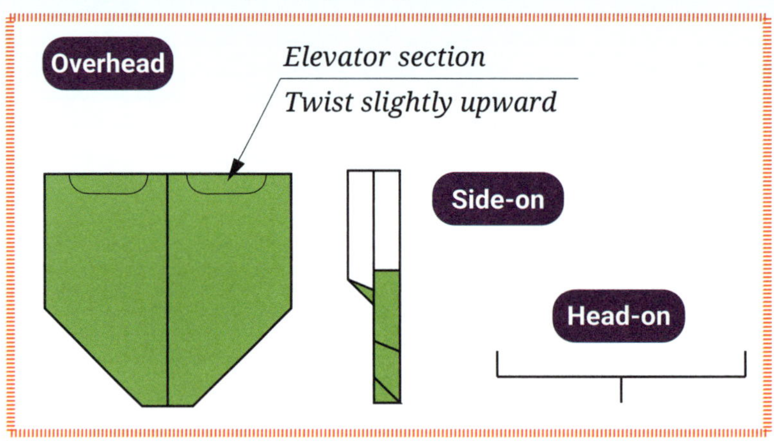

NEXUS KING I

The shape is similar to the Sky King (page 45), but the overlapping layers on the wings prevent deformation, resulting in a more stable flight performance.

Paper Shape .. Rectangular

Difficulty .... ★★★★

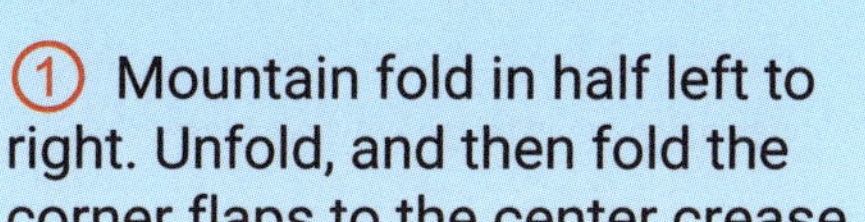

① Mountain fold in half left to right. Unfold, and then fold the corner flaps to the center crease.

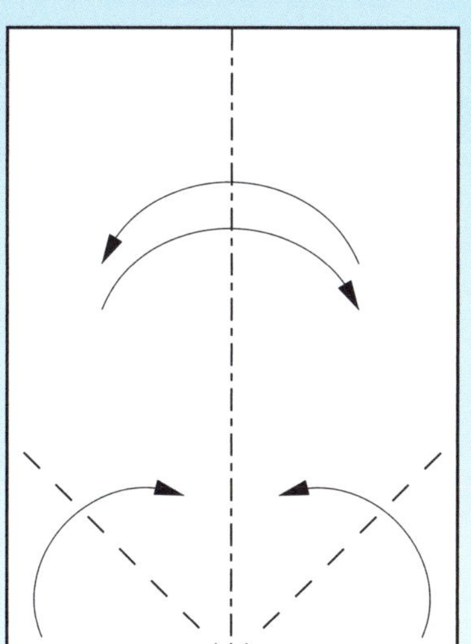

② Fold and unfold bottom to top.

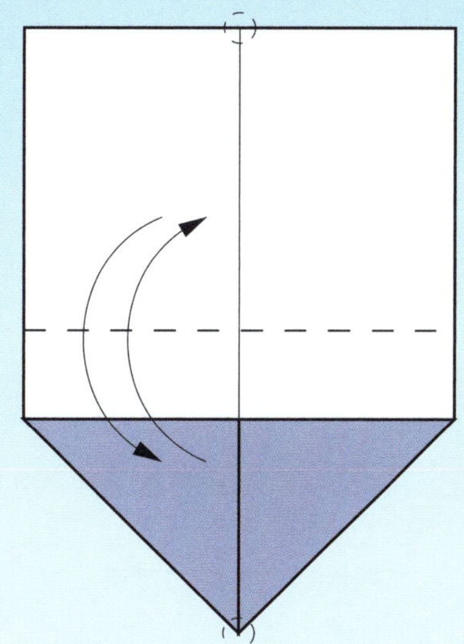

③ Fold as indicated, and then unfold.

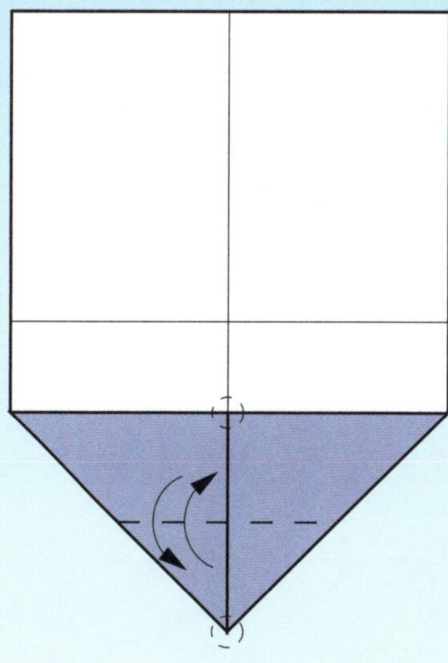

④ Fold as indicated, and then unfold.

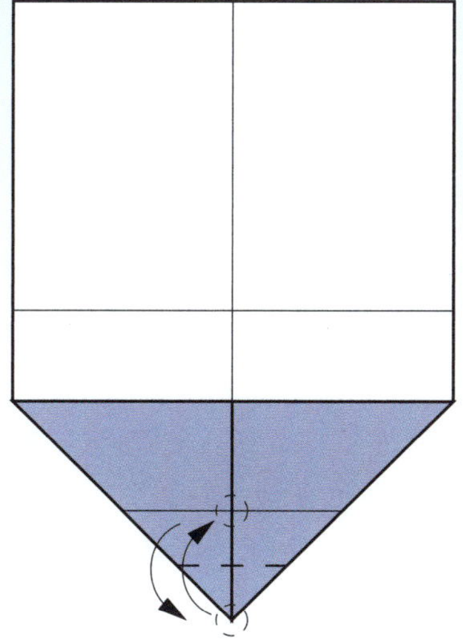

⑤ Fold as indicated.

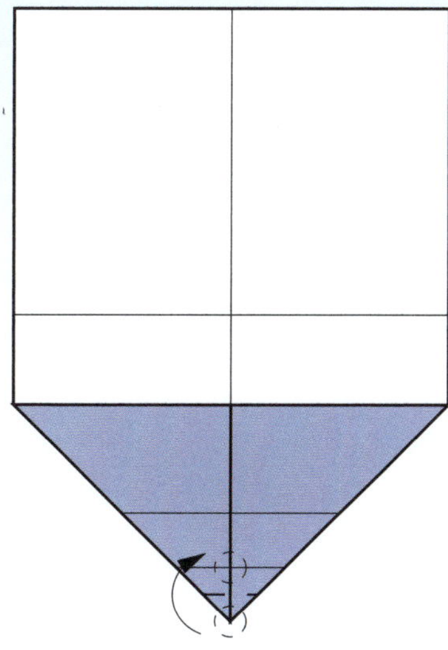

⑥ Fold at the indicated position.

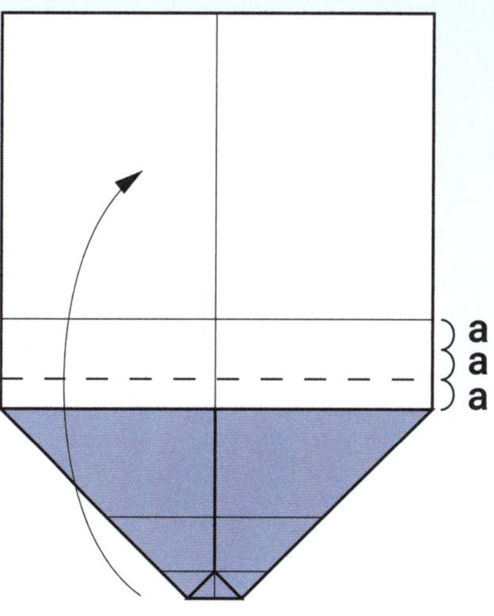

⑦ Turn the paper over left to right.

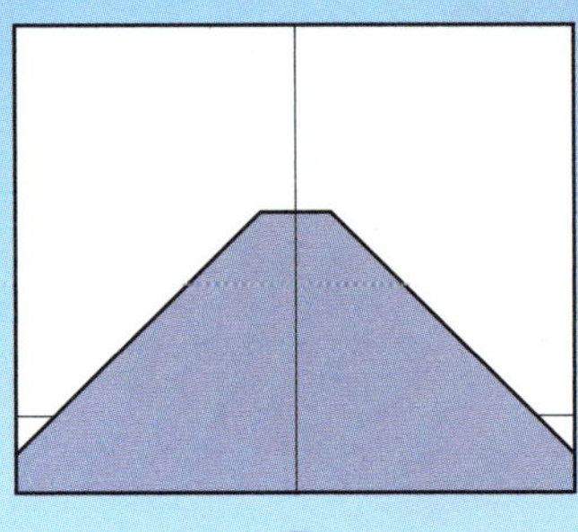

⑧ Fold the corner flaps to the center crease. Unfold both.

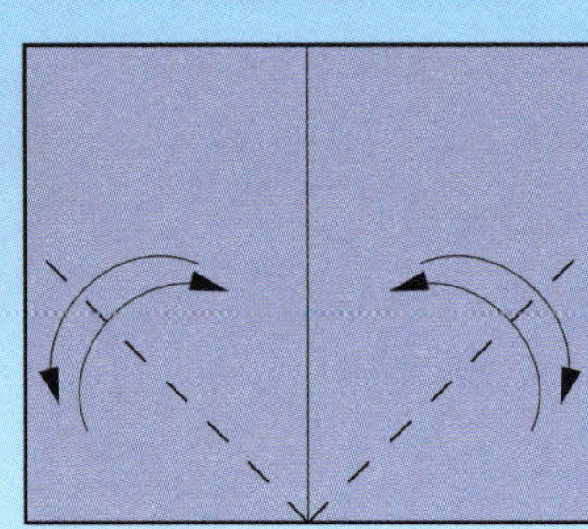

⑨ Fold as indicated, then unfold.

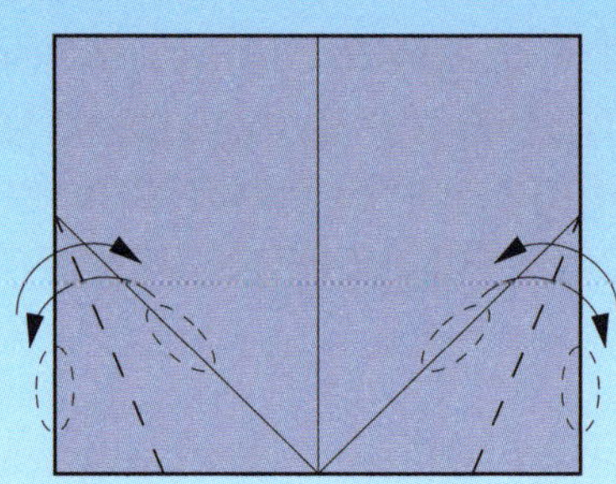

⑩ Fold the flaps so they match the shapes shown in step 11.

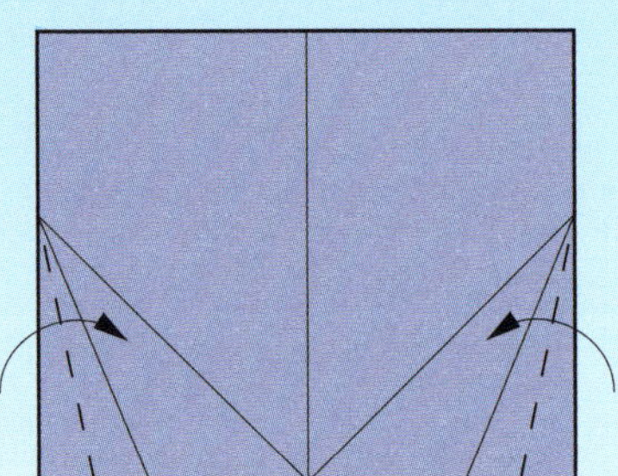

⑪ Use the creases made in step 9 as guidelines.

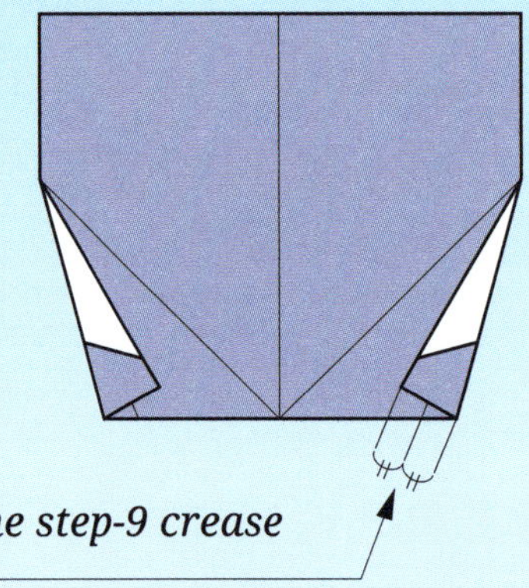

⑫ Open up pockets and squash so the edges are parallel to the "b" lines. Look ahead to step 13 for the shape.

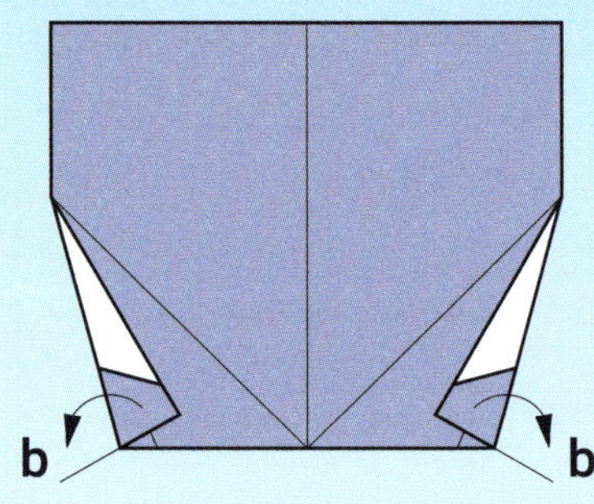

⑬ Step 12 completed.

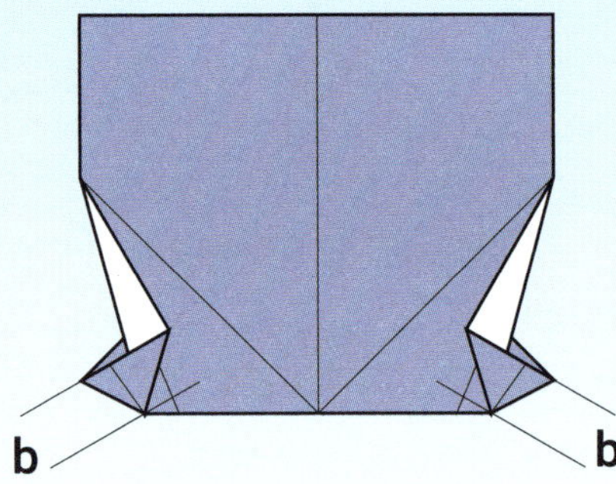

⑭ Refold along the creases made in step 8.

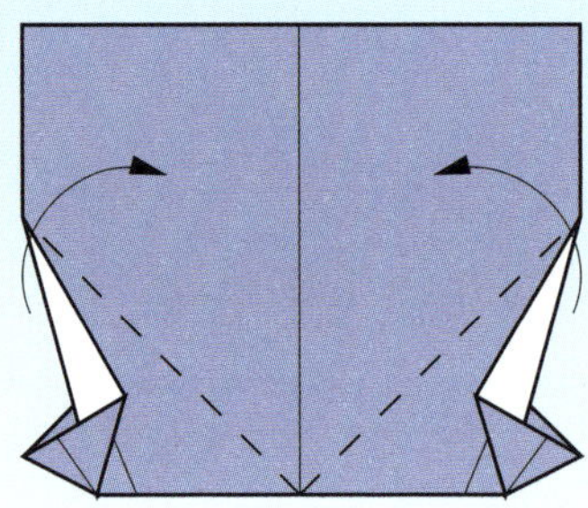

⑮ Turn the paper over.

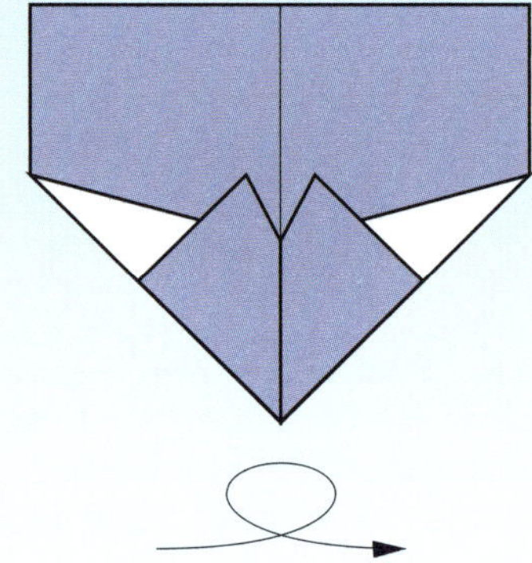

⑯ Fold the bottom point up as indicated, and then unfold.

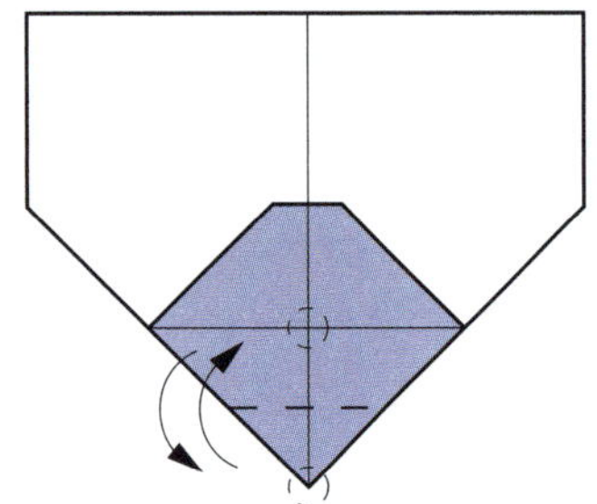

⑰ Fold in half to the back.

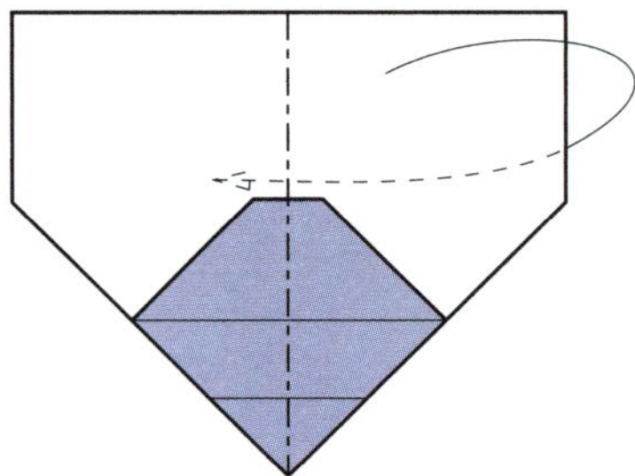

⑱ Fold the nose. (Refer to the enlarged diagrams to the right.)

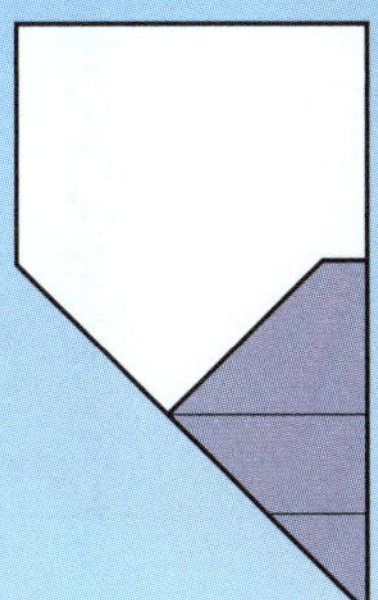

⑲ Fold the top layer to the width of "c." Fold the opposite side in the same way.

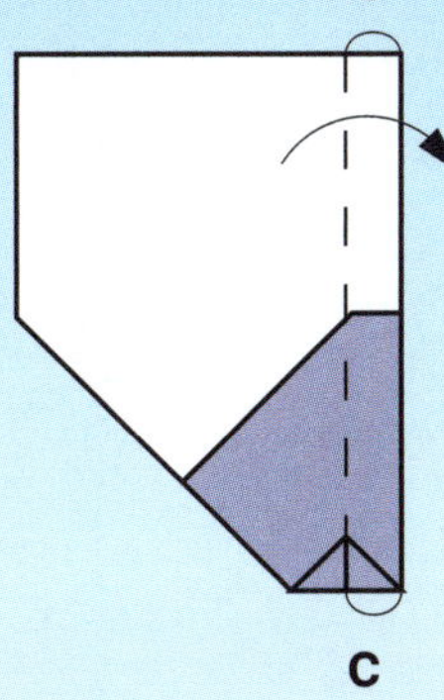

⑳ Fold the top layer to the width of "c." Fold the opposite side in the same way.

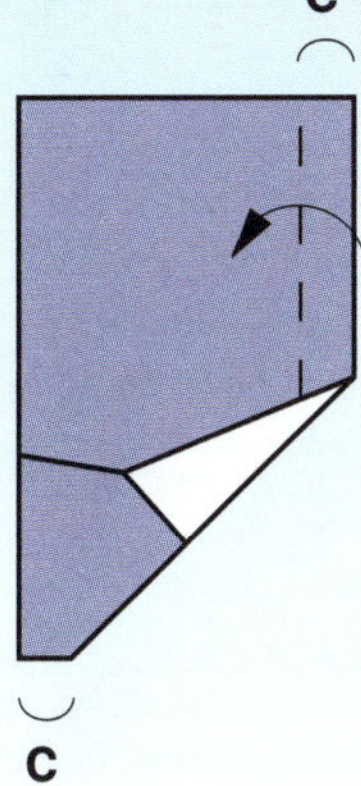

Open out the wings as shown in the 3D diagrams to the right. Completed.

Zoomed-in Diagrams (Rotated View):
How to Fold the Nose

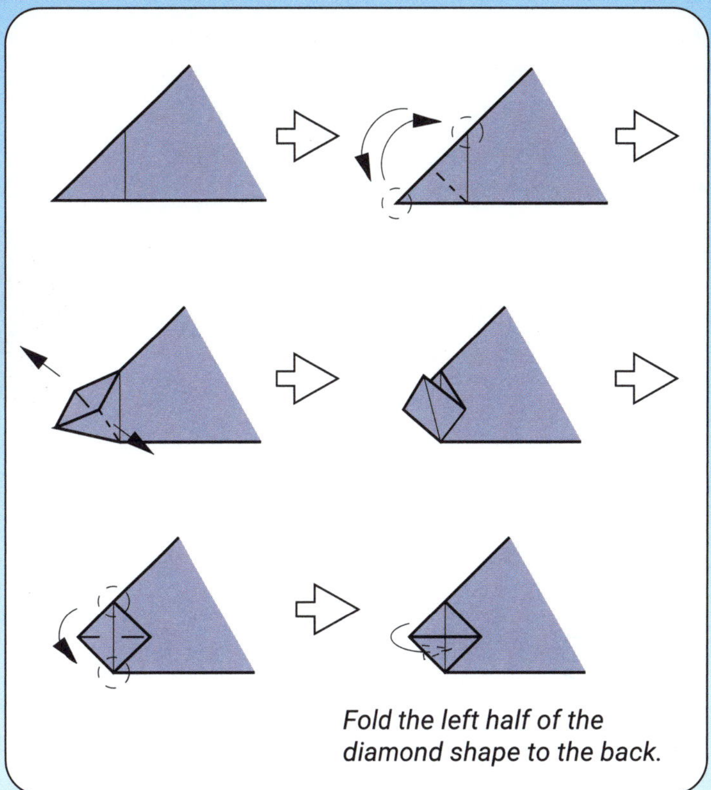

Fold the left half of the diamond shape to the back.

Check after folding ▶ **Nexus King I 3D Views**

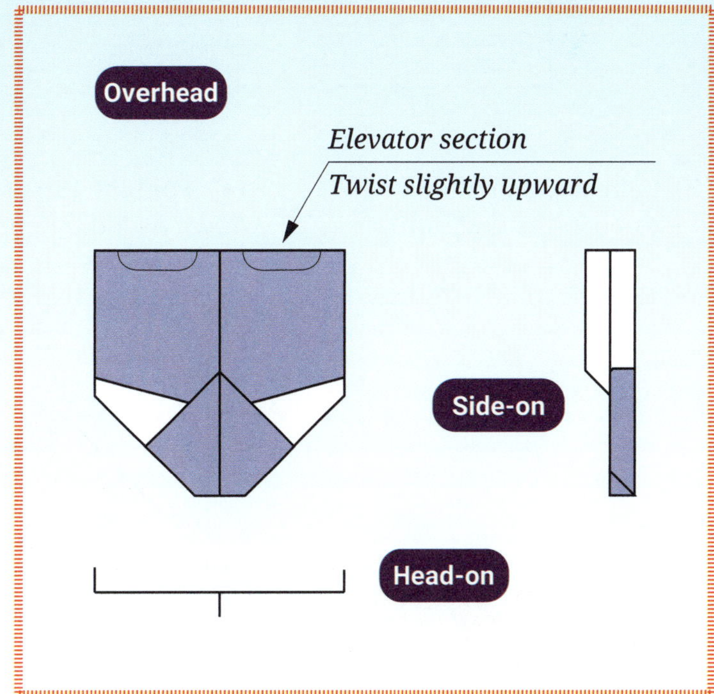

NEXUS KING II

This plane has a slightly more forward center of gravity than the Nexus King I (page 47) and features wings that are 5% larger. This design allows it to be thrown even higher.

Paper Shape .. Rectangular
Difficulty .... ★★★★

① Mountain fold in half left to right. Unfold, and then fold the corner flaps to the center crease.

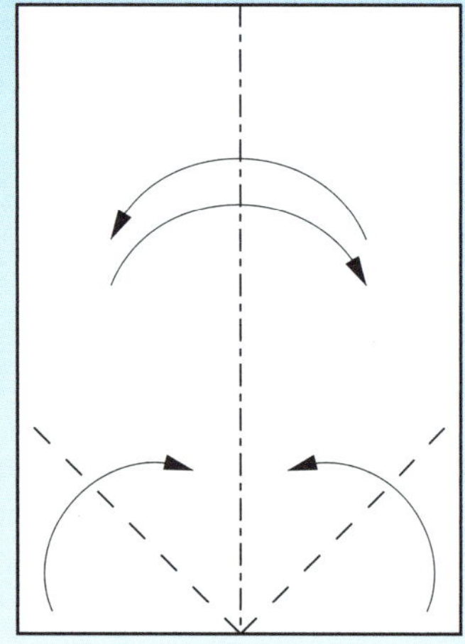

② Fold and unfold bottom to top ("a"). Then, fold so that the indicated "b" locations meet. Unfold.

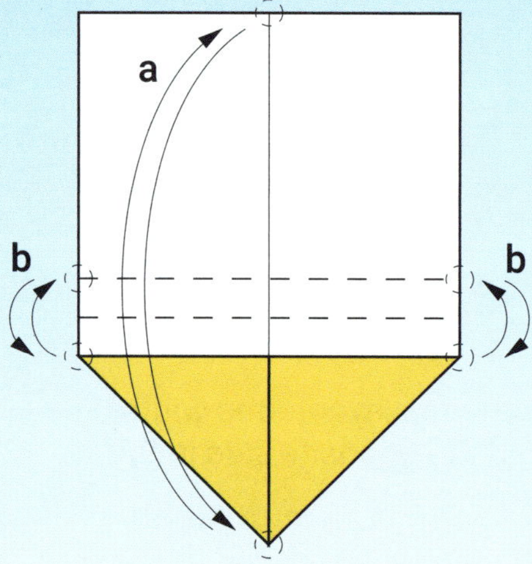

③ Fold at the position indicated in the diagram.

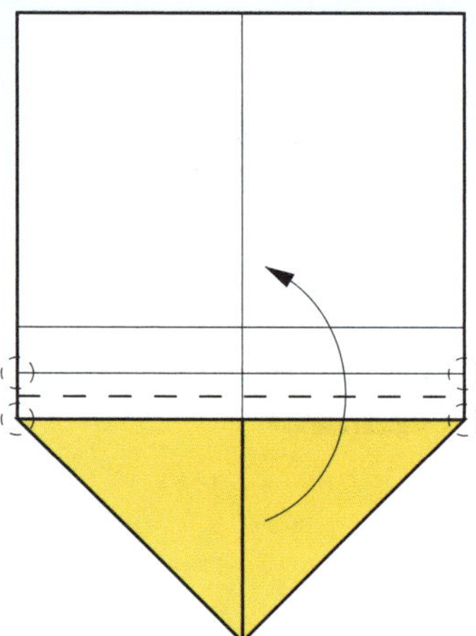

④ Fold the top of the flap down as indicated. Unfold.

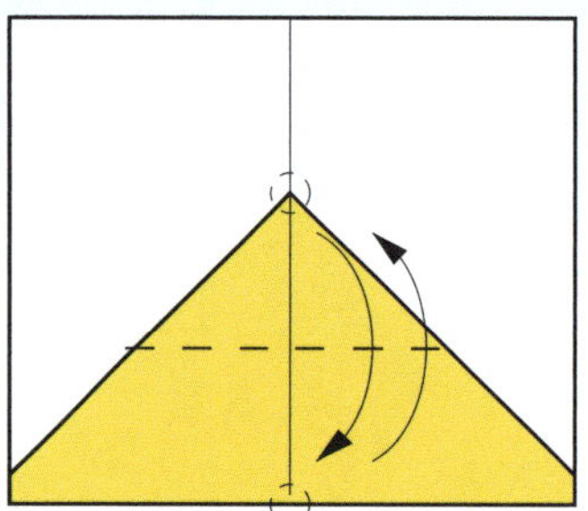

⑤ Fold the top of the flap down as indicated. Unfold, and then fold it to the back.

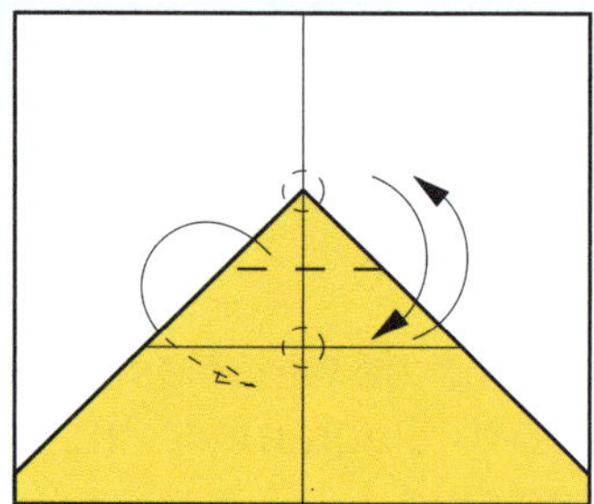

⑥ Turn the paper over left to right.

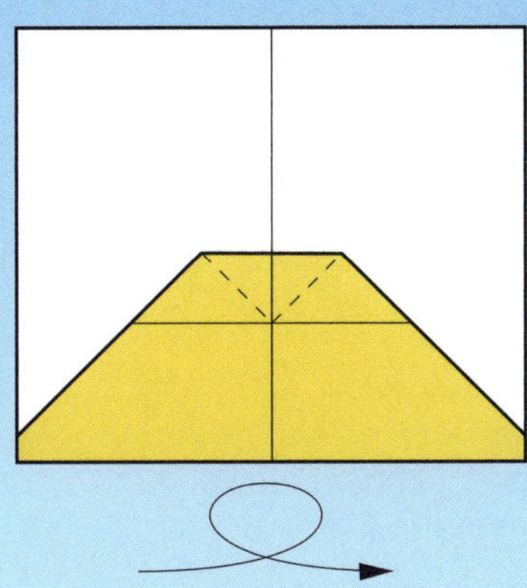

⑦ Fold the corner flaps to the center crease. Unfold both.

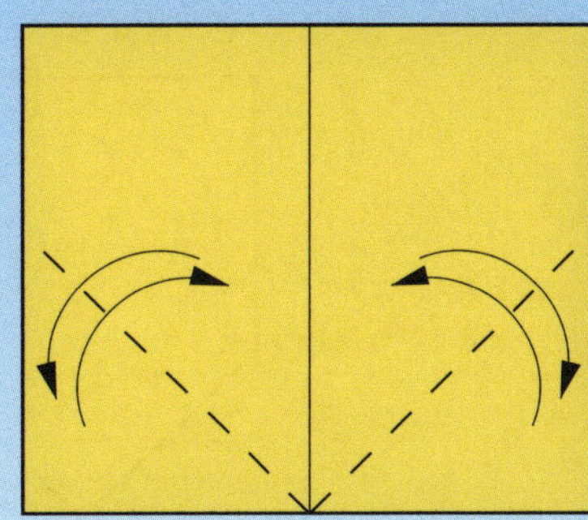

⑧ Fold as indicated.

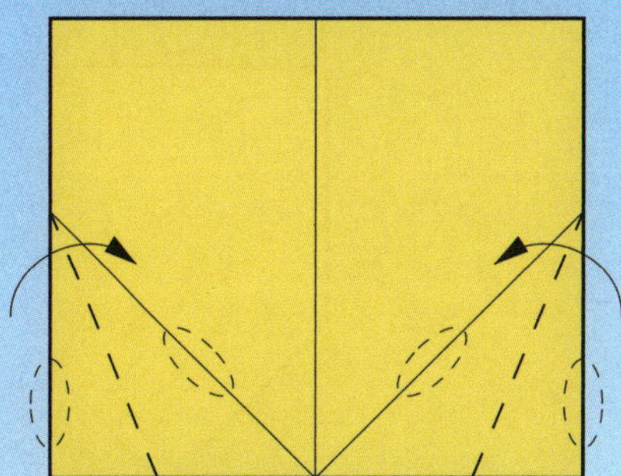

⑨ Open up pockets and squash to the outside as indicated. Look ahead to step 10 for the shape.

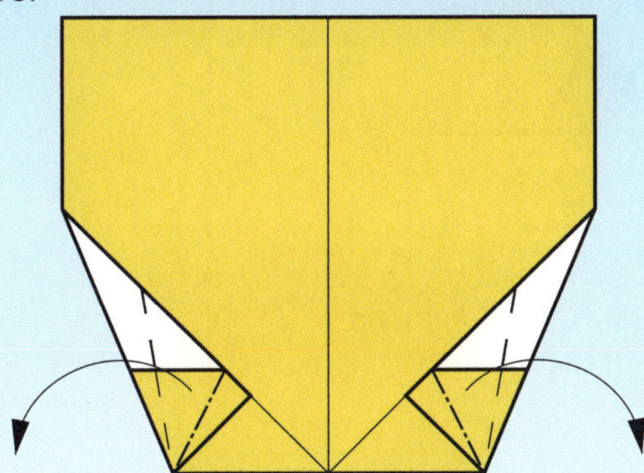

⑩ Fold as indicated.

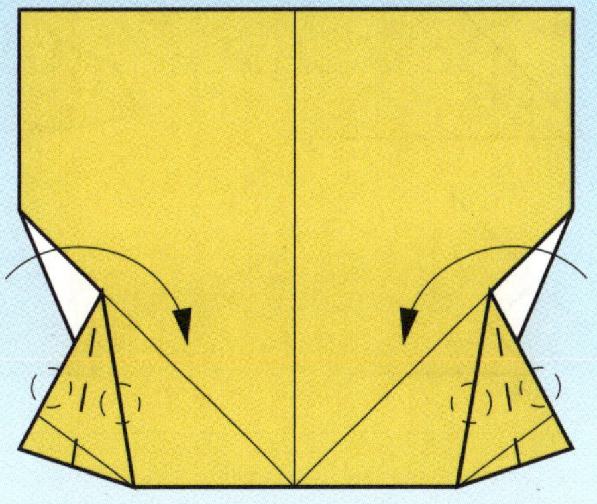

⑪ Refold along the existing creases from step 7.

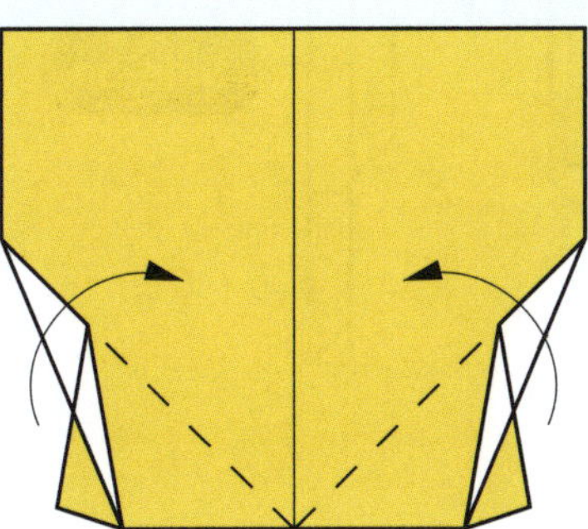

⑫ Turn the paper over.

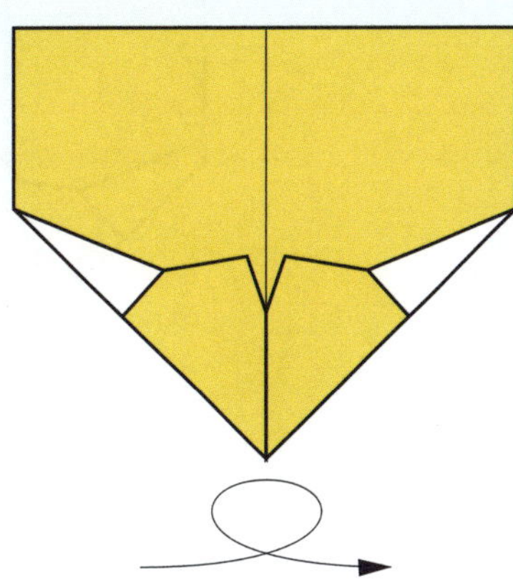

⑬ Fold up the bottom tip as indicated, and then unfold. Fold in half to the back.

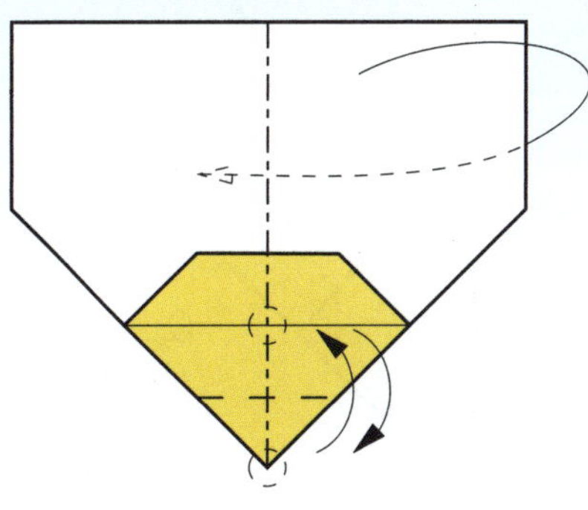

⑭ Fold the nose. (Refer to the enlarged diagrams below.)

⑮ Fold the top layer to the width of "c." Fold the opposite side in the same way.

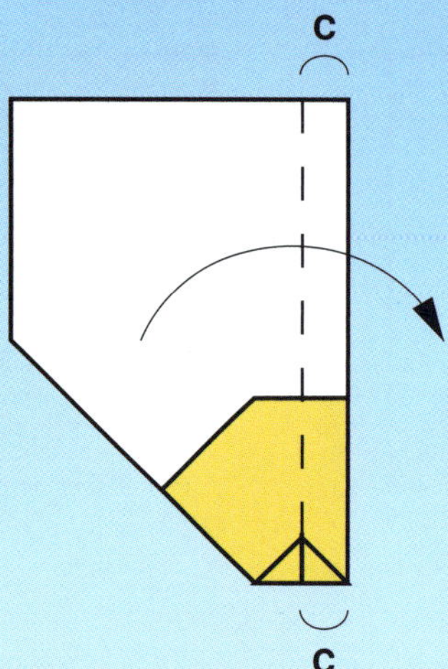

Zoomed-in Diagrams (Rotated View): How to Fold the Nose

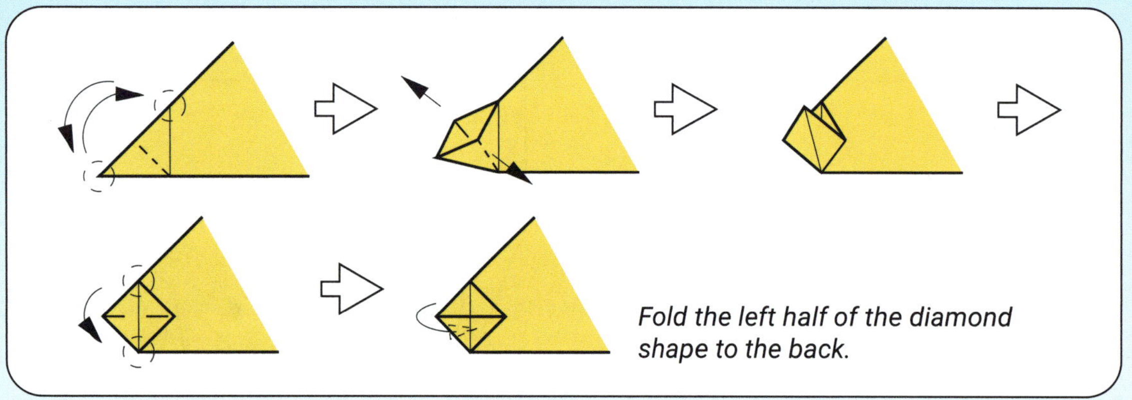

Fold the left half of the diamond shape to the back.

⑯ Fold the top layer to the width of "c." Fold the opposite side in the same way.

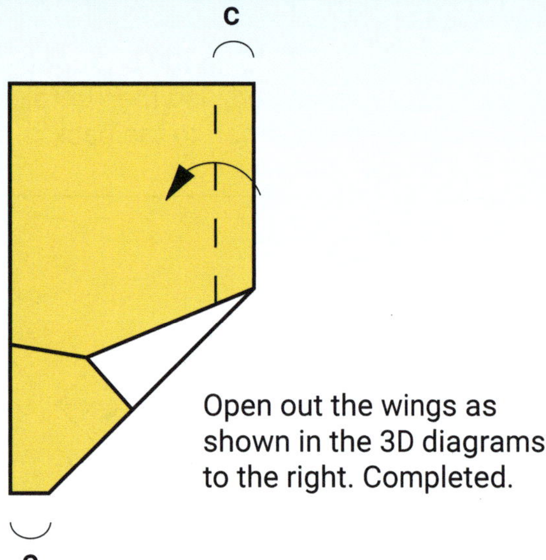

Open out the wings as shown in the 3D diagrams to the right. Completed.

Check after folding ▶ **Nexus King II 3D Views**

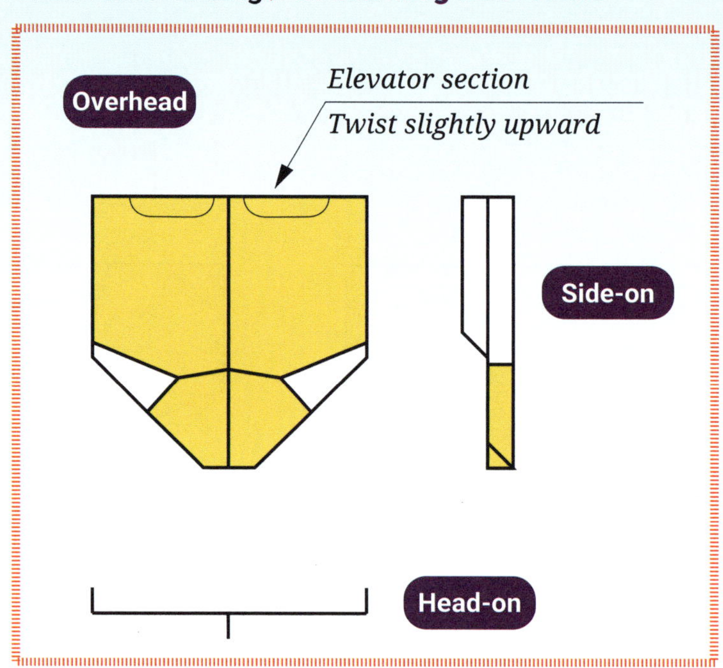

NEXUS KING MAX

By enlarging the rear part of the fuselage and angling the winglets, the wings are less likely to twist. This design is especially effective in high humidity conditions.

Paper Shape .. Rectangular

Difficulty .... ★★★★

① Mountain fold in half left to right. Unfold, and then, fold the corner flaps to the center crease.

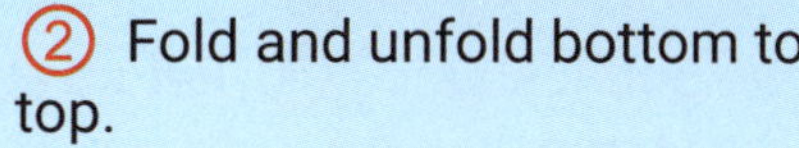

② Fold and unfold bottom to top.

③ Fold at the indicated position.

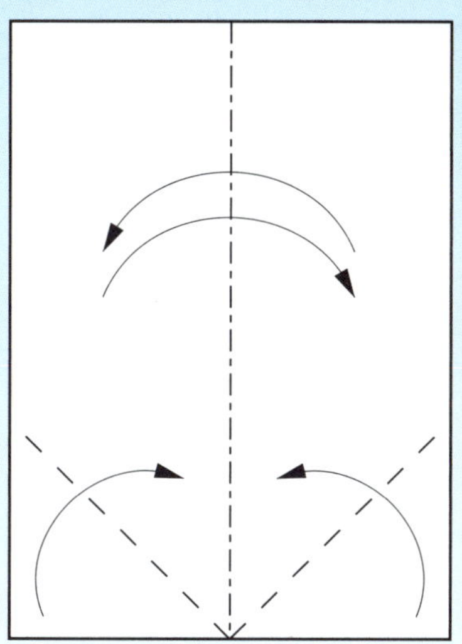

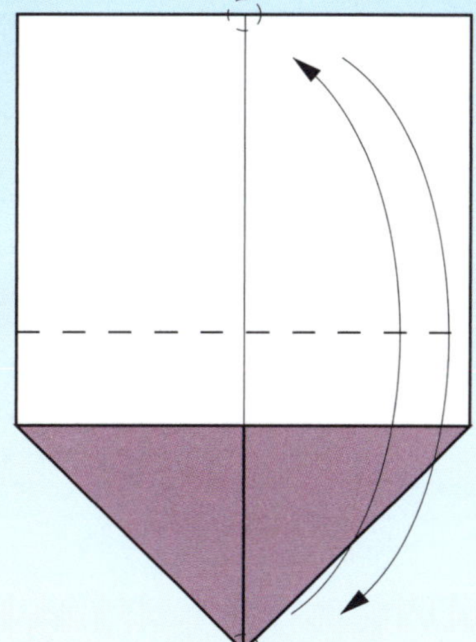

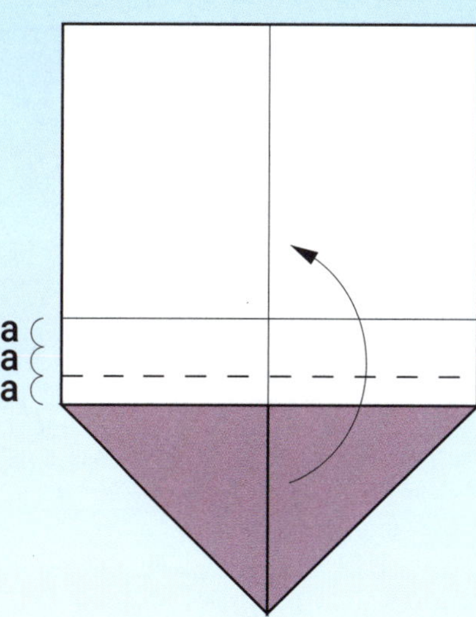

④ Fold the top of the flap down as indicated. Unfold.

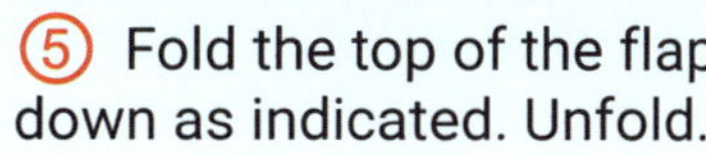

⑤ Fold the top of the flap down as indicated. Unfold.

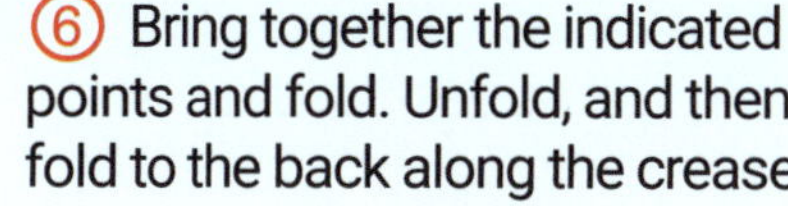

⑥ Bring together the indicated points and fold. Unfold, and then fold to the back along the crease.

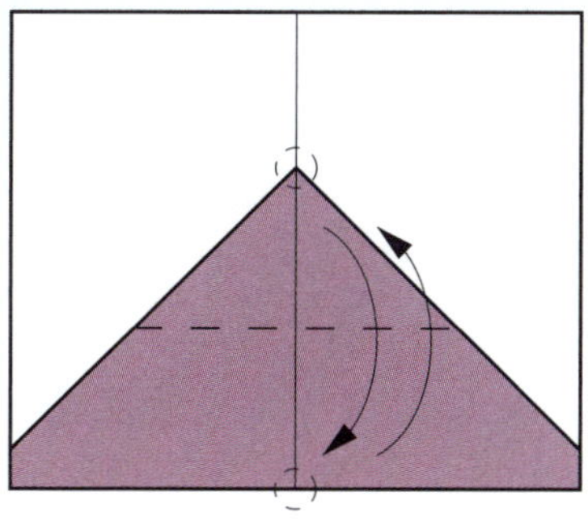

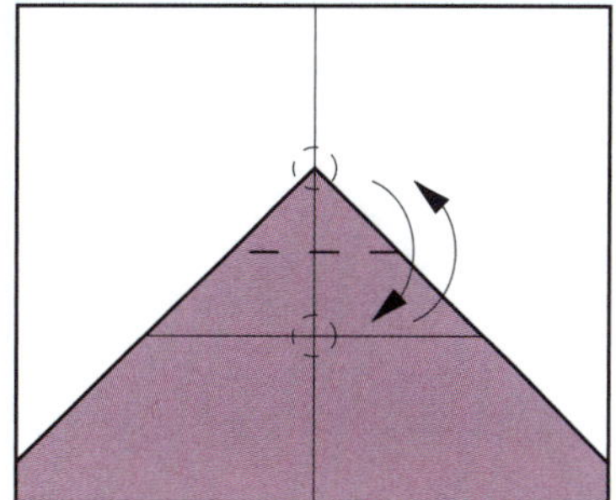

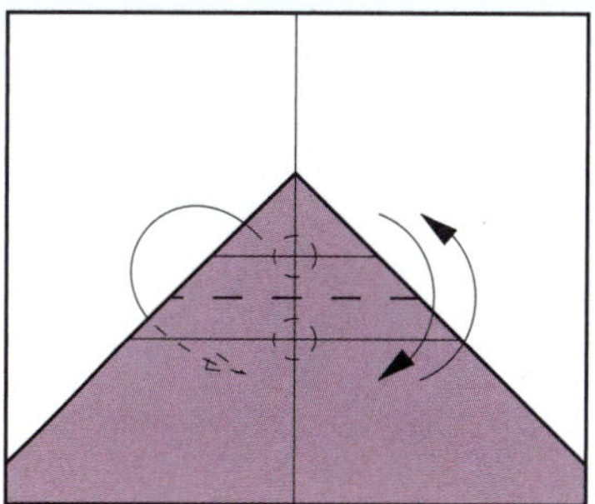

⑦ Turn the paper over left to right.

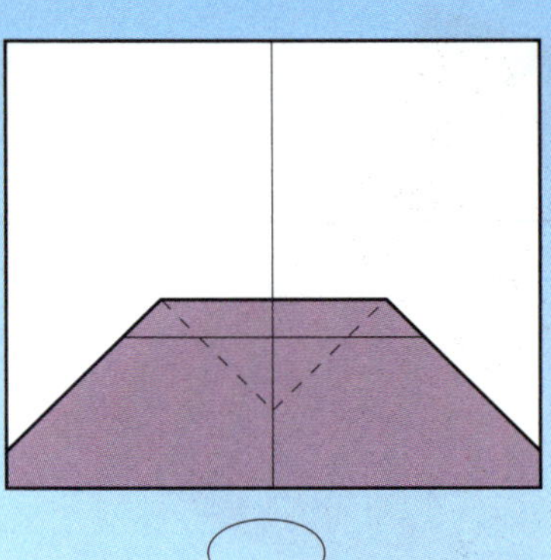

⑧ Fold the corner flaps to the center crease. Unfold both.

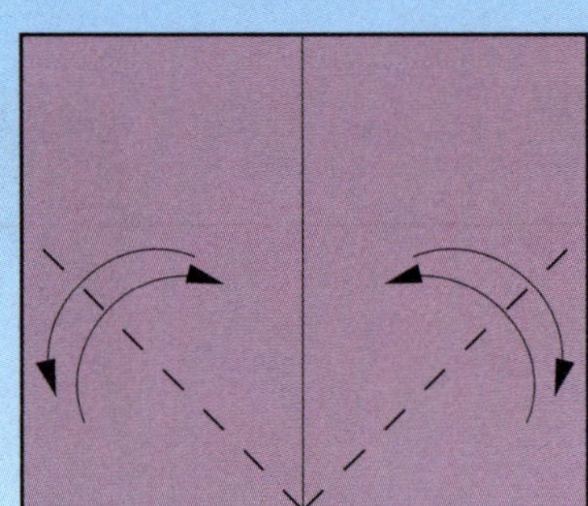

⑨ Fold as indicated.

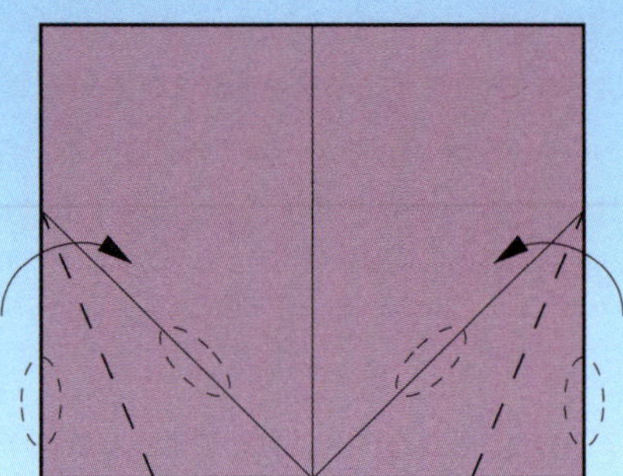

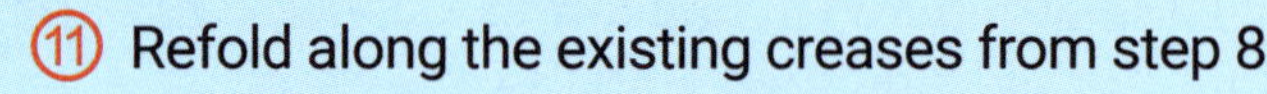

⑩ Open up pockets and squash to the outside as indicated. Look ahead to step 11 for the shape.

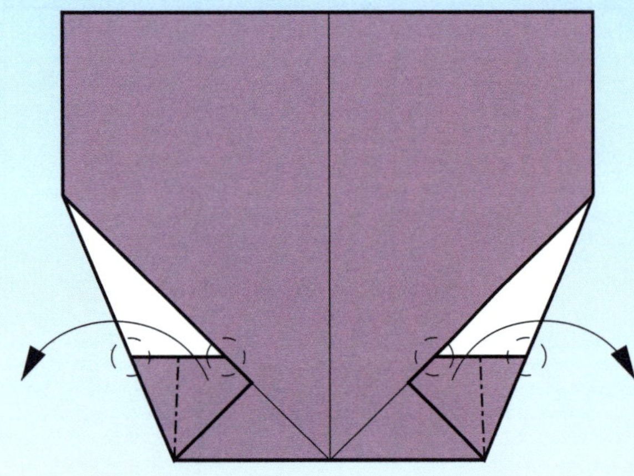

⑪ Refold along the existing creases from step 8.

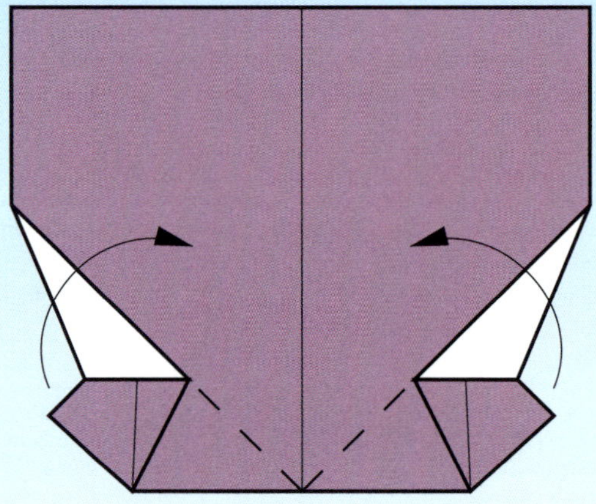

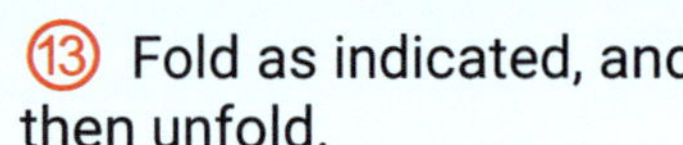

⑫ Turn the paper over.

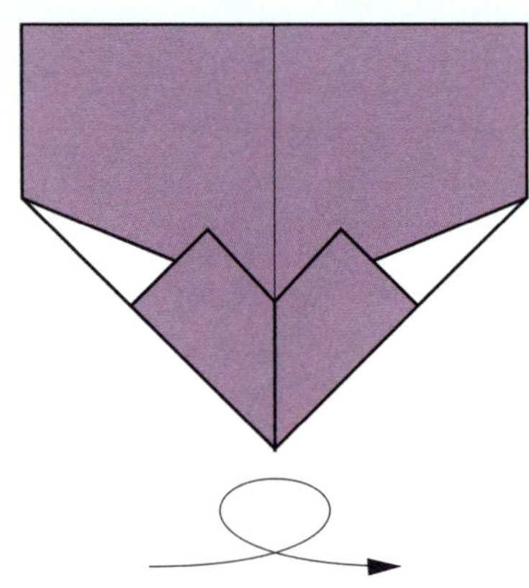

⑬ Fold as indicated, and then unfold.

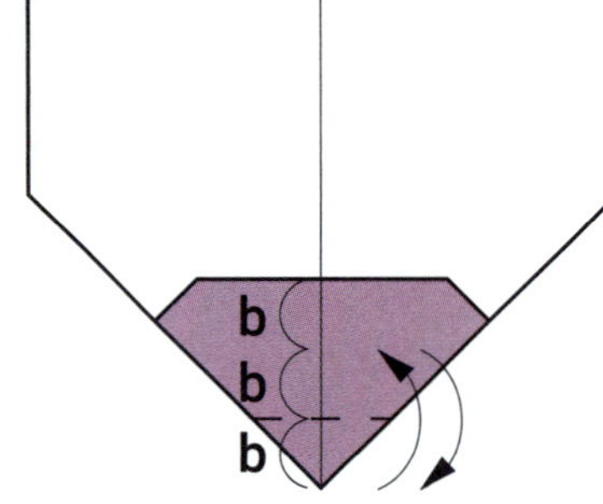

⑭ Fold in half to the back.

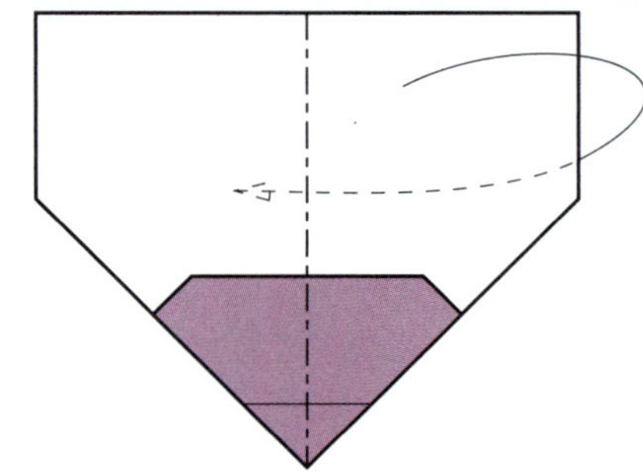

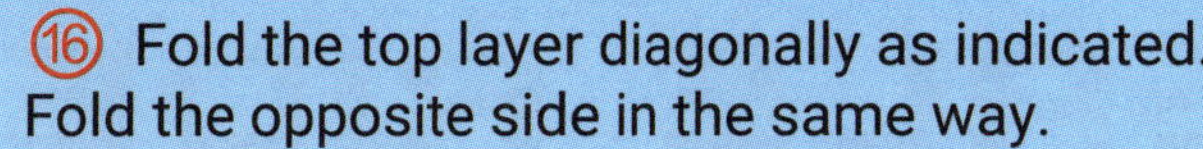

⑮ Fold the nose. (Refer to the enlarged diagrams below.)

⑯ Fold the top layer diagonally as indicated. Fold the opposite side in the same way.

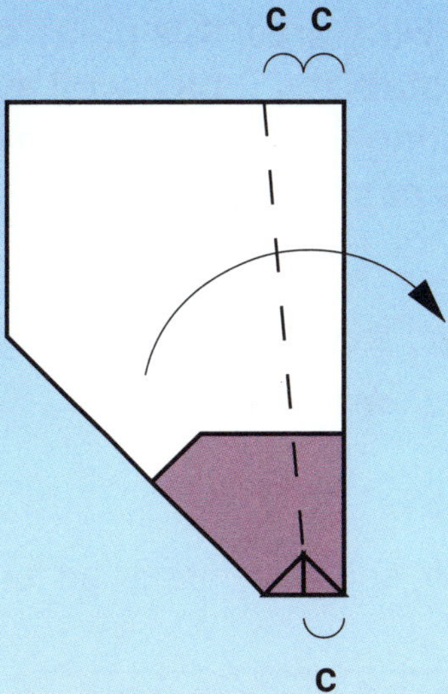

Zoomed-in Diagrams (Rotated View): How to Fold the Nose

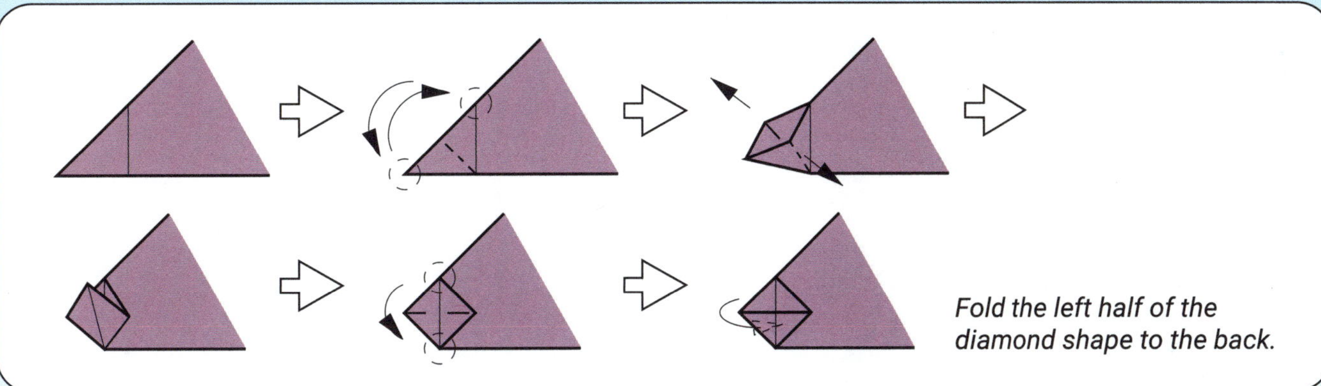

⑰ Fold the top layer to 150% of the width of "c." Fold the opposite side in the same way

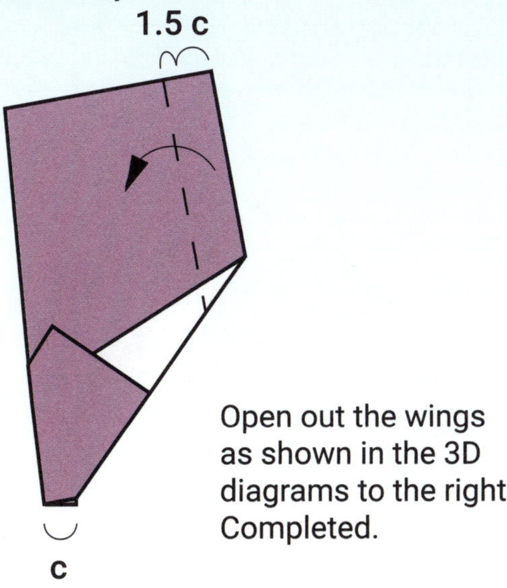

Check after folding ▶ **Nexus King Max 3D Views**

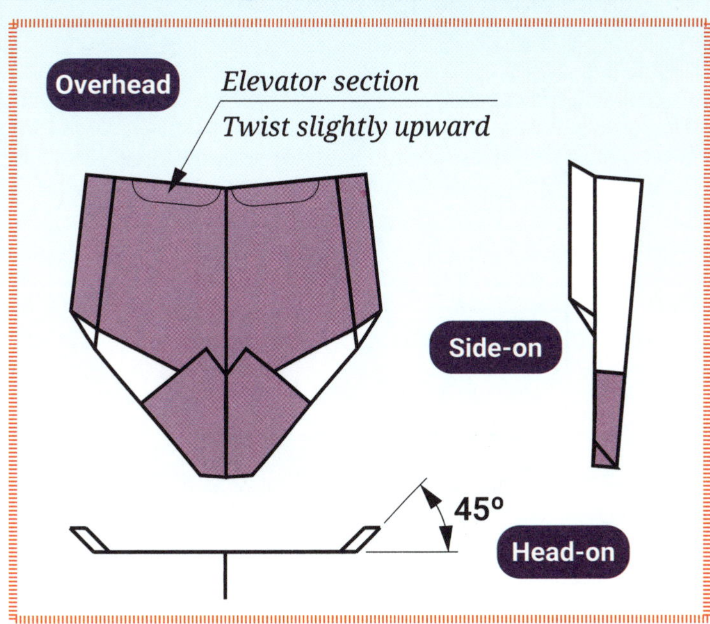

GALE RIDER

With a large wing area, this plane offers exceptional stability. It flies well even without twisting the elevators, making adjustments easy.

Paper Shape .. Rectangular
Difficulty .... ★★★★

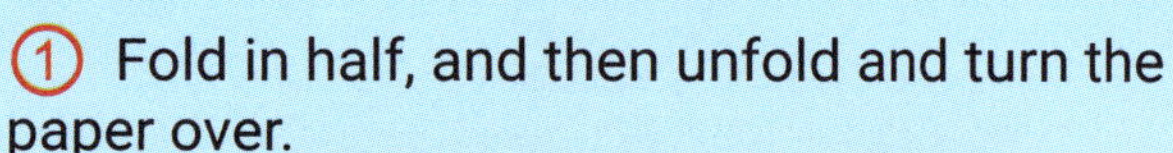

① Fold in half, and then unfold and turn the paper over.

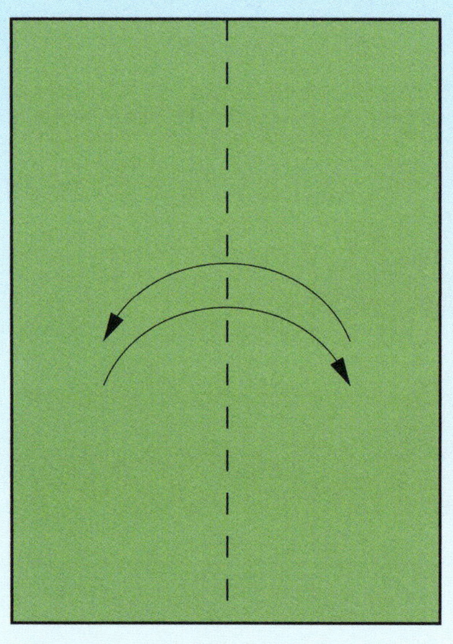

② Fold the corner flaps to the center crease.

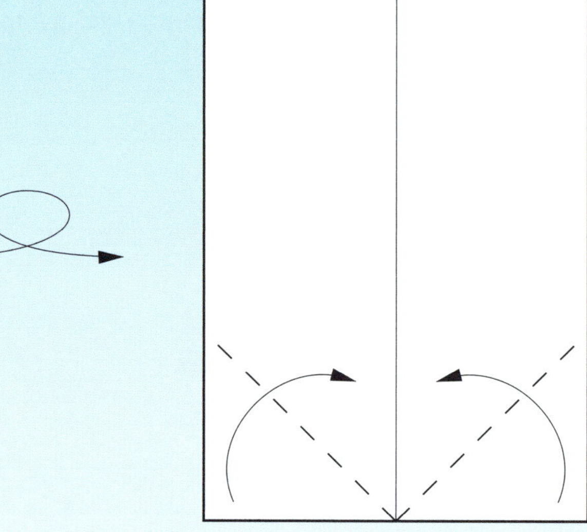

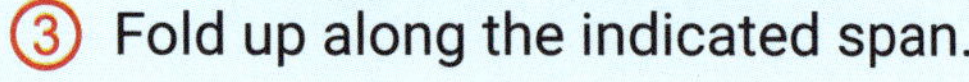

③ Fold up along the indicated span.

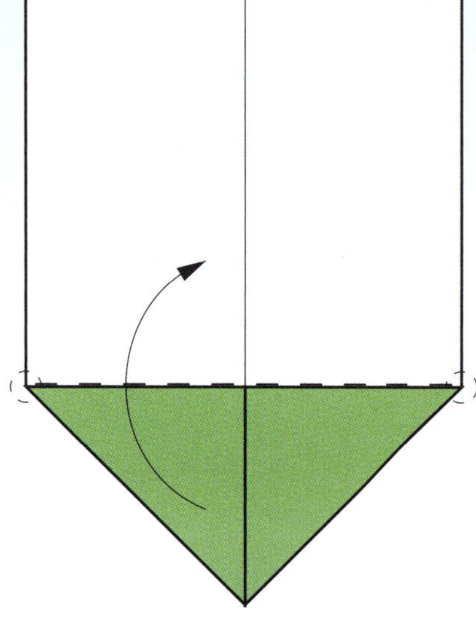

④ Fold the corner flaps to the center crease. Unfold both.

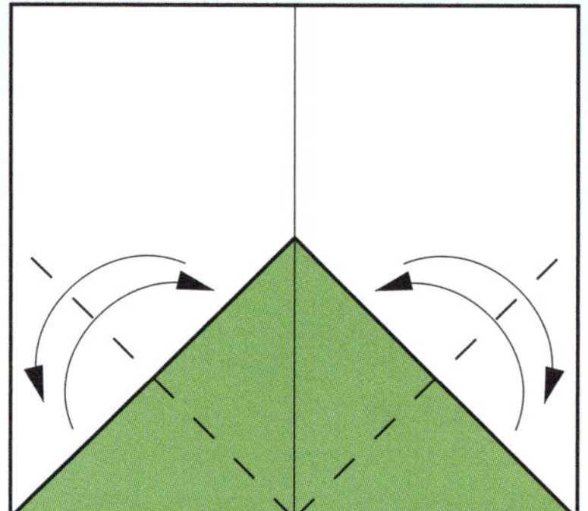

⑤ Fold as indicted, and then unfold.

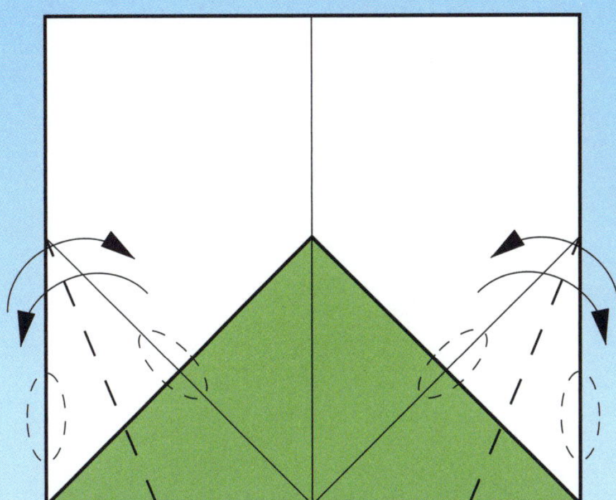

⑥ Fold as indicted.

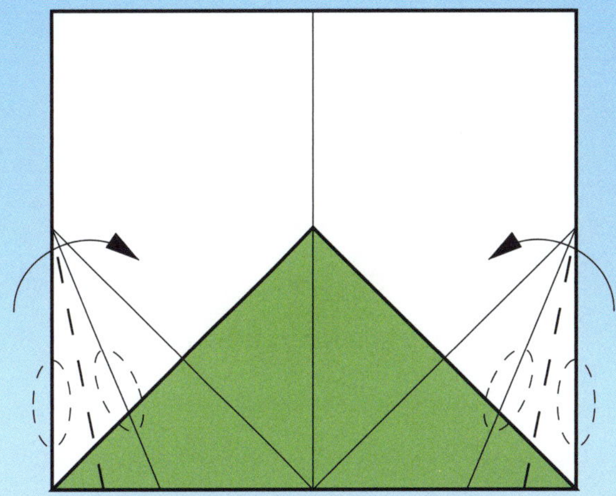

⑦ Refold along the 2 sets of creases made in steps 4 and 5, wrapping the paper.

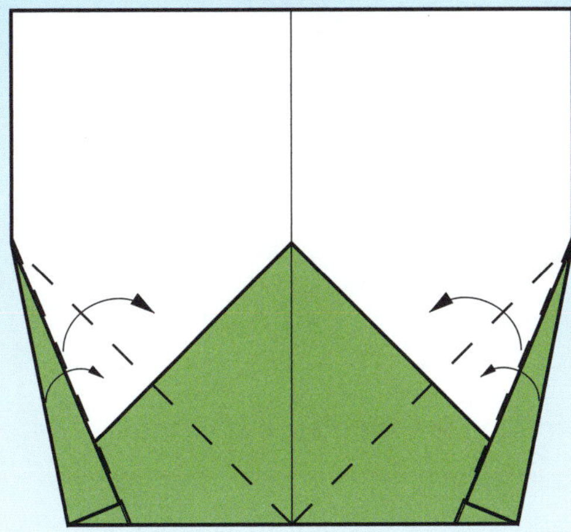

⑧ Fold the flap down as indicated.

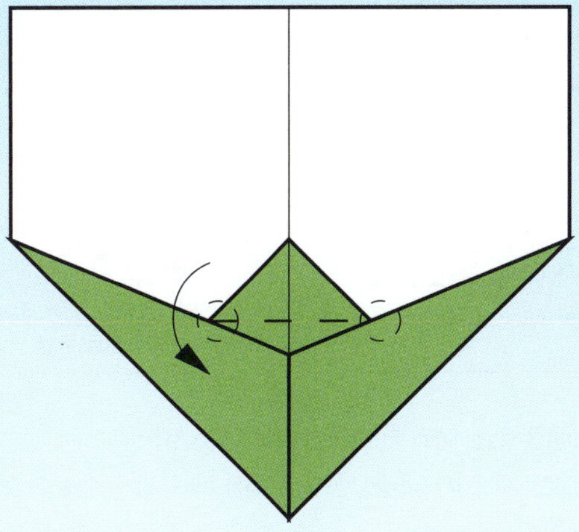

⑨ Fold at half the width of "a," and then unfold.

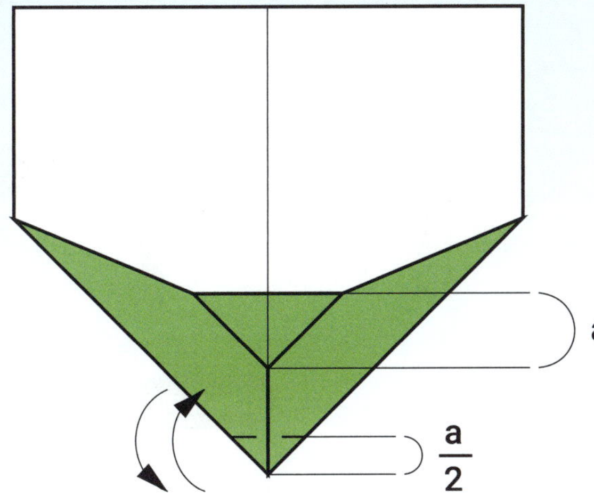

⑩ Fold in half to the back.

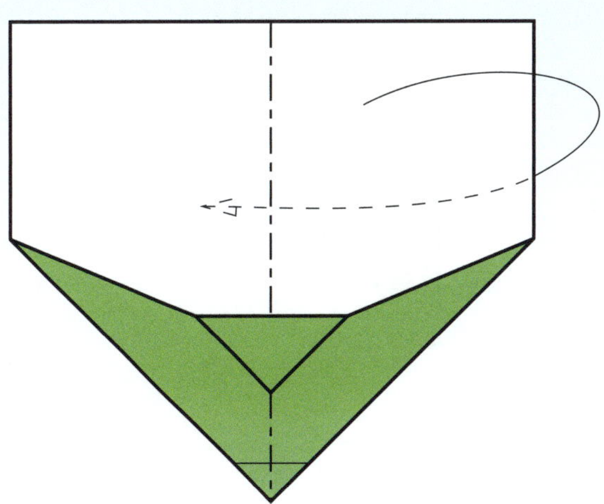

⑪ Fold the nose. (Refer to the enlarged diagrams below.)

⑫ Fold the top layer diagonally as indicated. Fold the opposite side in the same way.

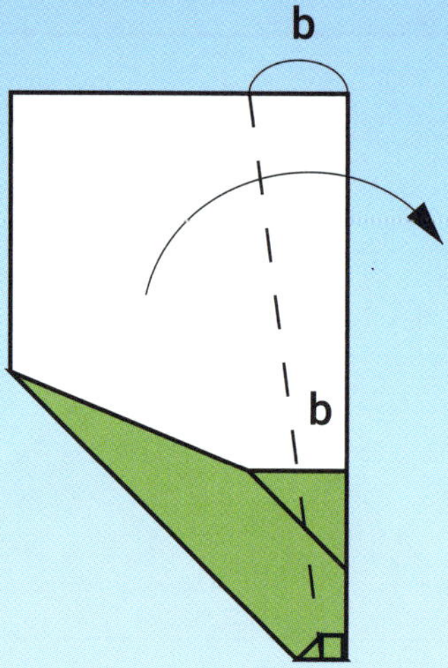

Zoomed-in Diagrams (Rotated View): How to Fold the Nose

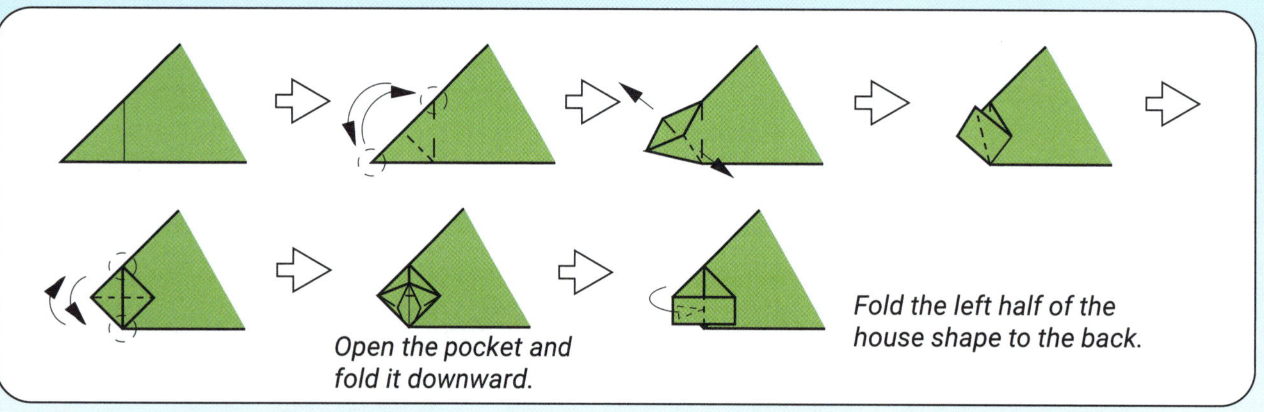

⑬ Fold the top layer to the width of "c." Fold the opposite side in the same way.

Open out the wings as shown in the 3D diagrams to the right. Completed.

Check after folding ▶ Gale Rider 3D Views

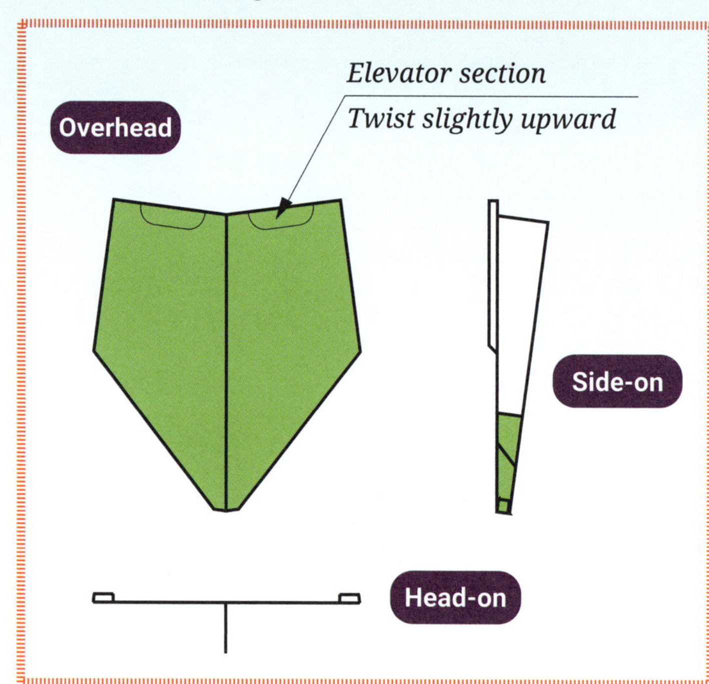

ZERO FIGHTER

This is the Guinness-World-Record holding paper airplane design that boasted an incredible indoor flight time of 29.2 seconds! Compared to the Sky King (page 45), it has a smaller keel and a vertical stabilizer.

Paper Shape .. **Rectangular**

Difficulty .... ★★★★★

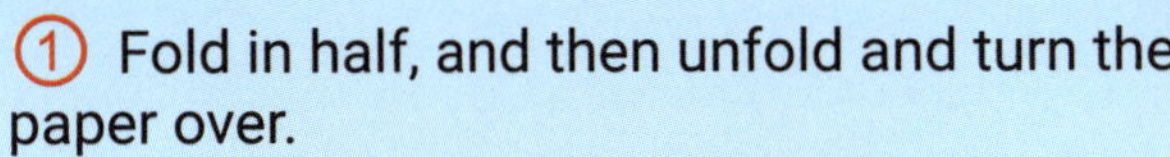

① Fold in half, and then unfold and turn the paper over.

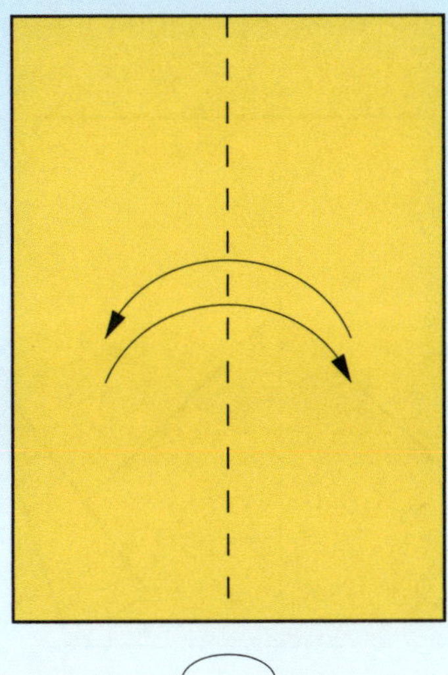

② Fold the corner flaps to the center crease.

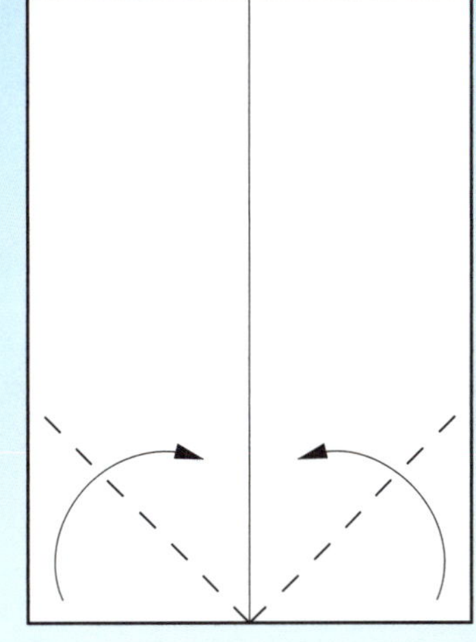

③ Fold and unfold bottom to top.

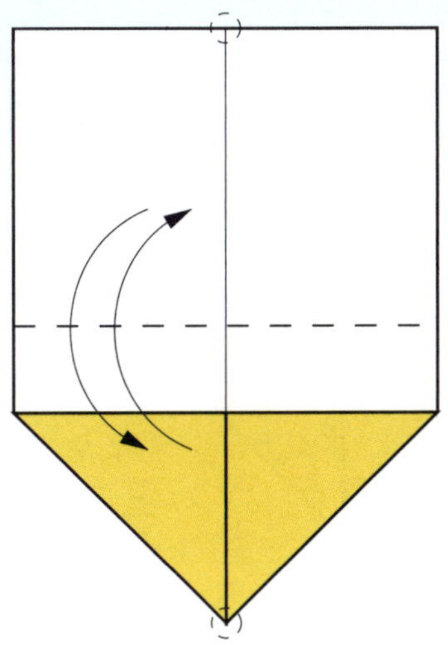

④ Fold at the indicated position, and then unfold.

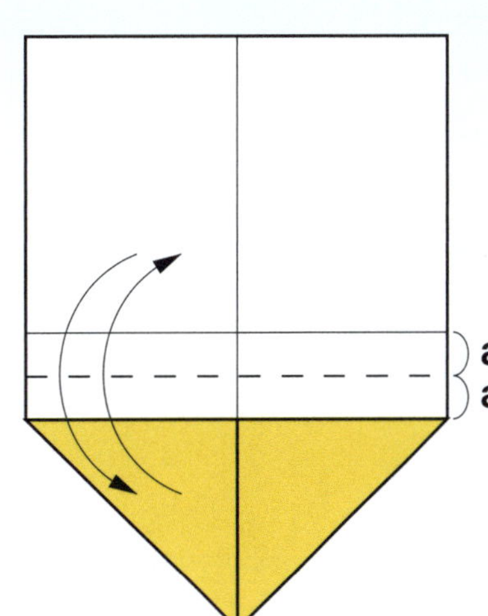

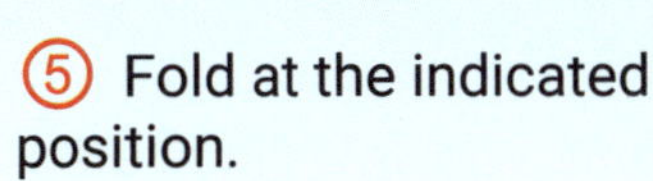

⑤ Fold at the indicated position.

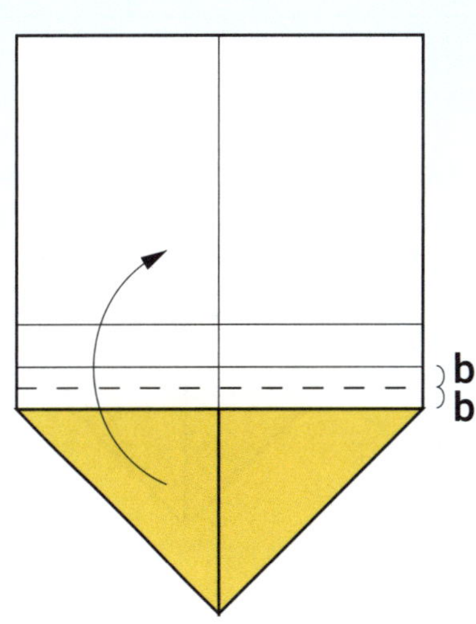

⑥ Fold the corner flaps to the center crease. Unfold both.

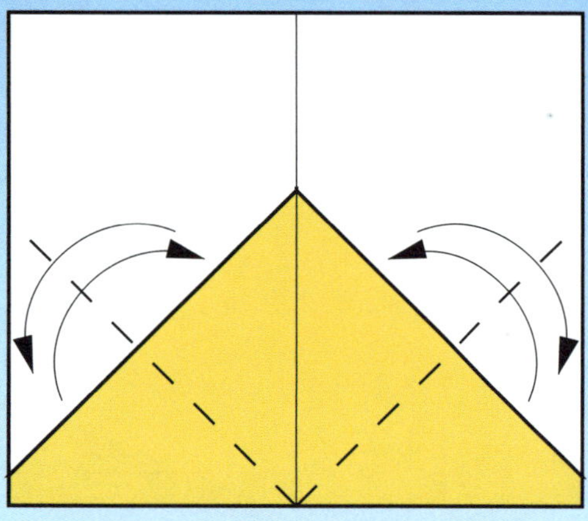

⑦ Fold as indicted, and then unfold.

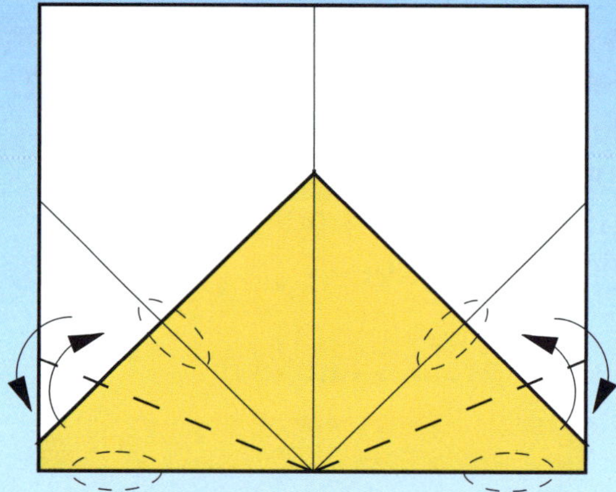

⑧ Fold the corners to the indicated positions.

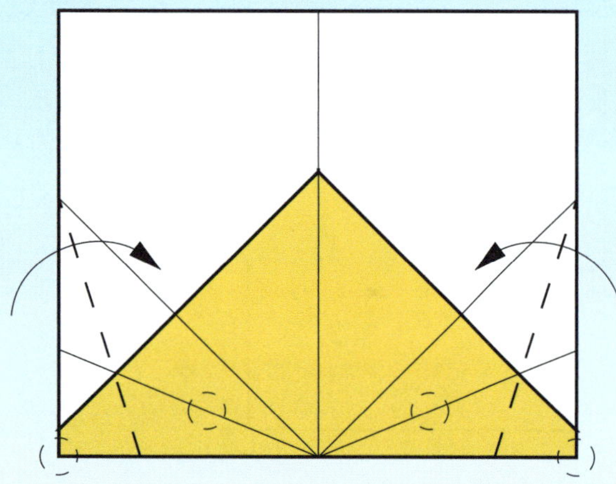

⑨ Fold along the creases made in step 6.

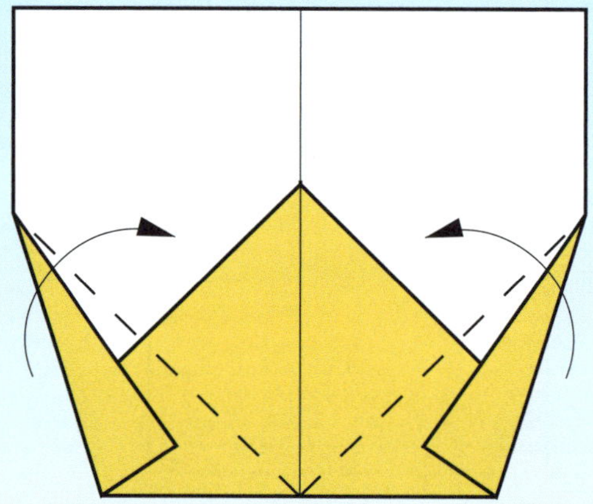

⑩ Fold the flap down as indicated.

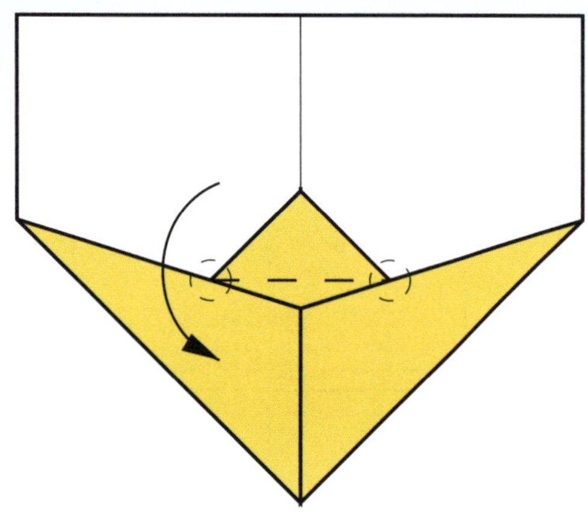

⑪ Fold at half the width of "c," and then unfold.

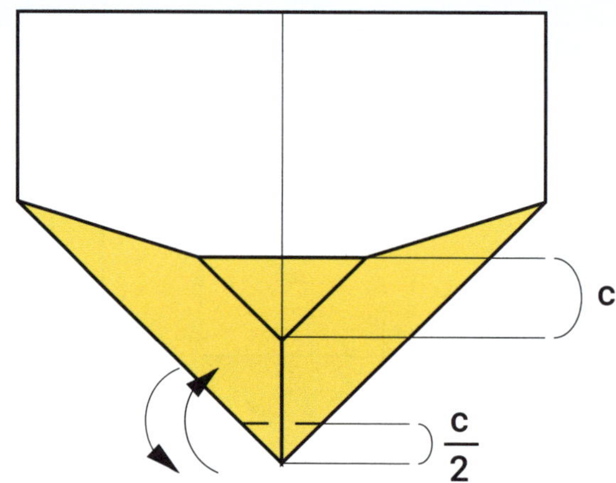

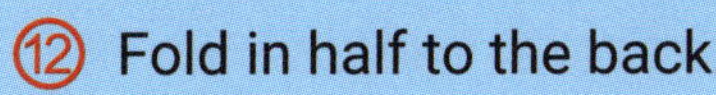

⑫ Fold in half to the back.

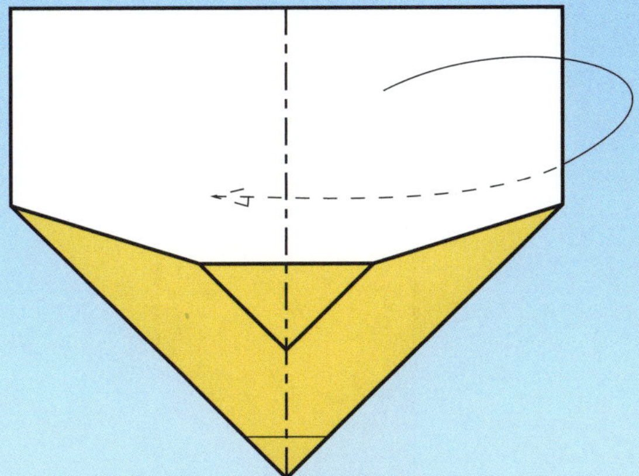

⑬ Fold the nose. (Refer to the enlarged diagrams below.)

Zoomed-in Diagrams (Rotated View): How to Fold the Nose

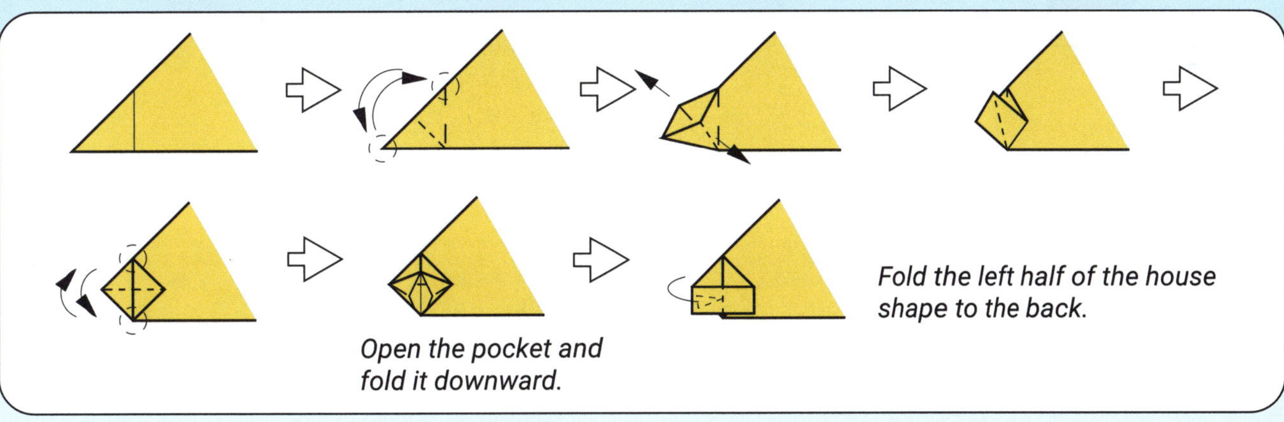

⑭ Fold the top layer to the width of "d," and then unfold. Fold and unfold the opposite side in the same way.

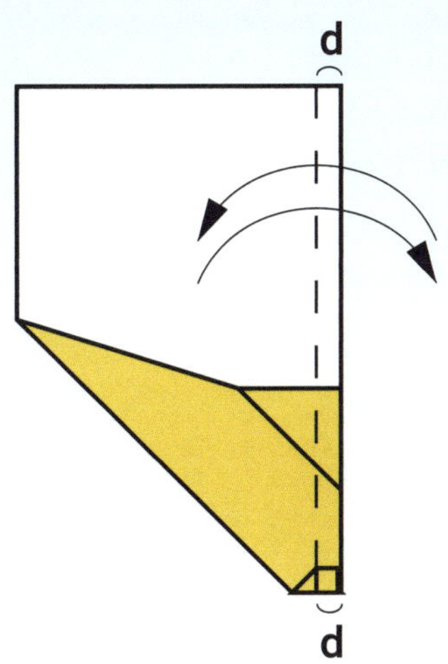

⑮ Fold the corner at d and 2d (twice the width of d), and then unfold.

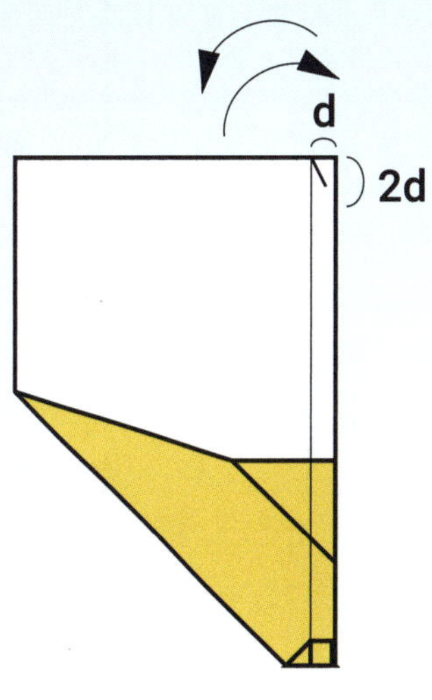

⑯ Inside reverse fold along the crease made in step 15. Refer to page 6 for instructions on how to do an inside reverse fold.

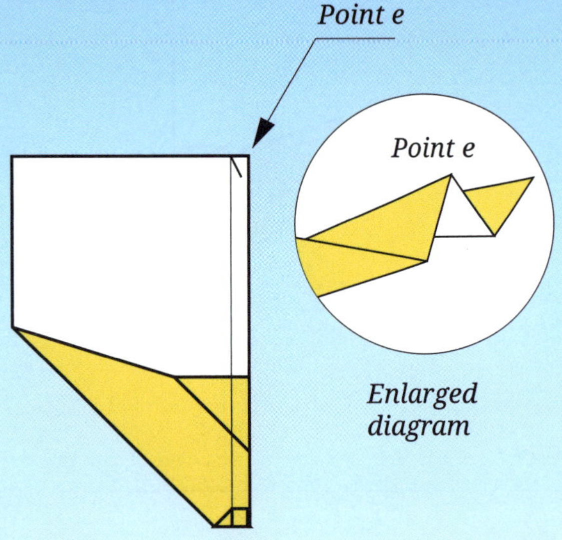

⑰ Refold along the creases made in step 14. Then, fold the top layer to the width of "d." Fold the opposite side in the same way.

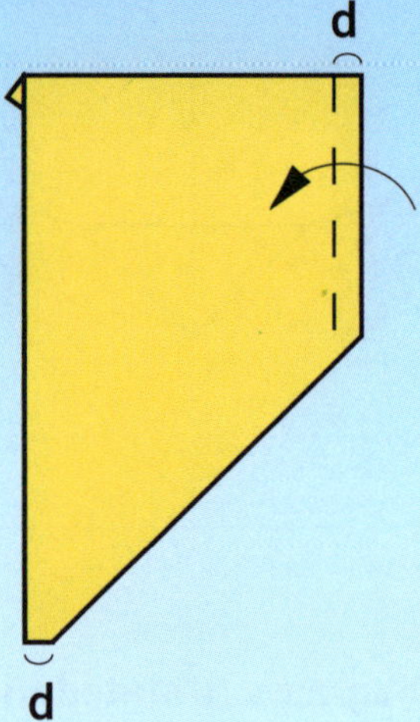

Open out the wings as shown in the 3D diagrams below. Completed.

Check after folding ▶ **Zero Fighter 3D Views**

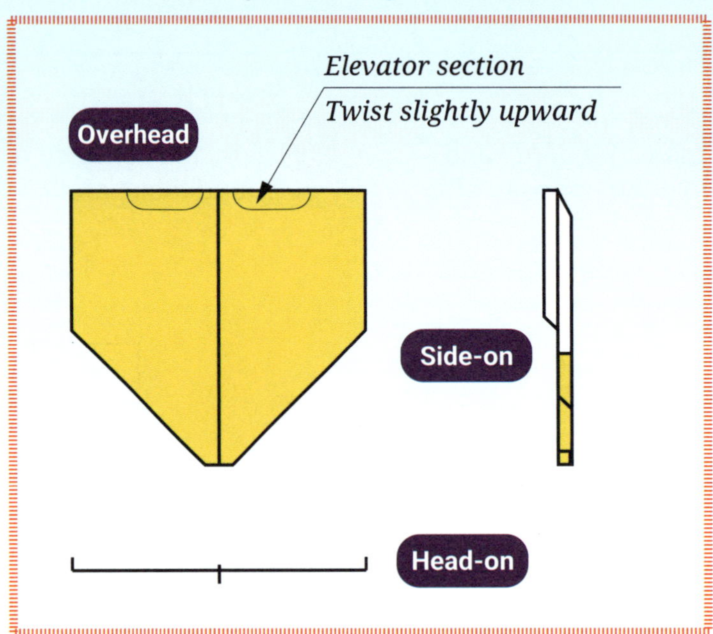

Origami Airplane Association

Established in 1995 following the publication of *Fly, Paper Airplane*, it now has an official competition rules set, hosts competitions and workshops based on those rules, and conducts lectures.

Website: http://www.oriplane.com/

Paper Airplane Museum

Opened on March 10, 2001, next to the owner's home, it is Japan's only museum dedicated to paper airplanes. It's a two-story building where the first floor displays hundreds of homemade origami airplanes and original works from paper airplane creators nationwide, and visitors can view videos in the video corner. The second floor has a large open space for origami airplane workshops, equipped with a wind tunnel experiment device to simulate the effects of wind on wings and the mechanics of lift. The walls display over 200 origami airplanes and works from paper airplane creators like Andrew Dewar and Yasuaki Ninomiya. Instructors are available when the museum is open, so paper airplane enthusiasts visiting Japan are encouraged to visit to develop their folding skills!

Address : 1396 Nakatsuhara, Mikicho, Fukuyama City, Hiroshima Prefecture 720-0004, Japan

Email : info@oriplane.com

Admission : 100 yen—less than $1 US (for ages 3 and up)

Hours : Every Saturday from 10:00 AM to 4:00 PM (for weekday and public holiday visits, please consult in advance via email or phone).

Toyomatsu Paper Airplane Tower

In the spring of 2003, the world's first paper airplane-dedicated tower was completed at the summit of Yonami Mountain, which is 2,175 feet (663 m) above sea level, in Jinsekikogen, Hiroshima. The steel structure has two floors, with an 85-foot (26-m) high observation deck on top. The first floor has a room for making paper airplanes, from which visitors can ascend to the observation deck. When the tower is open, visitors can fly their own folded paper airplanes from the observation deck. The building incorporates a solar panels on its roof and, together with the wind turbine installed in the park, it supplies its own electricity demands. On March 22, 2003, the first All-Japan Origami Airplane Championship final was held here. There are plans to regularly hold national and world championships.

Address : 381 Shimotoyomatsu, Jinsekikogen Town, Jinseki District, Hiroshima Prefecture 720-1704, Japan

Admission : 300 yen—less than $2 US (elementary school students and up) includes 5 sheets of eco-friendly paper (use of paper other than the provided eco-friendly paper is not permitted).

Hours : The tower is open Monday, Friday, Saturday, Sunday and public holidays. From May to September, 10:00 AM to 6:00 PM. In October, November, March and April, 10:00 AM to 5:00 PM. Closed from December to February. Open daily during Golden Week and the summer vacation period (late July to the end of August).

Takuo Toda's Career Highlights

1976 : Began developing original paper airplanes under the guidance of origami artist Eiji Nakamura.

1993 : Held the first paper airplane exhibition at the Fukuyama Art Museum, attracting 5,721 visitors.

1996 : Organized and supervised paper airplane competitions in Germany, Saga and Kagoshima.

1997 : Conducted a flight experiment from the Arc de Triomphe, broadcasted by Fuji TV.

1998 : Hosted a paper airplane exhibition at the Kawanoe Paper Town Museum in Ehime.

1999 : Successfully flew a nearly 10-foot (3-m) giant airplane, achieving a flight time of 35 seconds and a distance of nearly 443 feet (135 m) (sponsored by Tokai TV, received the Director-General of the Science and Technology Agency Award). Gave a lecture at the Aerospace Fair '99 in Nagoya.

2001 : Opened the Paper Airplane Museum.

2002 : Broke Ken Blackburn's indoor duration record for a pure origami airplane with a new record of 18.1 seconds (from 17.1 seconds).

2003 : Supervised the script and taught Kimura Takuya how to fold and fly paper airplanes for the TBS drama *Good Luck!!* Held the "1st All Japan Origami Airplane Contest."

2004 : Taught paper airplane making in Pokhara, Nepal. Updated the world record at Tokyo Dome (19.24 seconds, broadcasted by Nippon Television). Supervised a paper airplane competition at the INPACT event with the support of the Ministry of Education, Science and Culture of Thailand (80,000 participants, attended by Thai royalty). *The Evolution of Origami Airplanes* (NHK Publishing) was included in the national high school mock exam language questions.

2005 : Held the "2nd All Japan Origami Airplane Contest."

2006 : Cooperated with Hiroshima Prefecture's Dream Delivery Project (giant paper airplane).

2007 : Held the first elementary school invitational tournament.

2008 : Conducted a successful public experiment of space origami airplanes at the University of Tokyo.

2009 : Broke the Guinness World Record for indoor flight duration (27.9 seconds). Sky King was selected as one of the top 50 best inventions by *TIME* magazine in the USA.

2010 : Updated the Guinness World Record for indoor flight duration (29.2 seconds).

2011 : Held a Guinness challenge contest as part of the 100th anniversary of aviation in Tokorozawa. Conducted a project to uplift spirits for the recovery from the Great East Japan Earthquake.

2013 : Contributed as a paper airplane expert on *Shimajiro: A Wonderful Adventure* (Benesse Holdings).

2014 : Participated in a large-scale experiment in Okinawa for the *New Year's Special Gift from Sanma & Tamao!*

2016 : Held the "7th All Japan Origami Airplane Contest" at Todoroki Arena.

2017 : Held the "1st JAL Origami Airplane Asia Contest" at JTA Dome Miyakojima.

2018 : Held the "1st JAL Origami Airplane National Contest" at Ota Ward Gymnasium.

Publications

Fly, Paper Airplane (Japanese and Chinese editions), *Well-Flying Three-Dimensional Origami Airplanes*, *Well-Flying! Origami and Paper Cut Airplanes*, *Playing with Origami Airplanes with Your Child* (all published by Futami Shobo), *The Great Collection of Origami Airplanes BOOK* (Japanese edition / English translation included), *Super Origami Airplanes* (both published by Ikada Publishing), *The Evolution of Origami Airplanes* (NHK Publishing), *Origami Airplanes* (Thai edition) (METC), *Paper Airplane Museum* (edited by the Japan Origami Airplane Association), *Origami Airplane Play* (Showa Grimm), *The World's Best Flying Paper Airplane BOOK* (Takarajimasha), among others.

Origami Airplane Association Competition Rules

Common Provisions

1. There will be two competition categories: one for distance and one for flight time.
    - Category for elementary school students and below
    - Category for general participants (middle school students and above)
2. The paper used should adhere to the following:
    - For distance competition, use A4 size paper (equivalent to 8.3 × 11.7 in / 21 × 29.7 cm)
    - For hang time competition, use A5 size paper (equivalent to 8.3 × 5.8 in / 21 × 18.8 cm).
    - Use of paper certified by the Origami Airplane Association is standard.
3. Construction and throwing of the paper airplane:
    - Must be made from a single sheet of paper by folding only.
    - Cutting the paper, attaching additional paper, adding weights, using tape, gluing, and sanding are prohibited.
    - Participants must make and throw their own paper airplanes (borrowing and lending of paper airplanes is prohibited).
    - Changing the airplane model within the number of allowed throws is permitted (you may change the airplane model with each throw). Note:
        - An official will inspect the airplanes before the competition.
        - If a paper airplane tears during the competition, participants may switch to another model (spare or newly made) and retry.
        - Disqualification will result if a violation is discovered after measurement.

Specific Rules for Competitions

1. Distance Competition
    - Compete based on the distance from the point where the paper airplane is thrown to where it lands and comes to a stop on the floor.
    - The paper airplane must be thrown by hand without any assistance from another person.
    - The running distance before throwing the airplane must be within 10 meters (approximately 32 feet, 9½ inches).
    - Throwing from a position higher than the main level of flat ground is prohibited.
    - The wingspan (width) of the paper airplane must be at least 8 cm (approximately 3 1/8 inches).
    - If the airplane hits a wall or obstruction, the landing point is measured.
    - Distance is measured to the nearest centimeter (less than 1 cm is rounded off).
2. Flight Time Competition
    - Compete based on the flight time from the moment the paper airplane is released from the hand until it lands on the floor.
    - The paper airplane must be thrown by hand from a stationary position without any assistance.
    - Running or fast walking before throwing is not allowed.
    - Throwing from a position higher than the elevation of flat ground is prohibited.
    - During the throw, at least one foot must remain on the ground.
        - Lifting one foot up to 5 cm (approximately 2 inches) is allowed once with a warning; subsequent occurrences will invalidate the record.
        - Lifting both feet off the ground is not allowed and will invalidate the record.
    - Hang time is measured with a stopwatch to two decimal places (e.g., first attempt 12.34 seconds, second attempt 9.56 seconds).
    - If the paper airplane touches or collides with a person, the time is measured until it subsequently lands.
        - If it gets stuck for more than one second, a retry is allowed.

Photo & Illustration Credits—

pp. 6–11 (Background) AlinaMD / Shutterstock

Books to Span the East and West

Tuttle Publishing was founded in 1832 in the small New England town of Rutland, Vermont [USA]. Our core values remain as strong today as they were then—to publish best-in-class books which bring people together one page at a time. In 1948, we established a publishing outpost in Japan—and Tuttle is now a leader in publishing English-language books about the arts, languages and cultures of Asia. The world has become a much smaller place today and Asia's economic and cultural influence has grown. Yet the need for meaningful dialogue and information about this diverse region has never been greater. Over the past seven decades, Tuttle has published thousands of books on subjects ranging from martial arts and paper crafts to language learning and literature—and our talented authors, illustrators, designers and photographers have won many prestigious awards. We welcome you to explore the wealth of information available on Asia at **www.tuttlepublishing.com**.

Published by Tuttle Publishing, an imprint of Periplus Editions (HK) Ltd.

www.tuttlepublishing.com

Kids Origami Hikoki Taikugata

English translation rights arranged with Ikadasha Publishers Co., Ltd. through Japan UNI Agency, Inc., Tokyo

ISBN: 978-4-8053-1874-4

Library of Congress Cataloging-in Publication Data is in process.

Distributed by:
North America, Latin America & Europe
Tuttle Publishing, 364 Innovation Drive, North Clarendon
VT 05759-9436 U.S.A.
Tel: (802) 773-8930 | Fax: (802) 773-6993
info@tuttlepublishing.com | www.tuttlepublishing.com

Japan
Tuttle Publishing, Yaekari Building 3rd Floor
5-4-12 Osaki Shinagawa-ku, Tokyo 141 0032
Tel: (81) 3 5437-0171 | Fax: (81) 3 5437-0755
sales@tuttle.co.jp | www.tuttle.co.jp

Asia Pacific
Berkeley Books Pte. Ltd., 3 Kallang Sector, #04-01, Singapore 349278
Tel: (65) 6741-2178 | Fax: (65) 6741-2179
inquiries@periplus.com.sg | www.tuttlepublishing.com

30 29 28 27 26 25 10 9 8 7 6 5 4 3 2 1
Printed in Malaysia 2509UM

GPSR Representative
Matt Parsons, matt.parsons@upi2mbooks.hr, UPI-2M PLUS d.o.o., Medulićeva 20, 10000, Zagreb, Croatia

Flight distance

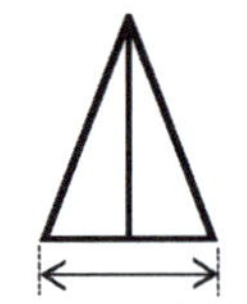

8 cm (approx. 3 1/8 in) or more

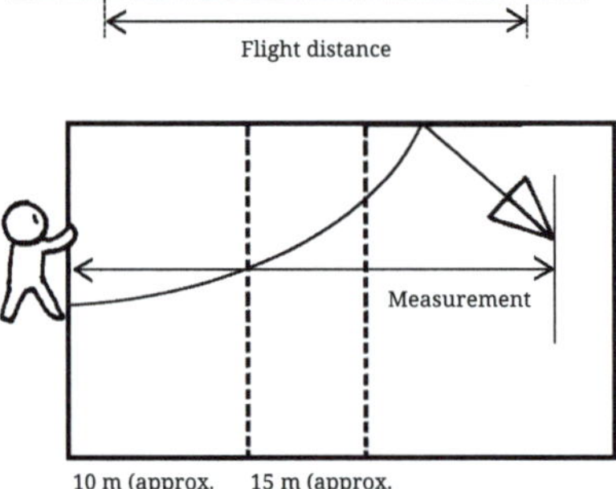

10 m (approx. 32 ft, 9½ in) 15 m (approx. 49 ft, 2½ in)

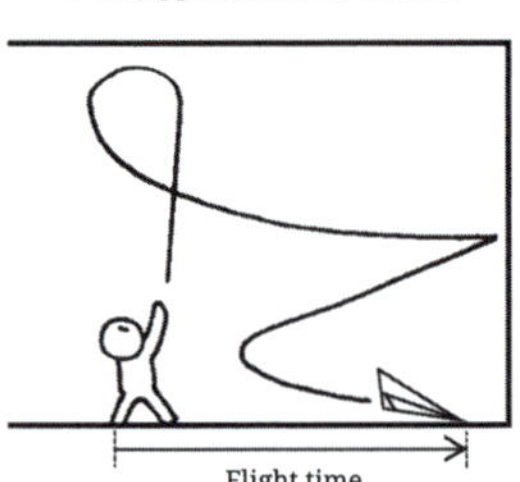

Flight time

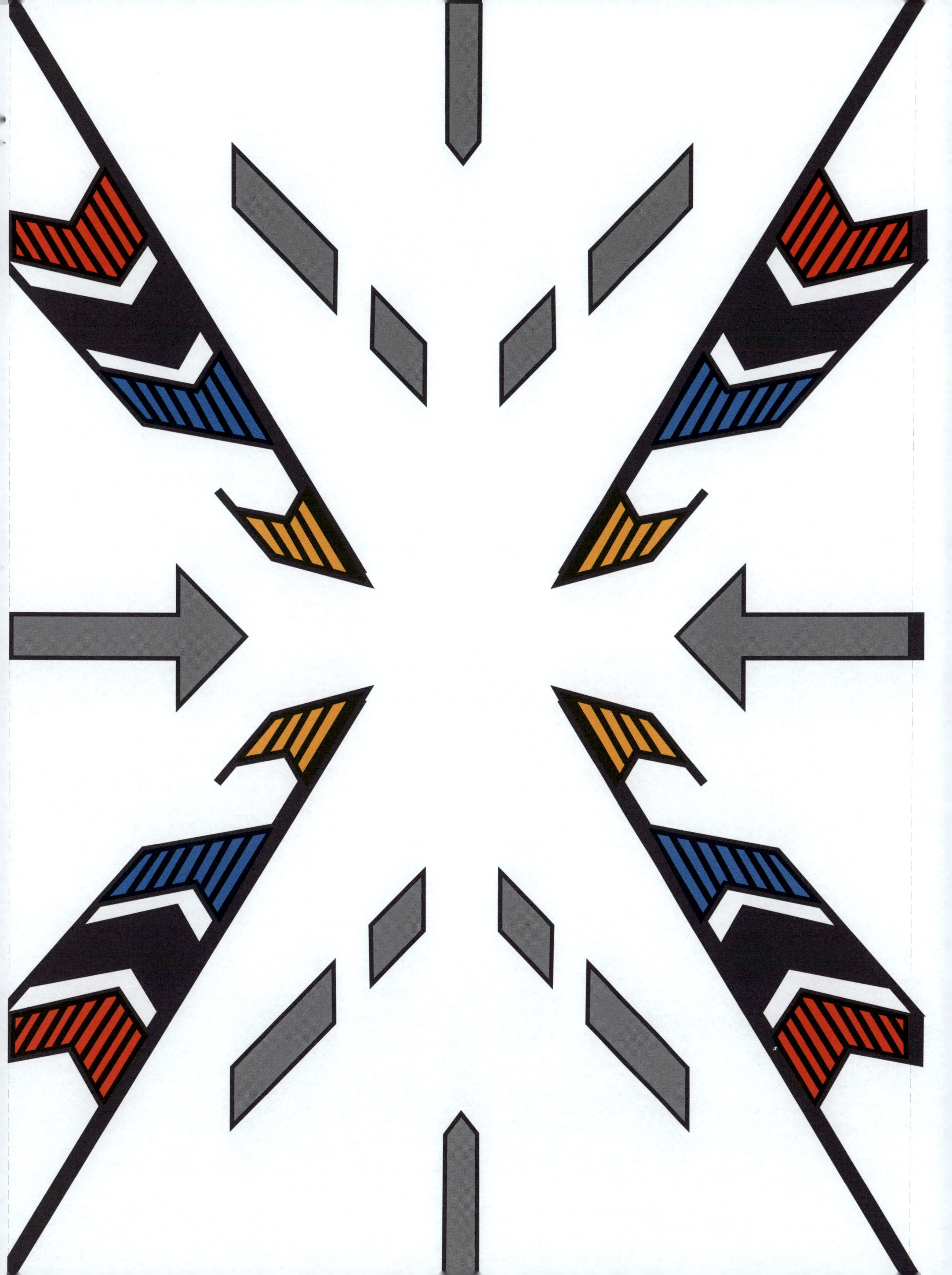

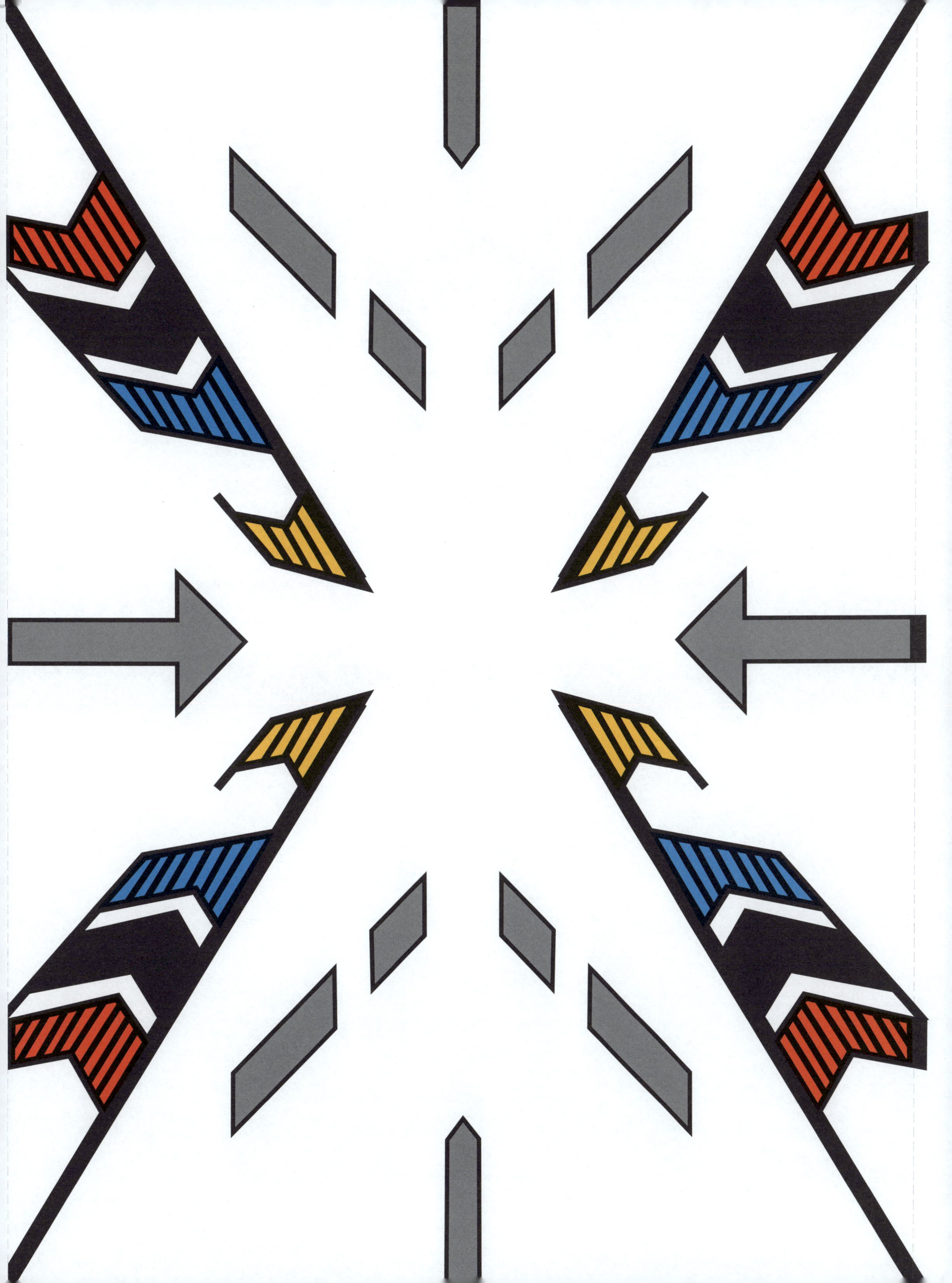

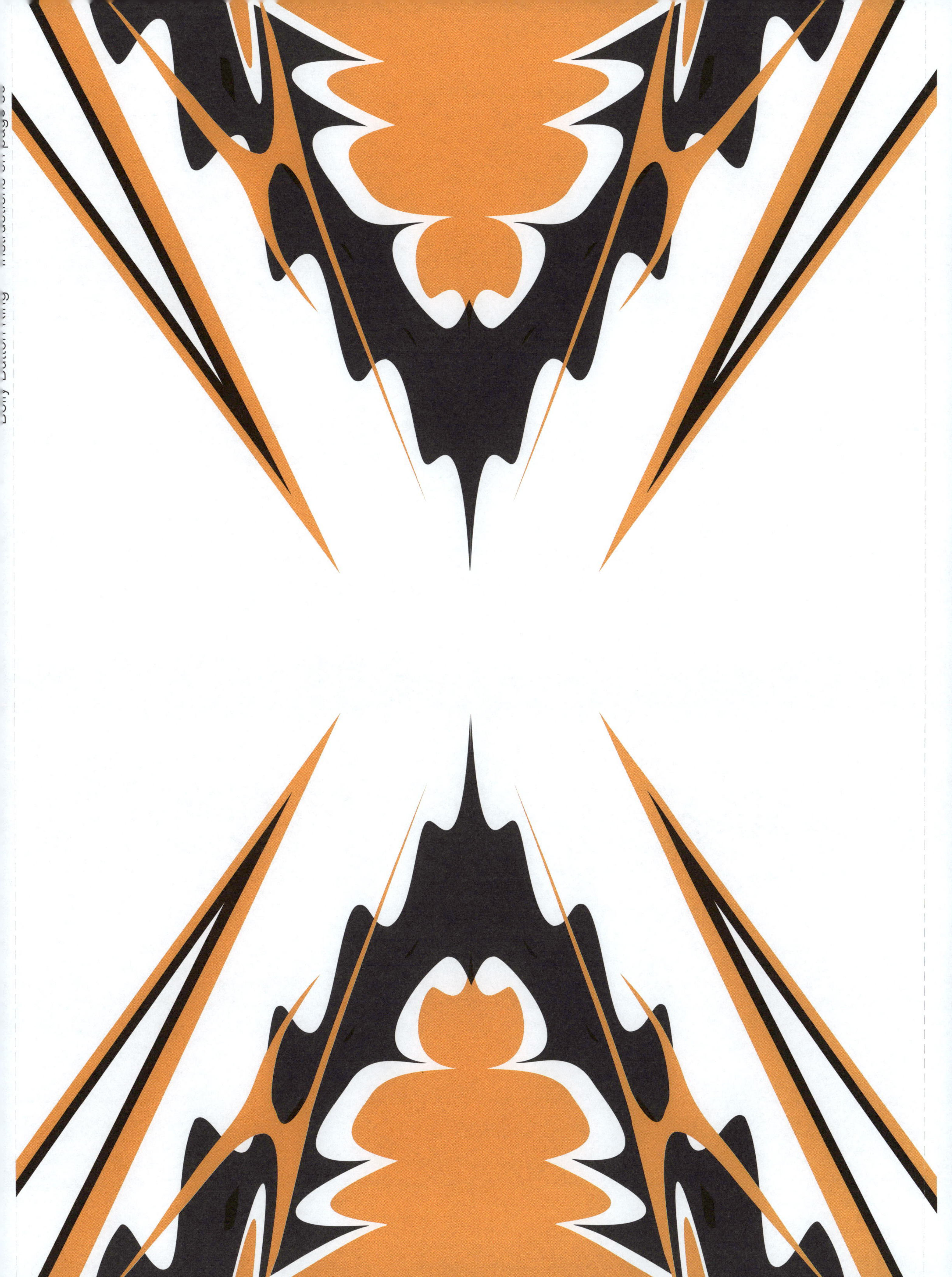